THE ULTIMATE SERVICE DOG TRAINING MANUAL

100 Tips for Choosing, Raising, Socializing, and Retiring Your Dog

KEAGEN J. GRACE

Skyhorse Publishing

Skyhorse Publishing books may be purchased in bulk at special discounts for sales promotion, corporate gifts, fund-raising, or educational purposes. Special editions can also be created to specifications. For details, contact the Special Sales Department, Skyhorse Publishing, 307 West 36th Street, 11th Floor, New York, NY 10018 or info@skyhorsepublishing.com.

Visit our website at www.skyhorsepublishing.com.

10 9 8 7 6 5 4

Library of Congress Cataloging-in-Publication Data

Names: Grace, Keagen J., author.
Title: The ultimate service dog training manual: a complete guide to choosing, raising, socializing, equipping, and retiring your dog / Keagen J. Grace.
Description: New York, NY: Skyhorse Publishing, 2020. | Includes index. |
Identifiers: LCCN 2019057977 (print) | LCCN 2019057978 (ebook) | ISBN 9781510703162 (paperback) | ISBN 9781510703179 (ebook)
Subjects: LCSH: Service dogs—Training. | Service dogs.
Classification: LCC HV1569.6 .G73 2020 (print) | LCC HV1569.6 (ebook) | DDC 362.4/048—dc23
LC record available at https://lccn.loc.gov/2019057977
LC ebook record available at https://lccn.loc.gov/2019057978

Cover design by Daniel Brount
Cover photos by Keagen J. Grace and Gettyimages

Print ISBN: 978-1-5107-0316-2
Ebook ISBN: 978-1-5107-0317-9

Printed in China

CONTENTS

INTRODUCTION

The service dog community is a diverse and eclectic collection of groups, individuals, and resources. Beginning with supporters, like donors, veterinarians, fund-raisers, breeders, and anyone who loves a service dog team, and progressing through programs, trainers, handlers, and puppy raisers, each facet of the community intertwines with the others.

Breeding, selecting, training, and owning a service dog, if diagrammed, would look more like a web as opposed to a straight line.

In the middle, there's the service dog, and woven throughout are the various pieces that go into the making of a good one. Some of them are linked (like puppy raisers, recipients, and formal training programs), whereas others, like breeders or suppliers, are connected only to the service dog.

Here's the fun thing: no matter where on the web you may fall, you share one thing with every other group, individual, or resource also on the web, and that's a passion for service dogs. Whether you value the freedom offered to a disabled individual, love a service dog yourself, or you're seeking state-of-the-art training methods for your organization, in some way, your enthusiasm for these unique and special canines is unmistakably clear.

Here's the other important thing to keep in mind: regardless of your position on the web, this book was written for you. If you are in any way connected to the service dog community, you'll find value in *The Ultimate Service Dog Training Manual.*

Some will find the most use out of the detailed training breakdown, whereas others will be more interested in the legalities and logistics of service dog ownership. Breeders or veterinarians who provide service dog programs or handlers will likely gravitate to the genetics, temperament, health, and trainers' sections, while programs and puppy raisers may find themselves returning to the book over and over to reference or research various aspects of the community.

Whether you're mostly interested in specific topics or you intend to read it cover to cover, please take a few minutes to review the organization scheme, features, and suggested use of this book. While you're certainly welcome to just dive right in, in order to get the most benefit from *The Ultimate Service Dog Training Manual*, you'll need to understand why the book is laid out the way it is and how to find the information you're seeking.

PROGRAMS

Formal organizations, groups, or teams specializing in the selection, upbringing, training, and placement of fully trained or started service dogs. Will receive the most benefit from the Selection, Training, and Socialization sections (pages 81, 129, and 136).

TRAINERS

Active, practicing, aspiring, or interested trainers of service dogs or service dog candidates. May or may not function as part of a program's staff. Will receive the most benefit from Training (page 129) and Socialization (page 136) sections.

OWNER-TRAINERS

Disabled individuals who aren't professional trainers or staff members of an organization who are planning to self-train working service dogs. Will receive the most benefit from the Legalities (page 19), Selection (page 81), Training (page 129), Socialization (page 139), and Logs (page 131) sections.

RECIPIENTS/OWNERS/HANDLERS

Everyone who receives a fully trained service dog from a program or trainer. Will receive the most benefit from the Overview (page 1), Training (page 129), and Care (page 199) sections.

PUPPY RAISERS

Volunteers or staff members who are raising service dog candidates for programs or trainers. Will receive the most benefit from the Socialization (page 136), Care (page 199), and Log (page 131) sections.

SUPPORTERS

Individuals, groups, organizations, teams, or companies who tangibly or intangibly provide support to any part of the service dog community. The most beneficial sections will vary depending on the type of supporter. Please see the table of contents or the index for specific topics.

1

SERVICE DOG OVERVIEW

SERVICE DOG BASICS

Service and working dogs have a lot of responsibility on their shoulders—they do extremely specialized, important work on a daily basis. Depending on each handler and their unique disability, the service dog could be the only thing able to protect them or even prevent them from death or injury. For these reasons, the training of any service or working dog is of utmost importance. The manners, behavior, and skills of any service dog should be above reproach, because at some point it may be necessary for strangers to direct the dog until the handler is able to resume management of the service dog. The dog's training should make that easy for anyone to do, without specialized knowledge.

An important note is that a service dog's training must mitigate their handler's disability. There are hundreds of tasks service dogs can perform. Federal law dictates, though, that the dog must perform trained task work that directly assists their handler. Merely having a disability and having a dog doesn't make a dog a service dog.

As an example, if a dog is trained to open doors, but the handler doesn't actually *need* the task, then that doesn't qualify as trained task work that mitigates the handler's disability. That's not to say that your dog can't perform work you don't actually *need*, as you and your dog should continue training and learning for a lifetime, but rather, that your dog *must*, in some form or fashion, directly increase your ability to function in day-to-day life through their training.

Chief considerations for any service dog are keeping your dog happy, healthy, and able to work for as long as possible. You should feed your partner the best food you can afford. Talk to your veterinarian about selecting a food. The better the food you can feed, the better your partner's nutrition, and the better they'll be overall. Health starts on the inside and is reflected by your dog's skin, coat, ear/eye health, weight, body composition, and many other factors. Most canine nutritionists recommend feeding a food with healthy ingredients and quality protein high in the ingredients list.

Don't feed your dog too much or too little—both create unhealthy conditions. A brace dog that carries too much weight, even if it's just a pound or two, has extra strain on their joints, which decreases their working life and ability to work safely. A mobility support dog that is underweight doesn't have the musculature to support the extremely physical nature of their task work and may be nutritionally deficient in a way that leaches nutrients from their bones, further increasing the risk of injury.

Any working dog should be kept lean, with good muscle tone. You should be able to see a clearly defined waist, but not be able to see hip bones, spine, or ribs. When you run your hands along your dog's ribs, it should feel like the back of your hand—bone structure readily able to be felt. If you see ribs, up your dog's food for a bit. If you have to push to feel ribs, decrease your dog's food for a bit. Your veterinarian can help direct this.

Brace and mobility support dogs specifically should be kept on a joint supplement, as their task work can be very physically taxing, and anything you can do to help keep their joints healthy is a plus. An excellent and economical choice is Nature's Farmacy's Phyto-Flex. A little bit of this stuff goes a long way, and it's much less expensive than many commercially available products or products available directly through your vet.

Preventative health care is strongly recommended. Your partner should be on monthly parasite prevention, including flea, tick, and heartworm preventatives. Keeping your partner free of fleas and ticks is necessary for public access, and your partner shouldn't work if they have internal parasites, as it can weaken them. Heartworm preventative is strongly recommended for most areas of the country, and regular worming as well to handle other internal parasites, such as tapeworms.

Your service dog must have the federally required rabies and DHPP vaccination, and you should be able to produce proof of this at any time. Working dogs are exposed to far more environments, animals, and potential health threats than household pets, and therefore also have more potential for them to bring illnesses into many more areas. Vaccines should be done in accordance with American Animal Hospital Association (AAHA) guidelines.

Keep in mind that while you can do your utmost to keep your partner healthy, other people may not do the same for their dogs, and working service dogs can come into contact with other dogs at any time, and/or be in areas where sick dogs have been previously, without the knowledge of their handler.

Make sure your dog has time to relax, play, recuperate from work, and just be a dog. You can enjoy a game of fetch or tug, snuggle while watching a movie, take up trick training for fun, or basically anything that gives your partner's mind and body a chance to rest.

Essentially, do all you can to keep your partner happy and healthy. Don't do anything to jeopardize their ability to work, or do anything that might injure them, even inadvertently. Service dogs are incredible, hardworking creatures, and they deserve all the best you can give them and more.

Things Handlers Want You to Know

Many people have a vague sense of awareness that service dogs "help" their person and that they're allowed to be in public, but there's a lot more to their handlers and teams than meets the eye. To help fill in the holes, here are the top ten things service dog handlers want every member of the public to know and understand.

1. My Service Dog Is Working

When you see my partner and me out and about in public, please understand that they're doing vital work for me, even if they don't "look like" they're working to you. Just like when you're working, they just want (and need) to be left alone to do their job. Please don't distract my service dog from their job by yelling at them, talking to them, using baby talk at them, touching them, touching their equipment, whistling at them, barking at them, or otherwise doing anything except politely ignoring them.

2. My Service Dog Is My Lifeline

Depending on my disability, my service dog may be the only thing standing between me and death. My dog is my lifeline and means the world to me. Please don't distract them from doing their job or tasks, because my life, health, and peace of mind, rests in their paws. If my service dog is distracted and isn't able to respond appropriately, it's possible I could become ill or injured. Please just ignore them entirely and let them focus on the job, which is keeping me safe.

3. My Medical History Is Private

Please don't ask me about my diagnosis, try to guess the reason I have a service dog, or ask me to disclose my private medical history. Oftentimes, disabilities are "invisible," meaning they aren't visually discernable to members of the general public. However, not being able to see my disability doesn't mean you should ask. Making inquiries about my personal information is not only uncalled for, it can feel very hurtful and invasive.

4. I Don't Always Want to Answer Questions

My service dog has made a huge difference in my life, but sometimes, I want to run a quick errand and go home, just like you. Please keep in mind that almost every person who sees me out in public with my service dog wants to ask me about their job, their purpose, their name, their breed, where they were trained, what they do, how old they are, and a plethora of other questions. Please don't be offended if I answer your questions quickly and move on.

5. Not All Service Dogs Are the Same

Service dogs come in all shapes, sizes, breeds, colors, coat types, and specialties. You cannot identify one by sight alone or by the presence of a vest or other gear. The only reliable way to tell if a service dog is well trained is via their behavior and manners. Unfortunately, fake service dogs are relatively common, and they do a lot of damage to legitimate teams. Please don't judge my obviously well-trained, well-mannered, quiet, well-groomed, highly responsive service dog based on the behavior of a yappy, untrained, or aggressive dog someone once claimed was a "service dog." Behavior tells all, and I ask that you not compare me to any other handlers or teams you may know or may have met, because not all service dogs are the same.

6. My Service Dog Is Loved

Please don't tell me you "feel sorry" for my service dog because they have to work all the time. My service dog is incredibly loved and does in fact enjoy "time off" to just be a dog. My dog does get treats, gets to play, and sometimes, when off duty, they enjoy getting the "zoomies" and running around in massive circles like all other dogs. My service dog is very well taken care of, and better off than most pet dogs because they're well-adjusted, highly trained, and well socialized.

7. My Service Dog Is Medical Equipment

My service dog is medical equipment, just like a wheelchair, crutches, or an oxygen tank. My dog is medically necessary. As such, the law allows them to accompany me in most public places. Generally speaking, if medical equipment and members of the general public are allowed, so is my service dog. Please treat them like medical equipment. You wouldn't walk up to someone you didn't know and start randomly pushing their wheelchair or talk to a little old lady's cane, so please don't touch, talk to, pet, or otherwise engage with my partner.

8. My Service Dog Is Protected under Law

United States federal law protects my service dog's access rights. Federal law allows my service dog and I access to places of public accommodation, like restaurants, businesses, entertainment venues, and most other places people are allowed to congregate, assuming the presence of my dog doesn't fundamentally alter the way the business operates. The only times my service dog could be excluded from a public place is if they are not housetrained or are out of control and

I'm not doing anything about it, and neither of those should ever be an issue. Certain venues where my dog could either be in danger or cause a significant change to daily activities or operations may exclude access or impose additional access requirements.

Common examples of such venues include zoos, tattoo parlors, amusement parks, laboratories, and similar places. A dog, even a well-trained dog, can distress some species of zoo animals to the point they become ill. The presence of a dog or dog hair may cause variations in laboratory results or experiments, though the general public is typically not allowed in this setting, either. Dog hair and bacteria common to canids might create a severe health hazard in a tattoo parlor.

9. There Is No Certification Required

There are no papers, documentation, ID, certification, or other required information of any kind for me to have my partner in public with me. Not only is there no documentation necessary, but it's illegal to ask for any. If you're a business owner and you're not certain my partner is a service dog, then you may only ask two questions: if my partner is a service dog, and what work my partner does for me. That's all—you cannot ask for my private medical information, request paperwork, or anything else. The legalities of this are discussed further on page 19.

10. I'd Rather Not Have a Service Dog

Please don't tell me you'd "like to have a service dog." In order to have a service dog, you must be disabled as defined by US federal law. Every time you say, "I wish I had a service dog," you're saying, "I wish I faced the same challenges you do!"

Also, please don't tell me you "wish your dog could go everywhere with you." Again, that requires so much more than you think it does, not the least of which is thousands of hours of training and socialization. It's not easy, and, while my partner is completely worth it, I'd rather not need her.

The Path to Becoming a Service Dog

Have you ever looked at a service or guide dog working in public and thought, *Wow! I wonder how they're so well behaved! My dogs won't even come when I call them!*

Here's a little secret: that dog was taught manners, basic obedience, and public access behaviors by someone who could be anyone. Not a dog trainer. Not a professional. Just someone who wants to help others, who loves the service dog cause, and who wants to give back to the community.

It's oft said in the service dog community that in the chest of every service dog beats the heart of a puppy raiser. Service dogs would not be possible without the hard work of all the volunteers who bravely offer their homes, hearts, lives, and time to a dog who will one day make a difference in the life of someone with a disability. You see, service dogs can't be raised and raised well in a kennel environment. In order to become service dogs, they have to be extremely stable, calm, and focused while in public, and the only way to do that is to have them in public from a very young age. They also need exposure to a home environment, which just isn't possible from a kennel facility.

The training that you actively see from working service dogs is actually just the tip of the iceberg. They have beautiful obedience, perform life-changing tasks for their handlers, and they're dedicated workers. What you don't see is the foundation—the hundreds and hundreds of hours of careful socialization and reinforcement for relaxed interaction with the world around them. All that foundation work is provided in the home and by the hands of a volunteer puppy raiser.

While puppy raising is a huge part of becoming a service dog, it's not the only piece. There are several stages to taking a brand-new ball of eight-week-old fluff from "blank slate" to "fully trained assistance dog." Puppies usually spend fourteen to eighteen months with their puppy raiser before returning to their program for evaluation and an additional three to nine months of dedicated task training. During task training, service and guide dogs learn the invaluable skills that will allow them to help someone who needs them, and then polish the basic training they learned as babies.

Every service and guide dog program has a distinct set of policies, guidelines, and protocols in place for selecting, raising, and training dogs placed through their organization. Some programs, like Guide Dogs for the Blind and OccuPaws, have an in-house breeding program. That means that the puppies and dogs in their program were bred by the program to be service or guide dogs.

Organizations that have in-house breeding programs carefully select parents who have the characteristics that make good service dogs—they're calm, tranquil, and relaxed. They're focused on their trainer or partner, but not to the point of it being overbearing. They're responsive and easy to train, but not over the top about food, toys, or rewards. They have excellent health, structure, and genetics.

Most organizations with breeding programs use "guardian homes" for their breeding stock. The dogs they're going to breed aren't placed as service dogs in the field, and they instead live with someone local to the program who loves them, trains them, and provides for their needs. When the program needs the male or female in question, the guardian home brings the dog to the facility or vet for breeding, and once breeding is done, the dog goes home to their guardians. In the case of momma dogs, they will oftentimes remain with the program until the litter is whelped, weaned, and placed.

Once the litter is born, and it's certain everyone is healthy and happy, many programs use a technique called "early neurological stimulation" to provide the puppies with safe and structured exposure to all kinds of sounds, surfaces, tactile input, touches, and experiences. Early neurological stimulation is also known as "bio sensor" or the "super dog" program.

Dr. Carmen L. Battaglia, a researcher and specialist in canine genetics and development, notes several benefits of ENS, including more tolerance to stress, greater resistance to disease, and better performance in simple problem-solving tests. There are other programs commonly used to provide very young service dog candidates with a solid base to help set them up for success, one of the more widely known and successful of which is called "Puppy Culture."

Puppies are evaluated constantly so that the program can best place them with a suitable puppy raiser. The program monitors activity level, learning style, and many other factors. In general, puppies go to their puppy raiser around eight to ten weeks of age, and they usually remain with the puppy raiser until they're fourteen to eighteen months of age.

Quality programs provide excellent support for their puppy raisers. Most require the puppy raiser to attend training classes and specific outings with their puppy. Commonly, they provide written material and guidelines, videos, or other information to help make raising a puppy easier. Oftentimes, there are program-affiliated clubs in the area so everyone who is raising a puppy can work together.

Puppy raisers are responsible for their puppy's upbringing, care, socialization, and training, unless otherwise noted by their program director. They house and crate train the puppy, get them used to training equipment, and transport the puppy to events, outings, veterinary appointments, evaluations, or anywhere else the puppy needs to go. Once the puppy can safely do so and has the proper skills, service and guide dog puppies in training go everywhere with their raiser—school, work, restaurants, movies, the mall, bookstores, etc.

If you do not work or study from home, your puppy will likely be able to go to work with you after a certain point of training, as long as you do not work in a sterile or high-risk environment. Most programs help you secure permission and formulate a plan to make bringing a puppy to work or school a smooth process.

While some programs will provide all the puppy's equipment, food, veterinary care, toys, gear, or anything else the puppy needs, some require the puppy raiser to pay for everything out of pocket. Good news, though—any money spent on a service or guide dog in training will likely be tax deductible! Make sure to keep good records and to keep all your receipts, if your program doesn't provide for everything.

It's very important to carefully follow the rules and guidelines of your program. Don't tell yourself, "Oh, it's just this one time; it won't matter," or "That's such a small thing! Surely it isn't important!" Service dogs, assistance dogs, and guide dogs aren't like other dogs. They must be free of temperament flaws, bad manners, and little habits that wouldn't matter in a pet. Something that doesn't seem so big to you could mean your puppy is career changed or unable to become a service dog.

For example, many people think it's funny to let their dogs chase laser pointers, but playing games with lights or laser pointers is expressly forbidden by most major assistance dog organizations. It can create a form of obsessive-compulsive disorder that can't be untrained, and it often results in the dog getting hyperstimulated or over-aroused by common things in the environment.

Many behaviors, tendencies, and traits can exclude a puppy from graduating from the program. A puppy who barks, growls, grumbles, whines, or vocalizes in public may not be able to become a service dog, though some behavioral issues can certainly be worked on. A puppy who learns to alarm bark likely won't graduate. A puppy who becomes overly excited about balls or toys may not successfully become a service dog. If a puppy in training is fearful, shy, timid, or scared of something and the issue can't be fixed, then the puppy in question probably isn't suitable as an assistance dog.

When it comes to shaping a service dog in training's behavior, most programs and trainers prioritize calmness, relaxation, and focus above all else.

People are sometimes concerned about the length of time puppies stay with their host family. Fourteen to eighteen months is a long time, after all. However, don't let the time commitment put you off helping to raise a service or guide dog in training. Puppy sitters keep a puppy for very short periods of time. Sometimes they have a puppy for a few hours (such as when a student has an exam they must focus on or a doctor's appointment the puppy isn't ready to attend), for a few days (perhaps the puppy raisers are going on an out-of-state or international trip), or for a few weeks (like during a puppy swap, which is where puppies are rotated to different handlers so they get used to working with others).

Puppy sitters are just as important as puppy raisers, and short-term raising of a service dog in training is oftentimes a great place to start! It allows you to get the training required to be a puppy raiser out of the way, gain some experience, and see if raising a puppy is for you and your family, without the year-and-a-half time commitment.

Other volunteer positions related to training assistance dog puppies include puppy drivers, puppy socializers, or weekend puppy parents. Puppy drivers take puppies to appointments, puppy socializers come and hang out with program puppies or play games with them, and weekend puppy parents take dogs who are in advanced training home for the weekend so that they retain their house manners and get some non-public-access time out of the training facility. It's important to note that not every program has part-time raising or volunteer positions, but it never hurts to ask!

Every organization has a different system and set of requirements for deciding when a puppy is ready to return to the program for advanced task training. Your program will communicate with you and make expectations clear. Typically, a puppy in training will exhibit calm, relaxed behavior in public, be responsive to basic obedience commands, and be mature enough to handle the intensity of advanced training. Some organizations have puppy raisers assist with some foundation skills like nudging drawers with their nose or hitting a touch lamp with their foot. Other programs do not allow puppy raisers to teach any skills related to future task training.

Many programs have specific milestones for training that puppies should achieve throughout basic training Others use an extensive set of field evaluations and tests, and still others make the decision regarding returning for the next training phase based on other factors.

Regardless of how it's decided that your puppy is ready to begin advanced training, when it's time for them to go, it's always hard. It's difficult to pour thousands of hours of love, time, companionship, and effort into such an amazing creature, and then have to give them up. However, the puppy that you've put so much heart and soul into will, hopefully, go on to give someone their independence, their freedom, their life back. These incredible working dogs make a huge difference to those they're partnered with, but without puppy raisers, it wouldn't be possible. So yes, you can expect the tears, but what you usually don't expect is that they're oftentimes just as much tears of joy and pride as they are sorrow.

Puppies who have returned to their host program spend several months undergoing formal training to be a service dog, assistance dog, or guide dog. There are dozens of potential tasks a service dog could learn, and guide dogs undergo some of the most rigorous training processes in the canine world. After they complete their advanced training, they are then partnered with a person who needs them. Both the new partner and the newly graduated service or guide dog undergo program-guided training so that they learn to function as a team.

When all is said and done, it takes approximately two years of hard, dedicated work to properly raise and train an assistance animal, regardless of what type of work the dog does. Make no mistake—it's not easy to train service dogs, but there's nothing like the satisfaction of knowing you had a hand in giving someone with a disability the opportunity to live their life to the fullest.

BASIC STANDARDS OVERVIEW

There are a few schools around the country that train service dog trainers. Most are small and began with experienced dog trainers (some began with training military working dogs, police dogs, or other working dogs) who moved into training service dogs for disabled individuals and then decided to help train trainers too. Bergin University offers extensive pre- and postgraduate coursework in training service dogs and assistance animals. Many well-known training programs around the country, including Canine Companions for Independence and Guide Dogs for the Blind, offer intensive apprenticeship programs.

Two more great resources for fledging dog trainers are the Association of Professional Dog Trainers (ADPT) and the Certification Council for Professional Dog Trainers (CCPDT). These organizations provide science-centric continuing education and evaluations for professional dog trainers.

There is no state or federally recognized certification for any type of dog trainer, including service dog trainers. Many schools and trainers offer apprenticeships so they can train new trainers. Those training programs may "certify" that they have passed their training course once they graduate.

The service dog community has come up with minimum training standards that most trainers follow. Assistance Dogs International and the International Guide Dog Federation are internationally recognized private organizations, and the small handful of organizations who have earned their prestigious accreditation are the gold standard of service dog training. Unfortunately, those programs aren't capable of supplying service dogs for every disabled individual. Without other private organizations and trainers, many disabled individuals would be denied service dogs.

About Service Dogs and the ADA

The Americans with Disabilities Act is written to allow disabled individuals to use their service dogs in public with as few barriers as possible. If access were not as open, every building, restaurant, and dry cleaner in the country could stop disabled individuals with their service dogs and demand proof of training. The ADA specifically states that if someone says their dog is a service dog they are to be taken at their word, regardless if it has been certified by a state or other authority.

The ADA states in section § 35.136 Service animals part (f) "A public entity shall not require documentation, such as proof that the animal has been certified, trained, or licensed as a Service animal."

The ADA is also laid out so that disabled individuals may train their own service dogs. Program-trained dogs can be very expensive—some may cost more than $10,000. It eliminates animals other than dogs and miniature horses and officially includes psychiatric service dogs which can help with severe depression and post-traumatic stress disorder (PTSD). In this case, though, access is contingent on the dog being trained in specific tasks to help mitigate the handler's disability; emotional support or comfort wouldn't qualify.

SERVICE DOG HISTORY

Humans have used working dogs for millennia, but it's only recently, within the last hundred years or so, that trained dogs have been used specifically to help individuals with disabilities. Dogs and humans have served as partners from the very beginning of time, though, starting with a symbiotic relationship between the earliest humans and wolves. The humans tossed scraps to the wolves, and, in turn, the wolves gradually drifted closer and closer to camp and helped sound the alarm when intruders were near. Eventually, the humans and wolves started hunting together, and their relationship deepened.

With time, dogs and humans developed a bond, and the first domesticated dog breeds started to emerge. Many of these creatures were still distinctly wolf-looking with prick ears, long muzzles, and very keen senses, but they helped pull heavy loads, keep livestock safe, and catch prey. Hound breeds came along next, starting with the long and lean racing hounds, and then as hound breeds started to diversify, the domesticated dog was well on its way toward no longer being "wild." The historical process of domestication and of specification (the process of breeding dogs specifically for certain looks and purposes) is complex, but fascinating.

After a natural alliance started to form between dogs and humans, and once humans started to breed dogs for specific purposes, it was only a matter of time before humans began to use dogs for work other than drafting, herding, and hunting. It's not exactly known when, exactly, dogs first started to perform service work for humans, although it's been speculated that it happened at some point early in building the relationship between humans and dogs. The History Channel did an exposé on the history of service dogs, and Jennie Cohen, the author of their online piece, "Assistance Dogs: Learning New Tricks For Centuries," notes that "the earliest evidence of such partnerships—a fresco in which a blind man is led by his dog, discovered amid the ruins of the ancient Roman city Herculaneum—dates back to the first century AD. European wood carvings and Chinese scroll paintings from the Middle Ages depict similar scenes."

Even earlier than that, a grave was unearthed around Pompeii containing the bones of a human and a dog together, along with a mural of a clearly blind man being escorted by a dog. That was around AD 79, and even though there's no doubt that individuals were somehow managing to get their dogs to help them with various disabilities, there was no systematic training process or widespread use yet.

At some point in the early 1300s, dogs were employed in ancient France as civil patrol partners. The dogs were partnered with specialized officers, and they patrolled the perimeter of the city of Saint Malo. No one knows precisely when this practice started, only that the canine patrols ceased in 1770 due to the death of a naval officer. This is one of the first recorded instances of dogs and humans partnering together, outside of hunting, herding, and drafting, to achieve better results than either canine or human could obtain on their own. There's no doubt dogs were used as guards and alarms long before this, but the French civil patrols provided specialized training to their dogs and officers, which is what sets this instance apart.

In the mid-to-late 1700s, a hospital in Paris began attempting to use dogs to help visually impaired individuals. While these dogs were not precisely "guide dogs," this was, nevertheless, the first systematic attempt to partner dogs with disabled humans so that the result would be increased independence or function. A few years later, a blind Austrian, Josef Riesinger, trained a Spitz-type dog to such high levels of guide work that people questioned whether or not Riesinger was actually disabled!

In 1819, the founder of the Vienna Institute For the Education of the Blind, Johann Wilhelm Klein, published a textbook that described and documented his methodologies for training guide dogs, which included the use of a rigid leash that provided feedback to the person on the other end and suggested that poodles and shepherds were the best breeds to use.

Throughout the 1800s, there were many documented attempts of people or organizations training guide dogs, particularly in Europe. However, it wasn't until the early 1900s that the modern-day guide dog, and thus service dog, movement actually kicked off. After World War I, thousands of soldiers were returning home from battle blinded, deaf, or otherwise severely injured. Blindness was one of the most common injuries, however, due to the widespread and crude deployments of poison gas.

In a post–World War I hospital, a German doctor, Dr. Gerhard Stalling, left a patient with his personal dog for a bit while he was attending to an errand, and upon his return, he noticed that the patient was far calmer, more relaxed, and more willing to comply with treatment and therapy. It was then that Dr. Stalling decided to test the idea of partnering the wounded soldiers en masse with specially trained guide dogs. He sourced his dogs from the hundreds of collies who had been trained to search for wounded soldiers and to serve as messengers for the ambulance and medical services.

While Dr. Stalling wasn't a dog trainer by trade or profession, he nevertheless began exploring means to produce functional guide dogs and, in 1816, established the first guide dog school. Based in Oldenburg, Germany, the school rapidly grew and soon had branches in nine other European cities. The school began turning out guide dogs to the tune of six hundred dogs a year, and within a short time, they were placing dogs not only in Europe but also in the United States, Canada, and the Soviet Union.

Dr. Stalling's school for guide dogs closed in 1926, but, by this time, other schools had opened and, using new and cutting-edge training techniques, were producing full-fledged guide dogs. Some of their work in training development and guide dog methodology is still used to this day, and the foundation they provided the guide dog training world proved invaluable as the service dog movement progressed. In 1926 to 1927, a wealthy American, Dorothy Eustis, traveled to Europe to spend several months studying the methods and training programs practiced by the training centers, and in October 1927, she wrote a widely circulated piece published in the *Saturday Evening Post* on what she had learned, observed, and seen at the European schools for guide dogs.

The article attracted the attention of a blind American named Morris Frank, who was quite excited about what he'd read. He reached out to Dorothy and told her he wanted to play a part in introducing these wonderful dogs to America. Dorothy was on board with the idea, and she trained her very first guide dog, Kiss, who was later renamed Buddy, for Morris. Morris and Buddy were believed to be the first American guide dog team.

In 1929, Morris and Dorothy founded the first American guide dog organization, The Seeing Eye, Inc. This school is one of the only modern guide dog training organizations in the world to have stood the test of time, and it is the longest continuously operating guide dog school in the world that is still training guide dogs today. By 1931, Dorothy had trained four guide dog instructors, two of which began working at the New Jersey-based Seeing Eye school. The other two instructors traveled to the European and British branches of The Seeing Eye, which was only one of many guide dog schools in Europe by this point.

In 1934, the Guide Dogs for the Blind Association, or the GDBA, was established.

In 1971, while she was traveling and working in the Middle East, Dr. Bonita "Bonnie" Bergin discovered that dogs could be trained to help people with disabilities other than blindness. In 1975, she brought the concept of service dogs as we know it today back to the United States. She founded the nonprofit organization Canine Companions for Independence to train and partner mobility assistance dogs, and now Canine Companions is the largest provider of service and assistance dogs in the United States. She conducted a vast amount of research on and related to the service dog field, which left the service dog world with knowledge on selecting potential candidates, evaluating them for success, partnering them with a disabled handler, and so much more.

Furthermore, Dr. Bergin went on to play in instrumental part in establishing Assistance Dogs International, or ADI, based on the belief that organizations who train assistance dogs of any kind, including service, guide, and hearing dogs, should have a platform from which they could communicate, share ideas, and come together. ADI, founded in 1987, provides standards, codes of ethics, and a benchmark for assistance dog programs of all kinds, all over the world. They also maintain a huge bank of resources and knowledge available for those in the service dog community.

Bergin also is responsible for founding several other service dog–related organizations, including one that works to provide grants for low-income individuals to get service dogs (the Assistance

Dog United Campaign) and another (the International Association of Assistance Dog Partners) that provides many benefits to working service and guide dog teams, including vouchers for routine health care and other needs.

She was asked by the US Department of Justice to assist them with the Americans with Disabilities Act (ADA), and in 1990, service dog laws as we know them came into being. When partnered with an individual with a disability, specially trained dogs were now able to accompany their handler anywhere members of the general public could go. The ADA was a huge step forward for disabled individuals, and there's no doubt in the world that Dr. Bergin was a pioneer in establishing the modern-day service dog movement in America.

Prior to the ADA, though, there was the Air Carrier Access Act of 1986, which granted access to all commercial airline carriers and planes to individuals with disabilities who travel with service dogs, and the Fair Housing Amendments Act of 1988, which prohibited housing discrimination based solely on a person's disability, including the presence or lack thereof of a service animal.

In 2009, International Assistance Dog Week was created to celebrate the incredible and near-magical work assistance dogs do, and to bring to light the way in which these special and highly trained dogs bring independence and peace of mind to their handlers and their communities. In 2010, the Americans with Disabilities Act was rewritten to further define "Service Animal" and to answer questions about their access, and those changes were enacted in March 2011.

Service dogs as we know them today didn't just happen—they're the result of tireless toil and work on the part of hundreds, if not thousands, of people, many of whose names have been lost to history. From the beginning of time, dogs have partnered with humans, but it's only recently they've actually worked to improve the lives of people with disabilities other than visual impairment.

Today, there are more than ten thousand guide dog teams in North America alone. There are thousands of other types of service dog teams, including medical assistance dogs, seizure assistance dogs, diabetic alert dogs, mobility support dogs, allergen alert dogs, psychiatric service dogs, and autism assistance dogs. There is no central registry or census of the service dog community, so no exact numbers can be provided.

History is still being written, and anyone currently in the service dog community is part of it. There's so much room for this field to grow and flourish, which is why it's especially important to always serve as an ambassador and to uphold high standards of behavior and training. What we do today affects the working dog teams of tomorrow.

SERVICE DOG LEGALITIES

North America

Every state in the United States determines its own service dog law and team access rights. Generally, whichever version of the law (federal or state) is most accommodating, with the most benefits or rights conferred, is used in any given state. However, regardless of what state law says, federal law and disability access rights trump it. Some states further regulate service dog teams and their access rights on the county or city level.

Assistance Dogs International (ADI) has a wonderful resource published that summarizes all laws pertinent to service dogs and arranges them alphabetically. It can be accessed online, downloaded and printed, or ordered and delivered to you, all via their website. You should always check the laws of any state you'll be residing in or traveling through, just so you're familiar. It's also important to note that different states bestow different access rights to service dogs in training. Some states grant them full access as if they were full-fledged service dogs, some specifically mention that they're welcome only with the permission of the business owner, and others don't mention them at all. Federal law does not mention service dogs in training, so state law should always be checked.

Federal

Most working and service dog handlers and trainers understand that federal law provides protection and access for service dogs in the United States. Still, it can be challenging to truly grasp all of it.

Before we jump feetfirst into murky legal waters, we need to lay out a few vital definitions and clarify some points. First and foremost, federal service dog law and state service dog law are very, very, different and it's vital that you know how the laws vary in your state, county, city, or town.

Federal service dog law applies all over the country and is the universally accepted standard in the United States. State service dog law may offer further clarification, add additional requirements, or outline expectations for various types of working/service dogs or for dogs in training. It is generally accepted that whichever law provides the most freedom for a disabled individual with a service dog in any given state is the one teams will abide by.

Next, there are several pieces of federal service dog law strewn throughout the legal system. In this section, we'll be referring to the Code of Federal Regulations (CFR). Other important service dog laws are contained in the Americans with Disabilities Act (ADA), Fair Housing Amendments Act (FHAA), and the Air Carrier Access Act (ACAA). We'll be addressing those at a future time. Here's a chart, though, that breaks down each resource and what it's good for:

	What Is It?	**Why Do We Care?**
CFR	Code of Federal Regulations (US federal law)	Provides the fundamentals of federal service dog law
ADA	Americans with Disabilities Act (A civil rights law)	Bestows public access rights to disabled individuals with a service animal
FHAA	Fair Housing Amendments Act (A civil rights law amendment)	Extends ADA protection to disabled individuals with service animals who are seeking housing in the public sector
ACAA	Air Carrier Access Act (Specific section of the CFR)	Ensures access to air transportation on all carriers for all individuals with service animals

C.F.R. § 36.202

C.F.R. § 36.202 - NONDISCRIMINATION ON THE BASIS OF DISABILITY BY PUBLIC ACCOMMODATIONS AND IN COMMERCIAL FACILITIES

Definitions for C.F.R. § 36.202 are provided by the ADA.

Accessible: Refers to a site, facility, work environment, service, or program that is easy to approach, enter, operate, participate in, and/or use safely and with dignity by a person with a disability.
Major Life Activity: Refers to activities that an average person can perform with little or no difficulty.
Person/Individuals with disability: (1) has a physical or mental impairment that substantially limits one or more major life activities; OR (2) has a record of such an impairment; OR (3) is regarded as having such an impairment.
Physical Impairment: Any physiological disorder or condition, cosmetic disfigurement, or anatomical loss affecting one or more of the following body systems: neurological, musculoskeletal, special sense organs, respiratory (including speech organs), cardiovascular, reproductive, digestive, genitourinary, hemic and lymphatic, skin, and endocrine.
Public Accommodation: Facilities whose operations affect commerce and fall within at least one of the following 12 categories: places of lodging (e.g., inns, hotels, motels except for owner-occupied establishments renting fewer than six rooms); establishments serving food or drink (e.g., restaurants and bars); places of exhibition or entertainment (e.g., movie theaters, theaters, concert halls, stadiums); places of public gathering (e.g., auditoriums, convention centers, lecture halls); sales or rental establishments (e.g., bakeries, grocery stores, hardware stores, shopping centers); service establishments (e.g., laundromats, dry-cleaners, banks, barber shops, beauty shops, travel services, shoe repair services, funeral parlors, gas stations, offices of accountants or lawyers, pharmacies, insurance offices, professional offices of health care providers, hospitals); public transportation terminals, depots, or stations (not including facilities relating to air

transportation); places of public display or collection (e.g., museums, libraries, galleries); places of recreation (e.g., parks, zoos, amusement parks); places of education (e.g., nursery schools, elementary, secondary, undergraduate, or postgraduate private schools); social service center establishments (e.g., day care centers, senior citizen centers, homeless shelters, food banks, adoption agencies); and places of exercise or recreation (e.g., gymnasiums, health spas, bowling alleys, golf courses).

Service animal: Any dog that is individually trained to do work or perform tasks for the benefit of an individual with a disability, including a physical, sensory, psychiatric, intellectual, or other mental disability.

Public Accommodations Shall Provide Access

(a) General. A public accommodation shall make reasonable modifications in policies, practices, or procedures, when the modifications are necessary to afford goods, services, facilities, privileges, advantages, or accommodations to individuals with disabilities, unless the public accommodation can demonstrate that making the modifications would fundamentally alter the nature of the goods, services, facilities, privileges, advantages, or accommodations.

According to the ADA, a "public accommodation" is any private entity that operates with the intent of allowing members of the public access for the purpose of business, entertainment, education, receipt of services or any other purpose. Most places a service dog team will visit or need access to are "public accommodations." So, the opening paragraph of federal service dog law states, pretty clearly, that public accommodations must allow an individual with a disability access with a service dog (or any other piece of equipment that mitigates their disability), as long as the service dog won't disturb the actual (not perceived) ability of the public accommodation to continue providing their service.

Referrals Are Acceptable

(b) Specialties—(1) General. A public accommodation may refer an individual with a disability to another public accommodation, if that individual is seeking, or requires, treatment or services outside of the referring public accommodation's area of specialization, and if, in the normal course of its operations, the referring public accommodation would make a similar referral for an individual without a disability who seeks or requires the same treatment or services.

(2) Illustration—medical specialties. A health care provider may refer an individual with a disability to another provider, if that individual is seeking, or requires, treatment or services outside of the referring provider's area of specialization, and if the referring provider would make a similar referral for an individual without a disability who seeks or requires the same treatment or services. A physician who specializes in treating only a particular condition cannot refuse to treat an individual with a disability for that condition but is not required to treat the individual for a different condition.

It is not "discrimination" if a public accommodation refers a service dog handler to another place of business, service, or entertainment if the public accommodation in question cannot provide the treatment/services the individual requests or needs. As an example, if you have a heart condition and you're visiting the kidney doctor, it's not discriminatory for the kidney doctor to refer you to a cardiologist. However, under federal service dog law, if you have a kidney issue, the kidney doctor cannot refuse to treat you because you're disabled or because you have a service dog.

Service Animals Allowed

(c) Service animals—(1) General. Generally, a public accommodation shall modify policies, practices, or procedures to permit the use of a service animal by an individual with a disability.

Public accommodations must allow service dogs who are accompanied by an individual with a disability.

Exclusion of Service Animals

(2) Exceptions. A public accommodation may ask an individual with a disability to remove a service animal from the premises if:

(i) The animal is out of control and the animal's handler does not take effective action to control it; or

(ii) The animal is not housebroken.

(3) If an animal is properly excluded. If a public accommodation properly excludes a service animal under § 36.302(c)(2), it shall give the individual with a disability the opportunity to obtain goods, services, and accommodations without having the service animal on the premises.

If your service dog is out of control (which includes any behavior that infringes on the rights of other customers/clients/visitors/patrons, including sniffing, begging, growling, whining, barking, wandering, jumping, or any other rude behavior) or your service dog is sick or eliminates in public, it's perfectly within a business's right to ask you to remove your partner from the premises.

If a business asks you to remove your service dog because of "out of control" behavior, they must allow you the opportunity to finish whatever it is you came to do without your partner present. Only the dog can be excluded for "out of control" behavior, not the handler as well.

Please note, due to separation of church and law, places of religious worship are not required by law to allow your service dog access.

Service Animal Under Handler's Control

(4) Animal under handler's control. A service animal shall be under the control of its handler. A service animal shall have a harness, leash, or other tether, unless either the handler is unable because of a disability to use a harness, leash, or other tether, or the use of a harness, leash, or other tether would interfere with the service animal's safe, effective performance of work or tasks, in which case the service animal must be otherwise under the handler's control (e.g., voice control, signals, or other effective means).
(5) Care or supervision. A public accommodation is not responsible for the care or supervision of a service animal.

Under US federal law, your service dog must be under your control. Unless your disability prevents you from using a harness, leash or "other tether," like a collar, wheelchair arm, vest, or other working gear, or your partner's job would be impeded by use of a leash, your service dog must be on-leash or otherwise attached to you. If your partner's job requires off-leash work or you are not able to leash your service dog due to your disability, your assistance dog has to be under your direct control with verbal or non-verbal commands/signals. Additionally, you and only you are responsible for your service dog—a business or employee is not required to watch or care for your partner while you're there.

Questions Businesses May and May Not Ask

(6) Inquiries. A public accommodation shall not ask about the nature or extent of a person's disability, but may make two inquiries to determine whether an animal qualifies as a service animal. A public accommodation may ask if the animal is required because of a disability and what work or task the animal has been trained to perform. A public accommodation shall not require documentation, such as proof that the animal has been certified, trained, or licensed as a service animal. Generally, a public accommodation may not make these inquiries about a service animal when it is readily apparent that an animal is trained to do work or perform tasks for an individual with a disability (e.g., the dog is observed guiding an individual who is blind or has low vision, pulling a person's wheelchair, or providing assistance with stability or balance to an individual with an observable mobility disability).

A place of public accommodation can't ask you about your disability, but they may ask the following two questions:

1. If your partner is required because of a disability (NOT "What is your disability?" or "Are you disabled?")
2. What specific, trained tasks your partner performs for you

There is no documentation, paperwork, license, or certification required as proof that a dog is a service dog, and businesses can't require that you produce any documentation. If it's obvious your dog is working as a service dog, under federal law, a public accommodation may not ask you to clarify your partner's purpose further.

Complete Access at No Charge

(7) Access to areas of a public accommodation. Individuals with disabilities shall be permitted to be accompanied by their service animals in all areas of a place of public accommodation where members of the public, program participants, clients, customers, patrons, or invitees, as relevant, are allowed to go.

Anywhere a person without a service dog would be allowed to go within a public accommodation, you're allowed with your partner. Having a service dog does not give you special access to anywhere members of the general public aren't allowed, like the kitchens in a restaurant or an operating room in a hospital.

(8) Surcharges. A public accommodation shall not ask or require an individual with a disability to pay a surcharge, even if people accompanied by pets are required to pay fees, or to comply with other requirements generally not applicable to people without pets. If a public accommodation normally charges individuals for the damage they cause, an individual with a disability may be charged for damage caused by their service animal.

You can't be required to pay a fee to have your assistance dog with you, even if people with pets are required to pay a fee. A public accommodation also can't make up special rules for you and your service dog to follow that people without a four-legged friend wouldn't have to abide by.

If your partner causes damage, however, it's reasonable for a business to charge you to repair the damage. Again, you and only you are responsible for your service dog's conduct, actions, and deportment.

Checkout Aisles

(d) Check-out aisles. A store with check-out aisles shall ensure that an adequate number of accessible check-out aisles are kept open during store hours, or shall otherwise modify its policies and practices, in order to ensure that an equivalent level of convenient service is provided to individuals with disabilities as is provided to others. If only one check-out aisle is accessible, and it is generally used for express service, one way of providing equivalent service is to allow persons with mobility impairments to make all their purchases at that aisle.

Stores are required to have check-out aisles that allow you and your partner to maneuver. If the only check-out aisle that allows you to move through easily with your assistance dog is a specialty one (like for customers with fifteen or fewer products, or card members only), then you must be allowed to use that aisle for all of your purchases, even if you normally wouldn't qualify.

Hotel Reservations

(e)(1) Reservations made by places of lodging. A public accommodation that owns, leases (or leases to), or operates a place of lodging shall, with respect to reservations made by any means, including by telephone, in-person, or through a third party—

(i) Modify its policies, practices, or procedures to ensure that individuals with disabilities can make reservations for accessible guest rooms during the same hours and in the same manner as individuals who do not need accessible rooms;

(ii) Identify and describe accessible features in the hotels and guest rooms offered through its reservations service in enough detail to reasonably permit individuals with disabilities to assess independently whether a given hotel or guest room meets his or her accessibility needs;

(iii) Ensure that accessible guest rooms are held for use by individuals with disabilities until all other guest rooms of that type have been rented and the accessible room requested is the only remaining room of that type;

(iv) Reserve, upon request, accessible guest rooms or specific types of guest rooms and ensure that the guest rooms requested are blocked and removed from all reservations systems; and

(v) Guarantee that the specific accessible guest room reserved through its reservations service is held for the reserving customer, regardless of whether a specific room is held in response to reservations made by others.

(2) Exception. The requirements in paragraphs (iii), (iv), and (v) of this section do not apply to reservations for individual guest rooms

or other units not owned or substantially controlled by the entity that owns, leases, or operates the overall facility.

Any place of nonpermanent lodging (hotel, campground, hostel, etc.) must be certain you can obtain an accessible room as quickly as a guest who doesn't need special accommodations. They must be able and willing to verbally explain the accommodations available so you can be certain any given room meets you and your partner's needs. Rooms that provide accommodations for individuals with disabilities must be held for guests who need accommodation unless all other rooms are filled. Finally, they must ensure that if you reserve a room in any fashion that provides specific accommodation for your disability, the room remains yours. It can't be given away or booked by anyone else for any reason. However, if you book your room with a third-party like Hotwire or Priceline, the hotel doesn't have to honor room accommodations. You must book your room directly with a hotel in order to receive assured accommodations.

There you have it, the CFR federal service dog law in its entirety. That's the base upon which all other service dog laws in the United States are built. The ADA, FHAA, and ACAA expand on the CFR to ensure access to anything not specifically covered under the Code of Federal Regulation, and state service dog laws clarify expectations even further. While it's wordy and difficult to sort through, in general, you may think of a service dog as durable medical equipment, like a wheelchair.

Canada

As America's northern neighbor, Canada sees a lot of Americans coming to visit. While service dog laws in Canada do not exactly mirror American laws, they're close. On a federal level, Canada provides protections to well-behaved service dogs accompanying a person with a disability. However, on the provincial level, service dogs and their access rights are more heavily regulated.

Some provinces, like Ontario, require teams to carry organization-provided ID cards, and others require dogs to come from an organization certified by Assistance Dog International (ADI). Before traveling in Canada, it's best to double check the service dog access laws of any province you'll be traveling to or through. If your partner is a bully breed, definitely check the laws of the province, as well as any regions (like counties) or towns you'll be in or traveling through, as bully breed bans are common throughout the country.

In order to cross the border from the United States to Canada, you'll need to be able to provide proof of a rabies vaccination, either via titer tests or a vaccination certificate. The certificate must be valid for the entire time you'll be in Canada.

Other Regions

When it comes to countries and regions outside of North America, service dog law and access rights can vary widely. It's always important to thoroughly research the laws of any country you're considering visiting, and to ensure that you're working with the most up-to-date version of the laws possible.

Remember, too, that requirements for flying with a service animal on foreign airlines and requirements for actually entering a given country or region (such as the European Union) can be quite stringent. Allowances may not always be made for in-cabin travel with a service animal, depending on the airline or country. If in-cabin travel is allowed, there may be a fee, and/or additional guidelines concerning vaccinations, microchipping, other health care and documentation of training or program completion. Lots of countries and international airlines require a dog to have graduated from an organization certified by Assistance Dogs International (ADI), and to possess a card or certificate from the organization, before they will acknowledge a dog as a service animal.

Once you've left the land side part of an airport and clear security with a ticket for another country, US service dog access laws no longer apply, and you will have to abide by the regulations and requirements of whatever country you're traveling to and/or connecting through.

Always thoroughly research the laws of any country you may consider visiting, and do so with lots of time before travel—some countries require documentation to begin months ahead of time.

Keep in mind that laws can change without notice, so any laws or guidelines printed below may not still be accurate. Always, always, always double check.

Europe

Regulations for travel with a service animal through and to Europe are mandated and upheld by the European Parliament. While each individual country in the European Union may have different laws and regulations in place, as a whole, laws for entering any EU country generally mirrors these requirements:

1. The dog must have an ISO microchip. ISO microchips are international standard chips, and while most countries in the world use only ISO chips, the United States is not one of them. ISO chips have a fifteen-digit chip number. If your dog has a microchip that has a ten-digit chip number (usually HomeAgain, Digital Angel, or FriendChip chips), then your dog will need to be chipped again with an ISO chip. An alternative to chipping your dog again is to travel with a scanner that can read your dog's chip.
2. Your dog must have a current rabies vaccination that was given at least four months prior to travel to the EU. Additionally, your dog needs a rabies titer test that shows results correlating to rabies immunity that was taken at least six months prior to the date of entry to the EU.
3. Your dog must have other routine vaccinations up to date, including DHPP.
4. Your dog must be treated for tapeworms no more than ten days prior to your entry to the EU.
5. You must have the required European Health Certificate and other health certificates completed by your veterinarian. If your certificate was issued in the United States, you must have it stamped with an official USDA stamp.
6. Depending on where you enter the EU, you may or may not need ADI-program-issued identification. Several EU countries only recognize ADI graduates as service dogs.

> For people who did not receive a dog from an ADI program, it is possible to obtain an ADI cert by testing with certain ADI programs. You'll likely have to call several to find an organization who will help you obtain ADI credentials.

Service dog status does not allow you to bypass the pet entry requirements. You must meet all requirements (vaccinations, microchip, titer, paperwork), or you risk customs issues or quarantine for your partner. If you plan on traveling regularly in the EU, you should consider undergoing the yearlong process to obtain a European Pet Passport. These documents can make travel a much smoother process.

Not all countries grant public access rights for service and guide dogs, or some only grant public access rights to guide dogs, or they require specific gear or identification for public access rights. It's recommended to carry an official letter in the language of the country you're in detailing what your partner does for you and why they're needed, so you can provide it to businesses or officials upon request.

Always ensure your partner is neatly groomed, presentable, and wearing easily recognizable gear. Rambunctious behavior from dogs is frowned upon in Europe, and it's vital you always remain in control of your partner, and that your partner remains quiet, calm, and in work mode when in public.

Central and South America

The procedures for entering Central and South America with a dog are complicated, convoluted, and regularly changing. Contact the embassy and department of agriculture of any country in Central or South America that you're considering traveling to for up-to-date requirements and regulations.

There will likely not be widespread acceptance of your service animal, and very possibly little public access rights. Keep in mind that in many central and south American countries, street dogs are a widespread issue.

Asia

"Officially qualified assistance dogs" are granted full and free use of streets and all public accommodations in Japan. An official identification card (likely ADI) is required, and the dog must be wearing proper gear, such as a vest or harness. Hearing dogs must wear an orange cape.

The process for entering Japan with a dog is difficult and requires lots of forethought and planning. Start early, and make sure to carefully complete each step as required.

Travel throughout other Asian countries carries other difficulties. Any country you wish to travel to with your service dog may or may not have varying regulations and requirements, and public access is not assured.

Middle East

There are strong cultural and religious connotations to having and working with a dog to be considered when traveling in the Middle East. While dog ownership is quite common, it's almost always in the vein of "property" or "working animal" and not as "pets." Within many sects of Islam and Judaism, dogs are considered "unclean" and oftentimes, as a result, are not well-received.

Entry to the Middle East with a dog carries vastly differing requirements depending on the country you're traveling to, and which countries you'll be traveling through.

Contact the embassies of all countries you'll be in or through and compile a checklist of requirements. Then, carefully meet the requirements, and understand that you may or may not have any access rights, depending on where you travel to.

2

SERVICE DOG TYPES/JOBS

ALERT DOGS

When most people think of service dogs, one of the "alert" type of service dogs is typically what comes to mind first. "Oh, you mean like those dogs who tell their handler about low blood sugar or that alert to seizures!" is often heard when someone first starts a conversation with someone unfamiliar with service dogs.

There are many different types of alert service dogs, but they share one key trait in that they all possess specialized training to recognize, identify, and alert their handler to changes in physiological, neurological, or environmental states that could have an effect on their handler's health or well-being. In order for a dog to be considered an alert-type service dog, they must reliably alert to the presence of whatever they're monitoring, be it blood sugar highs or lows, allergens, or radical shifts in body chemistry, and they must not offer the alert behavior in other circumstances.

As an example, if a diabetic alert dog is trained to pick up a small, soft toy that dangles from their collar whenever they smell a change in their person's body chemistry that signifies low blood sugar, then the diabetic alert dog must not pick up that toy when there is no dangerous shift in blood sugar. Otherwise, the alert is not reliable. This is important regardless of what type of alert dog the service dog in question may be—alerts need to be trained, proofed, predictable, and reliable.

Lots of people report that their dog just "knows" when they're about to show symptoms of their disability, be it a migraine, seizure, blood sugar shift, or something else. The intuitive nature of many dogs means that they very well could be cueing in changes in their handler's body, but it's not enough for the dog to simply know, or to know some of the time.

In order for a dog to be any type of service dog, they must have specialized training. When it comes to alert dogs, their training must allow them to reliably respond to changes in their handler's body or in the environment in a predictable, defined, and set fashion, meaning that the way that the dog notifies their handler of something important is always the same. It isn't sometimes a nose nudge, sometimes a paw on the handler's foot or arm, and sometimes the dog sits and stares. The alert behavior must be consistent.

There are many different ways alert dogs are taught to let someone know that something medically important is happening. Here's a few of those ways:

- Dog sits and stares at handler with a strong, unwavering, intense stare
- Dog downs with head on handler's foot
- Dog sits and places a paw on handler's knee
- Dog nose punches handler in the leg
- Dog continually nudges handler's hand with their nose
- Dog gently tugs on an item of clothing
- Dog picks up soft toy attached to collar and holds it
- Dog stands with muzzle pointing to surface on which allergen has been detected
- Dog lays head on lap, arm, or in hand (chin rest)
- Dog does a tight spin in place, and then lays down

Any trained behavior can be used as an alert behavior, but it should typically be quiet (no barking or whining as a trained behavior) and unobtrusive. An exception would be in a life-threatening medical emergency where the handler is unresponsive. In that case, many dogs are taught to "escalate" their alert—they perform their designated alert behavior for a certain period of time, and if the handler does not respond, then they begin to alert vocally, both to attempt to rouse the handler and to alert anyone around of the danger their handler is in. The dog should be taught to perform the chosen alert behavior whenever they smell or sense whatever it is their handler needs to know about.

The benefit to partnering with an alert dog is not the alert itself, but the extra time gained from the dog alerting the handler before the handler would otherwise be aware of the issue. Each alert dog has a different function to perform and each provides lifesaving benefits and peace of mind to their handler and their handler's family.

Allergen

Allergen alert dogs are trained to detect life-threatening allergens in the environment, and to alert their handler to the presence of said life-threatening allergens. Peanuts and shellfish are common triggers for allergen alert dogs. When the dog locates the source of the allergen using their hypersensitive sense of smell, they alert so that their handler can avoid the area or the area can be cleaned and made safe.

Diabetic

Diabetic alert dogs are trained to use their extremely sensitive noses to smell dangerous shifts in blood chemistry (high or low blood sugar) and to notify their handler of the need to test their blood sugar or take medical action to stabilize their sugar.

They are not a replacement for regular testing or for medical equipment, but they often serve as an "early warning" system for diabetics who have radical and rapid shifts in blood sugar, or who have dangerous lows throughout the night. It's been proven time and time again that diabetic alert dogs can be aware of shifts in blood sugar a whole fifteen to twenty minutes prior to when it can be caught on a meter.

Medical

Medical alert dogs use their senses and, in many cases, intuition, to sense an impending medical crisis and to notify their handler of the imminent danger before their handler would otherwise be aware of it. While medical alert dogs commonly use their sense of smell, they may also be clued in via audible or visual signals that the handler is on the brink of undergoing a medical crisis.

While some disabilities allow the dog to undergo systematic alert training (like with allergen alert dogs or diabetic alert dogs), that's not always the case, especially when it comes to neurological disorders or cardiac conditions. It's not always known what, exactly, a medical alert dog is seeing, smelling, or hearing that tells them their handler is in danger, but it's thought that it has to do with the bond between dog and handler.

When a dog begins alerting, their alert is then trained so that it becomes automatic, reliable, and consistent.

Psychiatric

True psychiatric alert dogs are few and far between, but these rare gems offer their people a valuable service that can't be replicated in any other way. Psychiatric service dogs often begin to key in on very subtle early signs of an impending psychiatric crisis, such as an increased rate of breathing, clenched fists or drumming fingers, slight rocking, or other cues specific to each handler. Whether their handler suffers from anxiety, panic attacks, PTSD, depression, a mood or personality disorder, or something else, the ability to know that they're entering the initial phases of a crisis allows the handler to attempt to use tools and coping skills, with the desire to slow or halt the impending crisis.

These dogs may also know trained commands that can assist the handler in situations that trigger their anxiety. For example, for a handler with PTSD, the psychiatric alert dog may be trained to turn their lights on, stand in front of or behind them to create space in a crowded environment, or to wake them up from a nightmare.

AUTISM ASSISTANCE DOGS

Autism assistance dogs and sensory processing disorder dogs perform similar jobs for different disorders. The differences between a child on the spectrum and a child with sensory processing disorder (SPD) are drastic, and while a child with autism oftentimes has a sensory processing disorder as well, the reverse isn't always true—a child with sensory processing disturbances may or may not have autism.

In a nutshell, autism is a neurodevelopment disorder that causes significant delays in communication, social skills, and development. A sensory processing disorder results from the body and brain being unable to accurately interpret input from any and/or all of the five senses, although visual, auditory, and tactile disturbances are the most common.

Oftentimes, the types of symptoms an SPD dog and an autism dog addresses appear to be the same, namely because the sensory processing side of autism is one of the ways in which an autism assistance dog can excel. The social and communication sides of autism are a bit more difficult for a dog to help with, so SPD dogs and autism dogs routinely end up grouped together, because their task work is typically quite similar.

Autism assistance dogs and sensory processing disorder dogs serve as anchors for people with autism or sensory processing disorders. This is relevant because individuals on the spectrum and those with SPDs can become overwhelmed with the environmental input around them, to the point that they feel as if they're drowning in all of the sensory input. Simply put, they hear, feel, taste, touch, and see everything; it can be hard to filter out the differences, and it's far more intense than a neurotypical (without autism) individual could ever imagine. Depending on the individual's level of disorder, meltdowns can occasionally occur, which may look different for each individual, but can be very scary, difficult situations to deal with, for children, for caretakers and parents, for family members, and for onlookers.

Enter the service dog. A common way to help soothe a child who is overstimulated, but who has not yet reached the point of a meltdown, involves using a weighted blanket or vest to provide "deep pressure stimulation" (DPS). DPS uses pressure, warmth, and weight to "even out" sensory input and to prevent the nervous system from continually escalating. For many children struggling with sensory issues, having their service dog lay across their legs or body is far more grounding and settling than the impersonal and sterile use of a blanket, and far less embarrassing than an aide or caretaker providing the pressure.

The dog also allows a child to "ground," or to seek a more comforting source of sensory input, by rubbing their fur or stroking their ears. In time, a child (or adult!) will learn to turn to their service dog for help before they reach the point of a meltdown.

For children with autism, connecting and communicating with the world outside of their heads can be very difficult. The impairment can prevent them from forming bonds with others, and more than that, it often results in a child being nonverbal, or being unable to use their words to communicate. Many families have reported their child on the spectrum saying their first words or holding entire conversations with their service dog!

Children with sensory processing disorders and those on the spectrum often have a deep-seated need for a highly structured routine and schedule. Partnering with a service dog can allow them to form a routine around something that can go with them to new places and environments, which can help ease the difficulty of doing so.

If their service dog routine remains the same, then it can often help the owner accept changes in other arenas. It also allows them to learn and practice self-care by tending to their canine partner, or to see it in action if the child is unable to directly care for the dog themselves.

Difficulty sleeping is one of the biggest issues reported by parents when it comes to autism and sensory processing disorders. Sometimes, the simple addition of a service dog to the bed or room can allow a child to sleep more or longer, or to remain settled if they are not sleeping, because they have soothing, familiar company and a source of grounding. Another common issue is that of "wandering," or a child bolting through any open door or gate. This behavior is extremely scary for caretakers, as many children with autism do not respond to their names, nor will they provide identifying information to any adult who finds them.

While responsibility for the well-being and safety of a child should never be placed solely on a service dog, it can help knowing that the child will not be alone if they do manage to Houdini their way away from a parent, aide, teacher, or caregiver. These types of service dogs often carry identifying or emergency information on or in their vests or on their collar, including, sometimes, the fact that the child is nonverbal. If the dog does not go with the child, then the dog may be trained to track the child.

The dogs can also be used to disrupt "stimming," or the repetitive physical movements children on the spectrum often use to demonstrate strong emotion. A T-shirt often seen in support groups is "I Get Flappy When I'm Happy!" and that's an example of stimming. Other behaviors commonly seen include rocking, head banging, biting their hands, or swinging their legs or feet. The dogs can be trained to interrupt these behaviors by gently nosing a child until the child engages with the dog instead.

A final note on these unique dogs—tethering. Tethering is much debated in the service dog world, and it involves leashing a child to the dog. There are several reasons programs or trainers do this, including the simple fact that the child may not be able to hold the leash for long periods of time, but the most hotly debated one is called "anchoring." If a child is prone to bolting, a large or giant breed, heavy-boned dog can be trained to lay down when they feel tension on their harness, thereby making it impossible for the child to run. The safety of the dog is often called into question, particularly if it's a larger child.

It is always important, with any task work, that the safety of the child and dog be put first. Oftentimes, tethering is the most efficient way to keeping the child and dog together, and it has nothing to do with anchoring.

Anchoring, if used, should only be done with a dog who is truly massive, and who possesses a gentle, low-key temperament that can't be shaken by anything. The child should be quite small, and the anchoring should be used to teach new coping skills, so that by the time the child is large enough that it would not be safe to anchor, they have already learned to turn to their dog for comfort and grounding before things get to the point of a meltdown or bolting.

Anchor dogs should not weigh less than sixty to seventy pounds for any size of child. A dog that is 100 to 120 pounds can work for a child up to about eighty-five to ninety pounds. For all children and adults bigger than ninety to one hundred pounds, a solution other than tethering is advisable, although for calmer individuals, a giant breed of canine can do this work.

BRACE AND MOBILITY SUPPORT DOGS

Brace and mobility support dogs are a type of service dog trained to provide their disabled handler with assistance moving from place to place.

Fun fact: Mobility support dogs were some of the first non-guide assistance dogs trained in the United States. This invaluable service is matched only by these dogs' ability to also help with other chores and tasks, like opening doors or retrieving dropped items. Due to the unique nature of their work, though, brace and mobility support dogs have special needs.

Brace and mobility support dogs, also known as mobility support dogs or mobility assistance dogs, are a special type of medical assistance dog primarily trained to assist their disabled handler with locomotion (defined as moving from one place to another by any means, including on foot or in a wheelchair). Mobility dogs may help people with impaired balance, gait, or coordination to safely walk or regain their footing after a fall; and they help individuals who use prosthetics or other assistive devices, including wheelchairs, gain unprecedented levels of independence, freedom, and mobility. They are also frequently trained to help their handler with everyday duties that their human partner can't readily perform because of their disability, or can only perform with difficulty. Some examples include picking up dropped items, retrieving out-of-reach objects, and opening/closing doors, drawers, and cabinets.

People partnered with a brace and mobility support dog may or may not be able to walk unassisted, and they may or may not be in a wheelchair. Some handlers use assistance devices in addition to their service dog, such as crutches, walkers, braces, canes, lifts, wheelchairs, or scooters, whereas other brace and mobility support dog users are able to rely solely on the assistance of their dog, free of other assistive devices.

No scenario is more or less valid or legitimate—the function of the brace dog depends on the needs of the handler and the handler's disability. The handlers, whether ambulatory or not, often need extra help balancing, remaining stable, getting around, summoning help, monitoring medical equipment/alarms, interacting with the environment, reaching items, maintaining independence, and communicating during emergencies. Mobility support dogs can be trained to help in all of those areas, as well as many others.

All dogs that are partnered with a person with a disability, and that also possess specialized training that directly reduces or mitigates the effect of that person's disability on their quality of life or ability to function like someone without a disability, are legally defined as "service animals." That definition includes brace and mobility support dogs, and many of the common tasks brace or mobility dogs perform (like assisting a handler to walk or pulling a wheelchair) are directly mentioned in the Americans with Disabilities Act briefing that details the legal rights of service dog teams, as well as in the "Frequently Asked Questions About Service Animals and the ADA" document provided by the Department of Justice.

Before digging too deeply into everything that makes mobility dogs so extraordinary, it's important to note that all of the behavioral/training standards and expectations surrounding the manners, conduct, appearance, and deportment of all service dogs also apply to brace and mobility support dogs. Assistance Dogs International is a great place to learn about the suggested level of training and skills for all service dogs.

However, while all brace and mobility support dogs are service dogs, all service dogs are not trained for brace and mobility. Due to the rigorous, intensive, and extremely precise nature of the work mobility assistance dogs perform for their handlers, there are a few additional recommendations and some very important details to consider; these details go above and beyond the usual service dog requirements and expectations when it comes to brace and mobility support dog selection, training, and upkeep.

In many cases, a brace and mobility support dog's handler's life, physical safety, and autonomy depend directly on the task work and training of their service dog. While it is always important that all service dogs possess the proper behavior, temperament, and training to succeed in their specific field, it's doubly important for brace/mobility dogs (and many other medical assistance/alert/response dogs), as their handler's health and well-being rests, solely or in part, on their service dog's ability to perform their job and perform it well. This is paramount in distracting or difficult environments and circumstances.

Lots of the task work these working dogs perform is extremely physical in nature and a brace and mobility support dog's given tasks can routinely require meticulous attention to detail, complex behavior chains, and an extremely high level of precision and exactness.

Beyond that, succeeding as a medical assistance dog of any kind, including mobility assistance dogs, usually requires the ability to perform, think, and problem solve independently of their handler or trainer's guidance. The dog must be able to not only learn the proper protocols, procedures, and tasks for mitigating and responding to their handler's disability, but they must also be able to implement them at home and elsewhere. The environment can range from regularly visited places to unfamiliar locales.

A brace and mobility support dog who is partnered with a person who is medically fragile might have to work during the chaos of an emergency. The dog may have set tasks that must be performed during such a medical emergency, and if they do not respond appropriately, the handler might become sicker or enter a deeply altered state of consciousness; they might be unable to summon help, or may possibly die. Some examples of emergency task work performed by brace and mobility support dogs include:

- Burrowing under an unconscious handler's legs or lying across their body to elevate their blood pressure.

- Nosing their handler over onto their side or into a recovery position.
- Dragging a handler who has fallen to a safe spot, or dragging a heavy piece of medical gear to the handler.
- Supporting an unsteady or injured handler as they struggle back to their feet or into their wheelchair.
- Standing over a fallen and unresponsive handler so that the handler does not get stepped on.
- Barking to alert bystanders of the emergency situation and continuing to bark at people and attempting to lead them back to the handler until someone accompanies the dog back to their unconscious, unresponsive, or symptomatic handler.
- Retrieving an emergency-only medicine that's stored in the fridge or elsewhere.
- Running to wake up another person who resides or works in the home and return with them to the disabled individual. This is often performed if their handler is unresponsive, or if their medical equipment is alarming.
- Calling an emergency response team on a special phone if the handler is unconscious, or if the handler's medical equipment has been alarming for a set time period without being turned off.

The service dog might even have specific work to do that involves the EMTs or medical personnel, such as opening the front door and leading EMS to their handler's location. Other common interactive tasks include delivering a medical emergency or ICE (in case of emergency) card to the closest person in uniform; guiding one of the first responders to the location where medications, supplements, or a prepacked hospital bag are stored; or retrieving a folder full of medical documentation/history, medically mandated response or treatment protocols, and contact info so their handler can receive rapid and appropriate treatment.

They may have to do their job while surrounded by strangers who may or may not be familiar with working dogs, disabilities, or proper medical response. They may have to perform several complicated, multistep tasks in a row. The brace dog may be required to notice subtle environmental cues and prompts—the consequences of missteps or failure on the part of the service dog, especially due to hurried selection, improper temperament, or incomplete training, can be detrimental. Depending on the disability, the ramifications could be life-threatening.

This cannot be stressed enough—all canine candidates selected and trained for brace and mobility support task work and any associated task work pertaining to their handler's safety must possess a number of characteristics. Namely, they need the proper structure, genetics, health, temperament, aptitude, reliability, capability, and training to succeed and flourish. It's also vital that fully trained and working brace and mobility support dogs receive the proper support, maintenance, upkeep, and care necessary to maximize the dog's safety and comfort while working. Furthermore, working brace dog teams need to be properly equipped and able to perform their job with the least amount of impact on the dog's health and longevity.

All of the above is a lot to ask of a dog, any dog, and the dogs that are capable of thriving in this line of work are few and far between. Those who excel are truly special creatures. That's what this chapter is truly about—finding, selecting, and training those exceptional ones. The specific considerations involved in the care, keeping, and maintenance of the fully trained brace and mobility support dog are also just as crucial as the acquisition process itself.

One notable piece of advice for anyone seeking out a potential service dog candidate for any type of work is that the evaluation and selection process requires a solid background in canine behavior and training. There are quite a number of characteristics, details, and possible red flags to look for when selecting a candidate. To that end, it is always best to consult a professional in this process for guidance and assistance in making the best selection for possible service dog candidates.

The Basics

There are many reasons for needing a brace and mobility support dog. The following are some instances in which these service dogs would be beneficial to an individual:

- People who have physical disabilities that cause irregularities in gait, stability, balance, movement, or ambulation, including cerebral palsy, multiple sclerosis, spina bifida, and many malformations or injury of the bones, joints, or muscles in the lower body or spinal column.
- People with disabilities that cause debilitating pain, dizziness, and/or severe fatigue, and as a result, reduce the ability to walk without assistance and/or to perform daily chores and duties—some types of migraines and fibromyalgia are examples.
- People who need assistance transitioning from one position to another, such as from sitting to standing, or from one spot to another, such as from a wheelchair to a recliner.
- People who need assistance standing up after falling, or help getting back into bed or into a wheelchair after falling.
- People who require medical assistance or who need the ability to reach others on an emergency basis as a result of their disability, and they need help securing that assistance—one example is someone with a neurological, cardiac, or metabolic disorder that results in unconsciousness and/or a marked inability to ambulate, who needs assistance getting their phone in hand or help calling EMS or another designated contact, and needs the ability for that help to be summoned whether or not they're conscious or able to reach a phone.
- People who require tactile grounding in order to orient and position themselves, or in order to ambulate, such as in the case of vertigo or another balance disorder.

- People who have a disability that results in reduced awareness or an altered perception of the environment, and/or that causes confusion, disorientation, or a reduction in physical or mental functioning, like some traumatic brain injuries.
- People whose disability, whether physical or psychiatric, is treated by doctor-prescribed medications with side effect profiles resulting in symptoms that could be considered a limiting part of the person's disability, including causing drowsiness, light-headedness, dizziness, impaired alertness, or otherwise affect the ability to safely ambulate or respond to emergency situations.

There are innumerable instances of disabilities and needs that aren't mentioned above that result in impairments or reductions in ambulatory ability and/or mobility. It's important to remember that not everyone is suitable for partnership with a service dog, even if they have a disability for which a service dog appears to be a perfect solution. Anyone who is considering applying for, obtaining, or training a service dog of any kind needs to consider whether or not service dog partnership is appropriate for them, their family, their disability, and their situation.

In addition to the safety of the handler, there are also a number of safety considerations for the service dogs themselves. Many brace and mobility support dogs wear a special harness with a rigid, upright handle that allows the disabled handler to more easily reach their dog and move with their dog while standing. A brace dog's harness is specifically made to be ergonomic and to fit both the dog and the handler for safety. The harness is made to fit the dog perfectly and allow the pressure of bracing to be safely borne by the dog's entire body. Mobility assistance dogs who pull wheelchairs, wagons, or small carts, or who carry heavy medical equipment like oxygen tanks, also wear specialized harnesses to safely perform their tasks. The required equipment, harnesses and such, cannot simply be thrust upon a service dog with the expectation that the dog will know how to adapt to it effectively. This is an essential part of their training. Like any other type of service dog, the training of a brace and mobility support dog can begin very early, even as early as a few weeks of age. However, brace work, wheelchair pulling, and other physically taxing tasks shouldn't be trained or used until the dog has finished growing and their growth plates have fully closed.

Joint health, soundness, and growth should be verified with X-rays by a reputable and knowledgeable veterinarian. If too much weight or pressure is placed on a growing dog, their joints could easily be damaged or the dog could be injured. Most mobility dogs don't begin fully working until they're at least two years of age, for these and other safety reasons.

Qualifications and Requirements

Due to the demanding physical nature of their work, brace and mobility support dogs are usually large, sturdy dogs with great structure and joint health. Regardless of breed or exact size, they must be in excellent physical shape. Any extra weight or lack of muscle tone in a brace dog increases the strain on the dog's joints, which can significantly reduce the dog's working life, safety, and comfort.

Like all service dogs, brace and mobility support dogs need to be free from fear, timidity, aggression, and reactivity, and their temperament should be extremely balanced, calm, and relaxed. It's vitally important that mobility support dogs, and especially brace dogs, not be easily startled. If they jerk or misstep their handler could fall or be injured.

Brace and mobility support dog candidates should be free from all joint and skeletal disorders, and they should be screened for genetic illnesses common in their breed. They should not have any characteristics that would automatically disqualify a dog from service dog consideration.

When selecting and training a brace dog, temperament, structure, and size are far more important than breed. That being said, there are some breeds that tend not to make good service dogs. Some breeds that are bred to follow their nose or eyes at all costs; breeds bred to be super intense, aloof or independent; and/or breeds known for aggression toward other dogs, small animals, or people for example. Always evaluate each candidate as an individual, but don't totally disregard breed tendencies.

Brace dogs should be, at an absolute minimum, at least twenty-three inches tall at the shoulders and weigh at least fifty-five pounds. If you aren't a child or extremely slightly built/short person, then your dog will need to be proportionately larger. A large man could require a dog that's twenty-eight to over thirty inches tall and that weighs over a hundred pounds.

A brace and mobility support dog's size should directly relate to their human's size, and/or the task work the dog will be doing. Dogs that will be pulling wheelchairs, carts, or wagons need to be at least sixty-five to seventy pounds, and athletically built.

A rule of thumb is that when your arm is in a resting position hanging at your side, your hand should be within six to eight inches, and definitely no more than ten inches, of your dog's withers if your service dog will be performing brace work while you're standing. If you use your dog for other mobility tasks or a different type of physical support, such as wheelchair transfers or assistance changing positions, then your dog's size should offer adequate weight, mass, and strength to perform the job safely without undue strain.

Structure is one of the most important considerations for a brace and mobility support dog. Ricardo E. Carbajal, chairman of the German Shepherd Breed Advisory Committee, states that "proper structure is the anatomical design that offers the least resistance to movement." He goes on to note that "a dog with good working drives but improper structure cannot take advantage of its hardware to perform to its fullest potential."

Breeds vary widely in their build and structure, but experts in the field agree that a dog optimally built for work and athleticism will showcase a smooth stride and appear to be well-balanced overall. Their back isn't too long or short, their legs aren't different lengths, they're not excessively light boned or heavily boned, they aren't overly muscular, and nothing about them is extreme.

They're squarely built, with a more or less level and strong top line, and front legs that, according to Dr. Carmen Battaglia, an expert on working and performance dogs, should "appear as two columns of support from the shoulder to the ground." The dog's back legs shouldn't appear to rotate in or out when the dog is standing and relaxed. Everything about the dog's build needs to appear sturdy, strong, and balanced, but not be limited by anything about the dog's skeleton, musculature, or joints. Anything that's "off" in a mobility support dog's structure could result in a less than optimal working life, or even in injury to the dog.

There are many breeds that are known for their athletic build and for structures that have been carefully honed over the years for performance, working, endurance, and soundness. Some of the breeds commonly used as brace and mobility support dogs include:

- Labrador retrievers
- Golden retrievers
- Standard poodles
- German shepherds
- Rottweilers
- Doberman pinschers
- Newfoundlands
- Bernese mountain dogs
- Many of the so-called bully breeds or bully breed mixes
- Dogs from the Molosser family of breeds—Great Danes, mastiffs, livestock guardian breeds
- Mixed breeds can excel as brace and mobility support dogs.

As long as a dog has the size necessary to safely perform the work, good structure, health, and genetics, and a great temperament with an aptitude for the work, it is suitable to be a brace and mobility support dog, regardless of breed.

Temperament and Traits

As stated earlier, service dogs should be free from timidity, anxiety, fear, reactivity and aggression in *all* situations. They shouldn't have excessive drive in any form—chase, prey, fight, toy, food, etc.

It's easy to go on and on about what a service dog *shouldn't* be, and all too easy to forget what traits they *should* possess. A good service dog, including a brace and mobility support dog, should be balanced, responsive, and quiet. They should be more interested in interacting with people than with other dogs, distractions, or the environment. They should be motivated by food or toys, but not to the point that they can't think, or that they can be distracted by the presence of either.

They should be relaxed and nonreactive, but not lazy. They should be social and friendly, but not overly interested in interacting with people who aren't their handler/trainer or with other dogs. They should be happy to be with people all day, but should be fine when left alone, and be free from anxiety, including separation anxiety.

Avoid "overly solicitous" dogs as well as dogs who appear aloof or extremely independent. If a dog would rather go off on its own than interact or be with a person, then that dog probably isn't an ideal candidate.

They should be happy to learn or work, but not so driven that they always appear wound up or tense. They should be able to walk and go and work all day but shouldn't require hours and hours of exercise. These dogs should be able to relax in most situations and environments, regardless of the amount of distraction or chaos around them, but they should also be able to quickly and accurately respond to their handler's requests, cues, and commands. They should be responsive and biddable, but not always on edge or coiled like a spring, waiting for the handler's next word. They should be trainable, which doesn't necessarily mean highly intelligent. Lots of highly intelligent breeds do not excel at service dog work, because they get bored doing the same thing day in and day out.

In a nutshell, everything about an ideal service dog candidate rests somewhere in the middle of two extremes. They're not aloof, and they're not overly attached. They're not lazy, but they're not always wired. They're not antisocial, and they're not overly social. They're not disinterested in food or toys, but they're not so excited by them they can't function. They aren't utterly disconnected from the environment, and they're not so overly engaged as to be easily distracted or uninterested in their handler. They're focused but not hyper focused. Truly a happy medium makes for an excellent candidate.

Particularly for brace and mobility support dogs, it's especially vital that the dog be relaxed, steady, and stable. Nothing should be able to distract the dog from its work. A large part of that is the formal training, but the ability to train a dog to that degree starts with its temperament and core traits.

Keep in mind, when selecting a service dog candidate, that what you see is usually what you get—this includes everything from physique to temperament and everything in between. If you have to "fix" something, or compensate for the deficiency, then a dog probably isn't the perfect candidate. There are enough things that disqualify a dog from serving in an assistance capacity that you shouldn't set yourself up for an uphill battle from the very start.

Genetics and Health

Selecting a candidate from a breeder who performs health testing is a great way to ensure your brace and mobility support dog won't suffer from a debilitating or disqualifying health issue down the road.

If you're looking for a candidate from a shelter or rescue, it's vital that you be prepared to perform health testing and X-rays (hip, elbow, and spine, at the very least) yourself. Yes, it's expensive, but it's more expensive to lose or be forced to retire a dog you've put thousands of hours into training due to an illness or structural flaw and then to have to start over from scratch. Though the screening and selection process can seem strict or rigid, its preventative measures are in place to make the overall investment as beneficial and successful for all parties as possible.

Training

There are dozens of organizations across the United States that train, or even specialize in, brace and mobility support dogs, so that training can vary widely, although it's also quite common for people to owner-train with the assistance of a reputable and skilled local trainer. No matter what work or tasks a brace and mobility support dog is trained to perform, there are some considerations that need to be kept in mind at all times, especially if the handler requires emergency assistance or response from their dog.

First and foremost, the dog's training must be extremely reliable. No matter the situation, a well-trained brace and mobility support dog will still be able to do their job. This can mean introducing all kinds of variables into the training process, including position changes, heavy distraction, or off-the-wall scenarios to help a dog "generalize" their task work.

As an example, most obedience trained dogs will "sit" when asked, when their handler is standing and the dog is in front of them, facing the handler. But what if the handler kneels, sits, or lies on the floor? What if the handler is facedown? What if the handler turns their back? What if the handler is at the bottom of the stairs, and the dog at the top? What if the handler FaceTimes the dog? What if the dog is in a "down" position and the handler asks for a sit? What if the handler whispers? What if the handler doesn't move their body/hands or offer any kind of physical cue?

Brace dogs may commonly have to perform task work while their handler is on the ground or in a position that isn't commonly encountered during routine training, and they need to be able to perform their trained responses without issue. Their training needs to be proofed against a variety of distractions, including the types of distractions commonly encountered during emergency situations (e.g., swarms of people, radios, sirens, flashing lights, loud, unfamiliar voices, strange places, etc.). The only way to do this is to gradually build the dog's understanding of the task work and commands and to build duration, distance, and distraction proofing into the behaviors.

A mobility support dog's training needs to be predictable and well-practiced. When given a cue, whether it's a verbal, physical, or environmental cue, the dog should immediately respond in a predictable and quantifiable way. When it comes to complex behaviors (like retrieving a beverage from the fridge or opening the front door and leading first responders back to their unconscious handler), the dog's training must be reliable to the point where the dog can perform it without assistance or guidance. Their handler may not always be able to help them, so they should be able to perform independently when required, and they should be able to uphold their training even if their handler isn't able to enforce it. As an example, if EMS transports the unconscious or injured handler, one of the paramedics should be able to put a leash on the service dog, walk them out to the ambulance, and load them up, and the dog should be able to calmly relax or perform necessary task work without EMS intervention or direction.

The ideology and framework laid out thus far for service dog candidate screening and selection, training and handling, handler needs and scenarios, etc., has been exemplified by brace and mobility support dogs. As you continue reading, keep these points of framework in mind, as most of them are applicable to other types of service dogs. Each specialty of dog will necessarily have their own unique needs, demands, training, scenarios, strengths, and weaknesses. They will have some requirements specific to their work and purpose that may not apply to others. However, the basics and general rules of thumb remain unchanged overall.

GUIDE DOGS

Guide dogs are partnered with individuals with varying degrees of visual impairment, up to and including total loss of vision in both eyes. They undergo some of the most rigorous training in the canine world—even more rigorous than that given to military working dogs—and their trainers complete years of schooling and specialty education in order to train them.

Guide dogs do not "see" for their person, contrary to popular opinion, but they do help their person navigate their environment more safely. A guide dog's job is to help their person avoid environmental hazards, including holes, curbs, stairs, or low-hanging obstacles like branches or wires. They help a person find turns and navigate familiar routes, and they assist their handler in finding a safe path. They indicate elevation changes, and, by responding to their handler's directional commands, can guide their handler along the safest route in the direction the handler wishes to go.

Handlers are trained in navigation and environmental mobility well before partnering with a guide dog. In fact, this handler training is often *required* before an organization will partner them with a guide dog!

Guide dogs wear special harnesses with rigid handles. The handle provides feedback from the dog's body and movements directly to the handler. If the dog is told to take a route that is unsafe, they will refuse to do so. This is called "intelligent disobedience," and it helps keep the handler safe from hazards they may not know are there.

HEARING DOGS

Hearing dogs are often small, active, inquisitive dogs who are trained to notify their deaf/hard-of-hearing handler of important auditory input in the environment. This can include things like:

- The handler's name being called
- Phone ringing
- Text message or email notification
- Doorbell sounding
- Someone knocking
- Approaching car
- Baby crying
- Alarms or timers
- Keys, phone, or coins being dropped

A hearing dog can be trained to alert to any important sound, and the sounds the handler wishes the dog to alert for are determined before training. These service dogs nudge, paw, or (rarely) lick their handler to alert to a sound, and usually, they're trained to take their handler directly to the sound in order to earn their reward. They will not stop alerting until their handler acknowledges the alert.

While having a hearing dog is very useful for deaf and/or hard-of-hearing individuals, it's not just about how handy it is—it's about safety. Not being able to hear a speeding car approaching or a fire alarm going off makes for a dangerous reality. Having a constantly roving pair of ears always by your side means you can relax a bit. Hearing dogs are custom trained for their partner and their partner's environment—no two teams are exactly alike. Hearing dogs can also be trained to respond to ASL or hand signals for those handlers who are nonverbal or who do not speak.

MEDICAL ASSISTANCE DOGS

The category of medical assistance dogs tends to be a bit of a catchall for any type of service dog that doesn't fit elsewhere. In fact, lots of other types of service dogs are also medical assistance dogs—any dog that possesses specialized task training to mitigate or assist their handler with a medical disorder is a medical assistance dog. It's quite the broad category!

Medical assistance dogs can be partnered with individuals who have:

- Seizure disorders
- Neurological disorders
- Migraines
- Cardiac disorders
- Mobility disorders not specified above
- Developmental disorders
- Skeletal or musculature disorders
- Postural orthostatic tachycardia syndrome (POTS)
- Many, many others

The tasks medical assistance dogs can perform can't be specified in generalities, as each dog will often have radically different task lists depending on what disability or disorder their handler has.

MEDICAL RESPONSE DOGS

Medical response dogs are a specialized kind of medical assistance dog that has been trained to respond directly to a medical crisis (or impending medical crisis). They may or may not also be medical alert dogs.

Medical alert dogs, once they recognize an impending episode based on recognition of symptoms pertaining to a specific medical condition, can also double as medical response dogs by then taking additional steps to help rectify the impending crisis. The differences between medical alert and medical response training depend on the triggers the dog has been trained to identify. An alert dog will notify the handler *prior* to an event, whereas a response dog takes steps once the event has occurred.

One example: A diabetic alert dog will notify their handler once their blood glucose drops below 70. A diabetic response dog will fetch an insulin kit or a pouch of blood sugar stabilizing candies or foods from the fridge and return it to their handler.

Medical response dogs can be trained to do many, many, different things. They may burrow under the legs of a child with POTS in order to help raise their blood pressure. They may offer tactile interruption of a seizure or help nudge a person over onto their side during a seizure. They may block a person suffering from a visual migraine from approaching stairs, or help lead them to a dark room, or fetch medication or a cold cloth from the fridge.

If a service dog is trained to take specific steps in response to something medical that is happening, they're a medical response dog. This includes dogs trained to go and retrieve a parent, guardian, or caretaker when medical alarms go off. These dogs are often grouped in with the alert dogs, but they are not, in fact, alerters. They're responders.

The technicalities don't always matter, but it can help when determining task work to know under which category any given service dog will fall.

PSYCHIATRIC SERVICE DOGS

Psychiatric service dogs partner with an individual who has one or more mental illnesses or psychiatric disturbances. They're commonly partnered with people who suffer from PTSD, anxiety/panic attacks, debilitating depression, or pervasive mood disorders, such as bipolar disorder.

Psychiatric service dogs are not dogs who merely offer comfort. Those are called emotional support animals, and they, unlike service dogs, do not have any public access rights as granted by law, though individual businesses/facilities may choose to allow them. Psychiatric service dogs, like all service dogs, must possess specialized training to mitigate their handler's disability. Psychiatric service dogs possess the same rights as all other service dogs, but, by the same token, they must also be upheld to the same training and behavioral standards.

In the case of psychiatric service dogs, their task work often takes the form of using deep pressure stimulation to soothe anxiety or panic, offering tactile input via nose nudges or pawing to force interactions, and retrieving medications or providing medication reminders.

They may retrieve dropped items for a handler who is unsteady on their feet due to medication, wake up a handler who is sleeping too deeply to hear an alarm, or turn on lights for an ex-soldier with PSTD. Task work can be highly varied.

SEIZURE DOGS

Seizure dogs are one of the more common types of service dogs, and there are three common types: alert, assistance, and response. Seizure dogs that alert to seizures notify their handler ahead of time that a seizure is impending. It is very, very important to note that at this time, seizure alerts *cannot* be trained. It is impossible to *train* a seizure alert. A dog can begin to alert naturally, given time and the opportunity to bond to their handler, but it cannot be trained.

Seizure assistance and seizure response dogs can be trained, however, and regularly are selected for extremely intuitive natures with the hope that they will begin to alert.

Seizure assistance dogs help a person who has a seizure disorder cope with the effects of medication, sensory input, or other aspects of their disability outside of the seizures themselves. A seizure response dog responds directly to a seizure as it is happening by helping keep a person safe, helping reduce the duration of the seizure via whatever means they are trained to do (some seizures respond to focused touch or licking, other seizures respond to pressure, etc.), and/or alerting a designated person or retrieving medication.

NOT A SERVICE DOG, BUT STILL A WORKING DOG

Service dogs and assistance dogs aren't the only dogs in the world that do amazing, life-changing work, but they are two of the few types of working dogs clearly defined and protected by federal law in the United States. Too many people don't understand the differences between many types of working dogs, though, and it's time to clear up some of the confusion.

When it comes to what is and what is not a service dog, federal law is very clear. A service dog, as defined in the US Code of Federal Regulations, is any dog who is individually trained to provide assistance to an individual with a disability.

For an overview of American laws governing service dogs, see the Service Dog Legalities section beginning on page 19. Service dogs, when accompanied by an individual with a disability of any kind, generally enjoy complete public access and may go with their disabled handler to almost any place nondisabled members of the public may go. While there are major exceptions (like sterile medical or laboratory environments, churches/places of worship, and a couple of others), in general, if a person with a wheelchair is allowed to be somewhere, a person with a service dog may also be there.

Service dogs may travel and live with their disabled handler free of charge, and it is illegal for most places of business or for public accommodations to deny a service dog team access—see more info on page 19.

In order to be a service dog with public access, a dog must meet three points of law:

- Be specifically trained to perform work or tasks that mitigate the handler's disability.
- Be accompanied by a person with a physical, mental, developmental, or other disability.

- Be house trained and under the direct control of the handler.

There are no other requirements (no documentation, no gear, no certification, no registration, no anything else) for a dog to be a service dog, and it's quite simple: if a dog is not task-trained, working directly for an individual with a disability, and under the direct control of the handler, it is not a service dog.

However, simply knowing a dog is not a service dog doesn't help you know what it *is*. To help you out, here's a brief overview of many of the other types of working dogs that commonly crop up in day-to-day life and in conversation.

Therapy Dogs

Therapy dogs do a valuable job by providing unconditional love, emotional support, and an understanding, listening ear anywhere they're needed. Many people are familiar with therapy dogs visiting hospitals, schools, universities, group homes, and libraries, but therapy dogs also provide a valuable service at funerals, disaster sites, or anywhere else emotions, grief, and tension may run high.

Therapy dogs are typically well-trained, sweet-natured, friendly dogs who are, first and foremost, pets. Their family trains them and has them certified via a therapy organization, and therapy dog teams are most often volunteers. Therapy dogs do *not* have public access, with or without their handler, and they may only enter buildings (that don't allow all pets to enter) with a direct invitation to the dog and handler or to the therapy dog organization.

Emotional Support Animals

Emotional support animals work with an individual who needs comfort. They require no specialized training, have no public access, and can be any species. The DOJ/HUD's Fair Housing Act does protect an owner's right to reside with their emotional support animal in accommodations that otherwise don't allow pets, and, with proper documentation, a person can fly with their emotional support animal.

Facility Dogs

Facility dogs are highly specialized therapy dogs who come in two types: dogs who provide extensive animal-assisted therapy, and dogs who live (or work extensively) on-site to provide comfort to residents, patients, or visitors.

Facility dogs who provide extensive animal-assisted therapy can often be found in physical therapists' offices, counselors' offices, or anywhere else a professional provides a specialized service to a lot of people. These facility dogs may help with the process of rehabilitation, provide practice for a physical therapy patient, or help a wounded child learn to trust again. Anytime dogs do specialized work for a professional's clients or residents, they're probably facility dogs.

Dogs who live on-site as a resident therapy dog are also facility dogs, and these can be found at nursing homes, residential facilities, group homes, and at many businesses. If a therapy dog is a "familiar face" at a business, he's probably a facility dog.

Facility dogs do not have any rights of public access outside of the office or building where they work.

Courthouse Companion Dogs

Courthouse companion dogs are specialized facility dogs who are trained to work with children (or adults) in a courtroom while they're giving difficult or painful testimony. Courthouse companion dogs work to lower tension, provide distraction, and give support during the difficult moments of deposition, testimony, and any other time they're needed.

Courthouse companion dogs are a little new on the scene, but their success is amazing, and, for the kids who use their services, there's nothing better to help them begin to heal and grow again.

Outside of the courtrooms in which they work, courthouse companion dogs do not have public access.

SERVICE DOG CONSIDERATIONS

Before partnering with a service dog, there are several important points to consider. While thousands of individuals with a disability benefit greatly from a partnership, it's not the solution for everyone. If you or a loved one is considering full-time service dog partnership, take some time to consider the ramifications of your decision.

In some cases, it is possible to prepare in advance for some of these challenges, and partnering with a service dog means a lifelong process of learning and evolution. Having strong support networks among friends and family and adequate primary care providers will also help a great deal. In other cases, the challenges of partnering with a service dog may not make it the ideal option for you.

You must know beyond a shadow of a doubt the benefits of partnering with a service dog will outweigh the disadvantages before venturing any further down the path of becoming a service dog handler, and whenever possible it is important to prepare for these challenges before making the commitment involved.

Partnering with a service dog is a huge step, and every person's needs, desires, limitations, abilities, and situations are unique. Each set of circumstances deserves due consideration. However, it's up to you to be honest with yourself. Frank and candid analysis/examination of you, your needs, your home life, your family, and your disability is a requirement for ensuring you're not making a choice that could set you back or hurt you, your relationships, your independence, or the service dog community. Keep in mind that your canine partner is a living being and that your decisions will also impact your service dog.

Give yourself plenty of time to explore your feelings and thoughts concerning partnering with a service dog. Don't make a decision hastily. It often helps to involve someone you trust in the brainstorming and soul-searching process. If, at the end of this self-exploration, you're not certain a canine partner is for you, it's probably best to wait before beginning the process or to spend some time learning more.

Questions to Ask Before Partnering with a Service Dog

Ask yourself the following five questions before making a final decision. Before beginning, you must understand there are no wrong answers to these questions—only answers that help you make the best decision for your needs and disability. The questions are designed to help you think and they're not meant to be answered with a simple "yes" or "no."

1. Am I financially able to take on the costs of caring for a dog for ten to twenty years?

Whether you decide to apply for a service dog via an established program or you opt to owner-train your partner, service dogs (or any dog, for that matter) are not cheap. The old saying, "There is no such thing as a free puppy," is completely true.

If you're applying to an assistance dog or service dog program, costs can vary widely. There may be application fees, travel, room and board costs, equipment fees, and, then, there's the actual cost of the dog. Many service dog programs charge more than $5,000 for a dog, and costs of $20,000 or more for extremely specialized or dual-trained service dogs are not unheard of.

There are very few grants or scholarship opportunities available to defray those costs, but fund-raising is always an option, and if you dig deep enough, you might find some assistance available. Service Dogs of America and the Assistance Dog United Campaign occasionally have assistance dog/service dog grants and scholarships available. However, you can't count on receiving assistance, and must carefully consider the costs of each program you interview. Consider speaking with a tax professional to discuss possible deductions related to purchasing and caring for a service dog.

If you decide to owner-train a service dog partner, you're responsible for the cost of the dog, all veterinary costs and testing, temperament testing, transport, initial training, advanced training, any necessary titling/certifications (like the American Kennel Club's Canine Good Citizen [CGC] or Canine Life and Social Skills [C.L.A.S.S.] or the American Temperament Test Society [ATTS] temperament test, should you decide to obtain those), all gear and equipment, and any other supplies required throughout the training process, such as food, poop bags, pet furniture, collars, leashes, harnesses, toys, supplements, and other "incidentals."

Additionally, it's not as simple as merely getting a dog from a shelter. Service dogs must possess a specific temperament and degree of trainability in order to succeed at the demanding work placed before them, and not just any dog will do. Finding the right dog to be your partner can take months, and often the only reliable solution is to obtain a well-bred puppy from a breeder known for producing service dogs in their lines.

Well-bred assistance dog candidates, depending on the breed, can range from $800 to $3,000 in purchase price alone. However, included in that price is the near-certainty that your potential partner is extremely likely to succeed and is physically, mentally, and genetically sound. You will have breeder support and backup, as well as access to extra resources, should you need them.

If you obtain a dog from a rescue, you must be certain they've been thoroughly temperament tested, are socialized, are trainable to a high level, and are medically sound. Hip and elbow certifications via a joint certification program like the PENNhip or the OFA is never a bad idea. Joint imaging and professional reading of the X-rays should be considered mandatory for any dog who's going to be doing brace/mobility support or any kind of weight-intensive task work like pulling a wheelchair or carrying heavy loads.

On top of basic hip and elbow certifications, you should determine if your rescue dog is free of genetic illnesses common in their breed or breeds. Nothing is more painful or costly than spending thousands of dollars training and bonding with your partner only to find they're going to be forced to retire years too soon due to genetic, temperamental, or structural infirmity.

For those who live in an area where Lyme disease is prevalent (northeastern US and upper midwestern states) or who are considering a service dog candidate from those geographic areas, budget in Lyme disease testing for any dog purchased, transported, or adopted from those regions. Lyme disease progresses quickly but in the early stages it is undetectable without medical testing. The tick-borne illness results in lameness, fatigue, a whole host of other symptoms and can, in fact, be deadly.

All in all, it's not unreasonable to expect to spend $1,500 to $2,000 finding, transporting, testing, and vetting a rescued service dog candidate, and that's before any of the training begins! Training itself can vary widely in costs, but you must include a professional, service dog–savvy trainer in your plans, even if it's only every now and again. Trainers typically charge per class (which can range from $65 to $200 for four- to eight-week sessions, depending on your location) or per hour (which typically runs $60 to $125/hour, depending on your location).

Finally, ask yourself if you are prepared to accept full financial responsibility for your potential service dog for the rest of their life? Whether you're going to train them yourself or you're receiving an assistance dog from a program, you and you alone are responsible for vetting, quality food, toys, any additional/necessary training, emergencies, working gear, preventative medication, grooming, joint or other supplements if necessary, bedding/crates/home items, doggy proofing, and many other incidentals. Veterinary health insurance can help defray the costs of routine and emergency vet care, so consider acquiring a policy as soon as you purchase your puppy or dog.

The price adds up quickly, but many trainers and experts estimate costs run between $1,200 and $1,600 a year at a minimum, every year for the rest of your dog's life, not including initial vetting, testing, and purchase.

2. Are you prepared to care or arrange for care for a dog every single day?

Partnering with a service dog is akin to having a toddler. Every day, without fail, your dog must be cared for. This means he'll need to be taken out several times a day, cleaned up after, fed a nutritious meal at least once a day, ongoing training maintained or improved, mental or physical exercise/stimulation, groomed as necessary, and treated as a companion and living creature, not merely as a tool or object.

Consider the complexity of this relationship—the service dog is a living, breathing partner with you in your health care and is also medical equipment that you must understand and interact with properly. Service dogs, like all dogs, have unique personalities, needs, and requirements. They require constant upkeep, and, no matter what, you must be prepared to meet their needs. It doesn't matter if it's raining, you're having a "bad day," there's four feet of snow on the ground, you're in the hospital, or there's a family emergency—your service dog *must* be cared for and provided for.

Carefully consider how a service dog would fit into your lifestyle and family. They're not an inanimate piece of equipment that always works flawlessly, and caring for them isn't always convenient. Even when it's difficult, hard, or stressful, you must be willing to accept full responsibility for your canine partner at all times—perhaps we should say *especially* when it is difficult, not simply the easy, enjoyable moments together.

Partnering with a service dog can have many advantages, but receiving the full benefit requires a degree of dedication many individuals can't provide due to their unique situations, busy lives, personality, or a plethora of other reasons.

Additionally, you must have plans in place in case of an emergency. What happens if you're sick? Your service dog is ill? You are unexpectedly hospitalized? You must have backup plans and support structures in place to ensure your partner always receives the necessary care.

3. Are you prepared to be the center of attention?

Working with and partnering with a service dog often places you smack in the center of the public eye. Everywhere you go, people will stare and point at you and your canine partner (as you know, most people love dogs). Many people find that having a service dog helps them better open up to the world and society, whereas previously others may have avoided interaction or not known how to start a conversation. Many people welcome this extra interaction and being able to connect over their dog, but some people aren't as eager, or may feel more introverted and less willing to be put on the spot.

When partnered with a service dog, you will never be invisible. People will stop and engage you in conversations, ask plenty of questions (many of which may seem intrusive or personal even if they aren't meant that way), tell you stories about how their dog would be just perfect for this kind of work, or how their uncle has a dog "just like yours," though really the only thing they have in common is they're both spotted . . . the list goes on and on.

Plus, people may judge you, especially if you have an "invisible" disability, and you must be prepared to calmly assert your rights and the rights of your service dog. Expect a degree of conflict and to have to educate people on the subject. You will be challenged, denied access, and forced to assert yourself for your own benefit and on behalf of the entire service dog community. You are an ambassador for the community, and your service dog might be the first people ever come into contact with. You must ensure your partner is always presentable, behaving well, on task, and an excellent example of what a service dog should be.

Partnering with a service dog carries responsibilities not only to the dog but also to service dog partnerships who will follow in your footsteps. You must do your best to ensure that you and your service dog leave an outstanding impression behind you. This may be a great deal of pressure, but consider that service dog use and recognition is still in its infancy, even with laws in place to ensure their validity, and the hard work you do as a "service dog diplomat" will certainly make this process easier for others in the future.

If you're unsure you are able to take on the added stresses that accompany working or training a service dog in public and being a constant ambassador/spokesperson, it may be wise to consider alternatives to partnering with a service dog. In other cases, knowing about this pressure in advance may make it possible to prepare for these challenges. The adage that "knowing is half the battle" rings quite true.

If you are already living with a disability, especially an invisible disability, you have likely already encountered some inquisitiveness and possibly rudeness. In some ways, having a service dog partner does not add more pressure or challenges, but instead shapes the form that those pressures will take.

4. Are you willing and able to accept the training and socialization obligations accompanying a service dog?

Partnering with a service dog is not a "one and done" deal no matter where or how you get your partner. If you receive your service dog from an assistance dog program, you're going to have to work very hard to bond with, learn to communicate with, and maintain your partner's training.

If you owner-train a service dog, you must accomplish a feat trainers work decades to hone and perfect: build training and socialization foundations from scratch and then maintain them. Still, just as a professional trainer must work diligently to improve their learning and skills with their canine charges, so too the owner-trainer must be willing to learn new skills, improve communication strategies, and so on. The process can be a monumental challenge, but the reward is well worth the efforts.

Service dogs possess highly trained, intricate, and specialized skills and degrees of training. The commitment to provide the practice time, boundaries, and training to ensure your service dog won't backslide in their training, public access, or level of socialization is imperative. The more your service dog knows or must know in order to work for you and mitigate your disability, the more vital it is that you work on maintaining and enhancing their skills as frequently as possible. The investment makes all the difference in the world for you as a team.

Service dogs are not robots, and they are not always perfect. Sometimes they have bad days, like any other living thing. On those days, you must be prepared to be mom, dad, teacher, coach, mentor, examiner, troubleshooter, judge, jury, principal, friend, partner, and sometimes even an impartial observer. The commitment is life-changing for you as much as it is for your service dog as a result of the willingness and perseverance every day to commit to taking care of each other. It is a true partnership.

You have to provide the structure, guidelines, and boundaries necessary for your partner to thrive and be able to serve you to the best of their ability. Being too emotionally invested, especially if your service dog is struggling or is pushing back, means you will likely miss the real issues and won't be able to fix them. The balance in maintaining and improving this partnership with your service dog is just like the very beginning of this whole process: finding the happy medium and setting yourself and your service dog up for success.

You must commit to upholding your service dog's training, skills, and behavior for the rest of their life. That may require you to seek additional, professional help or assistance from your support network. Service dogs must uphold very stringent standards, and sloppy or ill-behaved service dogs wreak havoc on the service dog community as a whole as well as being ineffective at assisting you with your disability. Professionalism is critical to success from and with your service dog. Strive for excellence and perform due diligence in training and upholding the standards set before you as a team.

Another consideration concerning training and socialization involves owner-trainers in particular. Professional service dog trainers spend years learning to train, socialize, ensure success, document, and work with service dog candidates, prospects, and partners. Not everyone possesses the proper training background or ability necessary to teach, perfect, and hone the behaviors, skills, and tasks required for working service dogs.

However, a straightforward solution for owner-trainers who don't have the necessary training, documentation, or socialization experience is to partner with a professional trainer willing to help guide them on their journey to partnering with a service dog. Teaching and training are both an art and discipline. Learning about training will be an ongoing experience, and often you may find it helpful to try and connect with a professional trainer who can mentor you in your process of learning to be a successful owner-trainer. Your service dog is being trained to be the best partner they can be for you. Giving them the best possible chance for success is a loving and necessary step in this process.

5. Are you prepared to deal with conflict?

While many people understand there will be access challenges while training, working, and partnering with a service dog, many individuals are not prepared for the other areas of conflict they will encounter.

As painful as it is to admit sometimes, the truth can be ugly. It is possible to lose friends or possibly even the support of family members, especially if you have an invisible disability. Not everyone is able to understand *why* you'd need or want a service dog, and some relationships may suffer. Naysayers and hecklers are an inevitability in life, and so too for service dog handlers.

Additionally, you may encounter strife at work, at school, and anywhere else you frequent. Business owners with whom you previously had an excellent relationship may begin to resent you and your service dog, even though they allow you access, as is required by law. You may occasionally receive varying degrees of (technically illegal) dismissive treatment or service ranging from merely rude to outright abusive. You must be able to remain poised and unflustered when faced with conflict.

Again, for many owner-trainers this is old news. You may already be living with a great deal of dismissive or rude behavior from less-informed individuals, and you may find friends and family retreat, even from people with whom they have a close, dear connection when they become disabled. But introducing a service dog to this complex emotional landscape is something to be prepared for.

It is important to be mentally and emotionally prepared to handle those blows when possible and to respond professionally and diplomatically, with courtesy and with poise, when you can. And keep in mind, just as your service dog is not a robot, neither are you. We all make mistakes, and if we learn from those mistakes, they only fuel our growth and abilities.

Issues That Make a Dog Unsuitable

Everyone knows that service dogs are supposed to be calm, well-trained dogs who work hard to help their human partners. However, too many people don't know what makes a dog unsuitable for service dog work. A popular quip in the service dog and assistance dog community is, "If you have to fix it, it isn't a service dog." So, without further ado, here are ten things that should immediately disqualify a dog, puppy, or candidate from beginning or completing service dog training.

1. Structural Imbalances or Issues

Service dogs work hard, and they have to keep up with their human partners in day-to-day life. Even dogs who don't do physical tasks like bracing, pulling a wheelchair, opening heavy doors, or carrying items often walk a lot, lay on hard floors for long periods of time, and must cope with the stress of frequent position changes. Dogs that do perform physically intensive work, especially any counter balance, bracing, mobility support, or pulling-based tasks, must be structurally sound and in great condition. Any structural imbalance, such as hip or elbow issues and dysplasia, back pain, malformed/deformed bones, or past trauma that resulted in broken bones means a dog shouldn't begin training.

If a dog is found to have structural imbalance during training, they should be career changed. It's usually best to ask your vet to x-ray any dog you're considering as a candidate and read the X-rays for joint and skeletal soundness.

2. Genetic Illness

Few things hurt as badly as pouring your heart, soul, energy, effort, money, and love into a dog, only to have them flunk out of training after three years because they develop a genetic disease. Dogs being considered for service dog work should have a series of tests done that determine whether or not the structurally sound dog in question has the potential of developing genetic illnesses common in their breed. While you can't test for everything, there is some peace of mind in knowing that the most common illnesses for the breed aren't present.

3. Vision or Hearing Problems

Service dogs must be able to see and hear cues given by their partner, and they must be aware of the environment around them. Healthy eyes and ears are a must for any dog being considered. Every year, the American College of Veterinary Ophthalmologists (ACVO) hosts an event to screen service dogs for ocular issues free of charge.

4. Unsuitable Size

While it's true that service dogs can be any breed, shape, size, or color, it's also true that their size must be appropriate for the task work they'll be doing. A forty-pound dog cannot do brace or counterbalance work for a 230-pound man, and they cannot pull a wheelchair. If you need a dog to open drawers and doors, then a twelve-pound terrier probably won't cut it, simply because they can't reach access buttons or any drawer/door that's not at floor level. The dog being considered must physically be able to safely do the task work you need.

5. Overweight or Obese

Overweight or obese dogs should not do service dog work. Being a working dog is taxing enough on a sound body, but additional weight means additional strain on joints, ligaments, and bones. Service dogs frequently change positions, squirm into small spaces under chairs and benches, raise up on their back legs, and perform other tasks that could injure an overweight dog.

Now, can a dog lose weight? Absolutely—but they should do so before beginning service dog training.

6. Timidity

Timidity is a huge flaw in a potential service dog. A service dog must be comfortable, settled, and content in all environments and in all situations. "Oh, he's just a little shy," or "Oops, sorry she growled; this is her first time," are not excuses.

If a dog is cringing, growling, or being avoidant, they are not comfortable, and they may not be service dog material. Excessive panting, drooling when there's no food, or refusing to take treats could also be more subtle indicators of stress, but not necessarily exclude a dog from eligibility.

That's not to deny that everyone has "off" days, including service dogs, but if a dog is fearful by nature, then they're unsuitable for service dog work.

7. Reactivity

Reactivity happens when a dog has an excessively strong reaction to a minor stimulus. For example, a dog may cringe and snarl when another dog passes them, or they may cower and hide when a person approaches. Reactivity can be minor or major, but regardless, it's a sign that there are situations the dog in question is very uncomfortable in, and it means they shouldn't be a service dog.

8. Aggression

Aggression in its most extreme form looks like a dog attempting to attack whatever they're aggressive toward—cats, dogs, people, small animals, children, bicycles, etc. It can also take the form of a dog snapping, snarling, growling, fixating on, going rigid and staring, etc. Whatever form it takes, it's dangerous and utterly unacceptable for any dog who needs to be able to work safely and calmly in a public arena.

It doesn't matter if you don't see children very often—even if you can maybe control your dog, you cannot always control the environment, and you do not know when or if a trigger will appear. Any aggression whatsoever immediately disqualifies a dog as a service dog, even if it only occurs infrequently or even once.

9. Excessive Drive and/or Energy

Service dogs work hard, and there are *so many things* they must learn—basic obedience, advanced obedience, public access skills, task training, and so on. Some drive, particularly food and toy drive, and some energy, are necessary for them to succeed.

That being said, if dogs are over the top about food to the point that they can't focus when it's around, or have so much toy drive that if they see a toy, they zero in on it, or they have so much energy that they never seem to just "relax," then those dogs probably aren't suitable as service dogs.

Some types of service dogs, like hearing dogs, use high-energy, higher-drive dogs and channel all of it into monitoring the environment and reporting back in to the handler, but for most types of service dogs, too much drive or too much energy means a dog just won't be able to work properly.

10. Aloof, No Desire to Interact or No Focus

Some dogs have no desire to interact with people, and that's okay. That's just their core personality. That being said, a dog that is very aloof, too independent, or who wants to get away from people and go exploring and sniffing at the first available opportunity probably will never be happy working as a service dog, nor would it be emotionally fulfilling for the handler or trainer to try to force this dog to change who they were.

Additionally, many of these dogs have no focus—they zip from one stimulus to the next and couldn't care less that there's a person around. Those dogs won't make it through service dog training and should not be considered for the job.

"Fake" Service Dogs

You're sitting in a café, enjoying a nice cup of coffee with your well-trained, well-mannered canine partner when someone waltzes in with a dog in tow. The dog is lunging at everyone who walks past, jumps up on the counter, gulps down a bagel, and then whirls around to start barking at people when they walk in.

The manager rushes forward and politely states, "We're sorry, ma'am, but we're going to have to ask you to take your dog outside. We don't allow pets."

Breezily, the woman waves him off and announces, "He's my service dog. He gets to go with me anywhere I go." The manager casts an appraising eye over the natural disaster of the dog who is now walking around and around his legs, tangling him in its leash, before hesitantly inquiring, "Do you have any papers?" He knows the law doesn't require ID for service dogs, but surely, for this dog, she's required to carry *something*, right?

The woman scoffs at the idea while reaching down to rub her dog's head. "I don't need any papers. Federal law doesn't require me to carry any. He's a service dog; that's all you need to know." The manager mumbles an apology and walks away. From the safety of the counter, he eyeballs the dog and owner as the woman allows him to run up to anyone, jump on their lap, and even kiss them or sniff their food.

Just before leaving, the dog squats on the floor and urinates. The dog's handler walks away from the mess and the manager sends a staff member to quickly clean it up. He considers calling the police but is afraid of getting in trouble for breaking ADA regulations and federal law. Finally, though, the woman leaves with her unruly dog in tow and he breathes a sigh of relief.

What other options did this poor, frazzled manager possess? Since the woman has produced the magic "service dog" words, it may have seemed he has no recourse but to back off and leave this self-professed "service dog" team be.

Fortunately for him, though (and the other patrons of the shop!), that's not the case. While federal service dog law is written to protect individuals with disabilities and their complete, unfettered public access with their (well-trained and behaved) canine partners, it also has provisions to protect businesses and other members of the public from "service dogs" in public who shouldn't be there.

Individuals with a disability have the right to have their service dog accompany them anywhere members of the public are allowed to be, but business owners and patrons have rights, too. There are two instances cited in federal law where a business may exclude a service dog: 1) The service dog is out of control and the handler isn't doing anything about it; 2) The service dog isn't housebroken and urinates or defecates inappropriately.

If a service dog team is asked to leave due to the dog's behavior, the business must provide the unaccompanied handler the opportunity to obtain goods or services. Only the dog can be excluded from the premises. If a dog's behavior infringes on the ability of other patrons to enjoy a safe, routine experience similar to one they would experience without a service dog on-site, then a business may be perfectly within their right legally to ask the team to leave. Before making that determination, though, check out the lists below detailing what service dogs in public should do and what service dogs in public shouldn't do. See page 19 for service dog legalities and more information on federal law relating to service dogs.

Service dogs in public should:

- Focus on their handler at all times unless doing trained task work.
- Possess a stable, even temperament without anxiety, reactivity, or aggression of any kind.
- Walk nicely on a leash without pulling, straining, lunging, lagging, circling, or foraging.
- Remain quietly by their handler's side when their handler stops without wandering or losing focus.
- Lie quietly under the table or beside their handler's chair without getting up or moving around excessively. Changing positions is fine; breaking stays to respond or engage with distractions or to wander off is not.
- Be able to recognize and ignore distractions.
- Be quiet at all times unless performing specific, trained task work. Unless working, service dogs should be seen by the public and not heard.
- Appear professional, well-groomed, and well-taken-care-of. Your service dog is both your representative and a diplomat for the service dog community and should leave positive impressions.
- Keep their nose to themself at all times, even if there are food, toys, products, or other interesting items readily accessible. Sniffing people, objects, or food is not only rude, it's a possible health hazard. Exceptions to this rule include allergen alert dogs or other service dogs who rely on their nose to perform their work. However, the service dog's sniffing should be directly related to task work and not random or merely "exploring."
- Respond quickly and readily to the handler's commands, cues, or directions. Service dogs should give off the appearance to anyone watching that they are highly trained and that they completely understand what's being asked of them.

Service dogs should possess outstanding obedience skills and above-average manners, and both should be readily apparent. A service dog's demeanor, training, and behavior should, without question, differentiate them from all but the best-trained pet dogs.

The canine must be able to do pertinent task work to mitigate their handler's disability. In order to be considered a "service dog" under US federal law, a dog must be partnered with an individual with a disability *and* perform specific, trained task work to mitigate that disability. Task work is not optional. If a dog doesn't perform task work, they're not a service dog—they're an emotional support animal, and not prepared for the complex role of a service dog in public.

Service dogs in public should *not*:

- Urinate or defecate inappropriately. If a dog isn't house trained, the dog isn't ready to be in the public domain, service dog or not. For younger service dogs in training, outings should be short enough to provide plenty of opportunities to make trips outside. "Accidents" are one of the few reasons a business can exclude a service dog team, and there are no reasons to have a service dog who isn't house trained. On very rare occasions, a service dog may truly be sick or have an upset belly and an accident is unavoidable, but those occurrences must definitely be the exception and not to be expected from service dogs on anything like a regular basis. If you know your service dog is ill, it may be wise to give them "sick days" so they do not embarrass you or create a negative impression of service dogs while recuperating.
- Pick food or objects up off the floor or steal (or even show much interest in) food or items that are sitting out. Exceptions include dogs who retrieve dropped items for their handlers or who are otherwise doing trained task work. In general, service dogs should not interact with distractions of any kind unless cued to them or otherwise working.

- Sniff staff members, patrons, floors, tables, counters, surfaces, products, shelving, or anything else unless the service dog is performing specific, trained task work, such as detecting allergens or other substances dangerous to their handler.
- Drag or pull their handler for any reason, unless the dog is performing specific mobility-related task work for their handler as evidenced by the presence of a brace mobility support harness, other task-related gear, or a wheelchair assistance harness.

A service dog's behavior should never appear "out of control," and there's a huge difference between a service dog providing counterbalance for their handler by leaning into a harness and a dog who is simply dashing here and there and yanking their handler toward distractions.

Service dogs should not wander or move widely out of heel position unless cued to by their handler. While service dogs aren't robots and can't be expected to maintain exact heel position at all times, neither should they range widely enough to infringe on the space, movement, or rights of other patrons or teams.

Service dogs should be responsive to their handlers' movements and focused enough to readily move with them without significant lags or delay. Service dogs should not be so engaged by or engrossed with the surrounding environment or distractions that they give the appearance of wandering, daydreaming, ignoring, or of just being generally untrained.

Service dogs should not break "stays," "unders," or other fixed-position behaviors to investigate distractions, explore, or otherwise move around. Exceptions include service dogs who must perform task work that requires them to take the initiative to respond to their handler's disability regardless of location or position or to retrieve assistance/medication/help. The service dog's decision to break position or disobey a "stay" should be a direct result of specific, trained task work. There's a huge difference between a dog who gets up because they're bored or distracted and a service dog who's obviously responding to their handler's disability or safety needs.

Service dogs should not be anxious, antsy, agitated, or aggressive in any way. A service dog should never make anyone interacting with her nervous or afraid because of her direct behavior. Service dogs should not stink, smell, or appear unkempt/ungroomed in any way. They should not engage with other dogs, people, children, or distractions unless allowed or instructed to do so by their human partner. There's nothing wrong with allowing a service dog to greet a friendly child or dog if the handler is comfortable with it, but it should be the handler's decision and choice, not the service dog's.

A service dog should not appear overly excited, unfocused, distracted, overstimulated, or otherwise out of control. There's no defined line in the sand on this one, but it's easy to know once you see it. This limit on behavior includes laying their head on stranger's knees, licking hands while passing by, or leaning against the legs of the person standing next in line. It's not "cute" or acceptable behavior regardless of whether or not the other person is okay with it.

Remember that training and handling your service dog means both the empathy and compassion needed with a pet or companion and also the discipline and consistency often needed when parenting a small child. Inconsistency or being overly indulgent can create significant problems for you and your canine partner down the road.

A service dog should never engage in any behavior or activity that could potentially be hurtful, harmful, leave a bad taste in someone's mouth. Their behavior should never cause the handler to have to apologize to the recipient. Many business owners fear excluding a poorly behaved team due to the "must provide access, or you're breaking the law" statements touted by those who drag their not-yet-trained dogs around with them in public, and with every instance their business, clients, or sense of control suffers due to a bad experience, the more all teams, even well-trained and professional ones, will encounter access challenges and issues.

Any individual who brings their untrained dog into the public claiming this is allowed because they're a service dog, whether they're still in training, or are in fact a fake service dog, negatively impacts or affects the service dog community as a whole and can cause major problems and issues for any and all real teams to follow in their wake.

Fund-Raising Options

Obtaining a service dog isn't without its costs, as we have discussed, and all disabilities add some degree of costs, service dog or no. Coming up with plans to fund-raise can be challenging.

While effective fund-raising takes time, energy, and passion, with a little creative thinking and planning, anyone can fund-raise for a service dog. When you're first beginning to fund-raise for a service dog, seek out organizations or groups who may be willing or able to assist you plan, host, or advertise events. Churches, scout troops, local lodges, or other service-based groups are excellent places to begin looking. For any events, activities, special occasions, or tournaments, be sure to either charge an admission/participation fee or to ask for an entry donation at the door. Some restaurants may agree to fund-raising events where the owner keeps the "door money" and the restaurant takes the profit from food and drinks.

Be sure to have fun along the way and don't get discouraged! Progress is progress, no matter how slow, and every donation adds up over time. A dollar may be only a dollar, but if one hundred people each give a dollar, then a difference is being made. Every drop in the bucket counts. Fund-raising platforms such as GoFundMe can also offer an easy way to track and raise money via social media.

Partnering with a Service Dog: Final Considerations

When it comes right down to it, no one can ask all the right questions. You and only you know whether or not a service dog is right for you and your lifestyle. At the end of the day, you're the one who's going to have to dig deep and accept responsibility for your choices. Service dogs bring peace, independence, security, and a new degree of ability to thousands of people, and if you're going to be one of them, congratulations, and welcome to the service dog community! If you're not, though, that's okay—assistance dogs are not right for everyone. Recognizing this is not a failure on your part.

Knowing yourself, your needs, strengths, and weaknesses, and knowing the needs and challenges that come with partnering with a service dog, will go a long way toward helping you make the best decision possible. We hope that this text has helped shed some light on behind-the-scenes insights, as well as stirred some questions to help you make a solid, informed decision.

3
SERVICE DOG SELECTION

SERVICE DOG SOURCE

Basic Considerations

It's time to look for your potential service dog. What traits should you look for? What's important? What doesn't matter? There is a sea of information, and a good deal of misinformation, that a service dog trainer or handler must sort through while picking a puppy or candidate.

As you make your way to the middle of a wriggling pile of puppies, it occurs to you that one of these tiny balls of fur is going to be your friend, your partner, your focus, your pride, your companion, your joy, and your worker. Not only will this puppy be all of the above, it's going to be the one meant for you. Musing over these thoughts as you allow the puppies to swarm over you, you idly pick one up and ask it, "Are you the one?"

Laughing as the puppy bites your finger, you gather the soft, fat critter into your arms, breathe in the intoxicating puppy aroma, and daydream about all the possibilities. The puppy wriggles for a bit in protest at being restrained but quickly quiets down, snuggles its head against your belly, and falls asleep. While you know that the service dog selection process is far from over, something in your heart says that this puppy is the right one.

The scenario laid out above is one that nearly every "dog person" is familiar with. Almost every single one of us has had a dog that "picked us." Sometimes, the dog's choice was a good one and sometimes, it wasn't. Therein lies the inherent problem. When the dog is allowed to choose their handler, the results are left in the hands of chance.

Picking a service dog leaves enough left to chance when everything is done perfectly, let alone when pieces of the equation are incomplete or missing. Even dogs who have been selected from an extensive line of well-bred service dogs, been trained and socialized to the utmost degree, and have undergone extensive medical testing to ensure soundness for work don't always make it to the completion of service dog training. This is a stark and daunting reality for some. Being a service dog is hard work, and very few dogs are suitable. Maximize your chances of picking a service dog successfully by carefully considering your needs and desires, and then working to find the perfect service dog candidate. Don't let a puppy pick you until you've narrowed it down to "almost no chance of failure."

The simple fact of the matter is that we, as the human members of a service dog team, are much more intelligent than our four-legged partners. The puppy that chooses you and tugs at your heartstrings may or may not be the proper puppy for your goals, needs, and ability level. You, as the human half of the team, must carefully consider several factors in order to choose a potential partner who has the most likely chance of succeeding as your canine lifeline and service dog.

The solution is not an easy or quick one. Be patient. Picking a service dog candidate involves careful research, a lot of time, and in-depth (and, at times, brutally honest) consideration of your goals, wants, needs, and desires. Settle in, though, and hang on tight. We're in for a whirlwind trip through the confusing world of service dog selection.

Picking a Service Dog Breed

Picking the breed or mix of your service dog is a highly personal decision. The first place to begin is with your partner's size.

Do you need a large, sturdy dog suitable for brace and mobility support? Or will a mid-sized dog be suitable? Do you need a small breed that's easy to transport and care for due to frequent hospitalizations or travel? Do you need an agile breed that's compact? If you travel frequently, a smaller dog might be much more manageable than a larger dog.

Once you've selected a size, consider the parts of your potential partner that you can never change, like grooming needs and activity level. If you do not like long hair, then you will not enjoy having to groom a long-haired dog or having to pay to have them groomed. Do not select a breed known for traits you simply can't see yourself ever learning to love.

Finally, consider the necessary traits common to all successful service dogs—calm demeanor, solid handler focus, friendly and without suspicion, aggression, or timidity, highly trainable yet capable of doing the same job day in and day out without boredom interfering, and a dog that is inherently driven to seek out and perform work.

Write out a Venn diagram with the three realms of breed selection—size, unchangeable attributes, and temperament—and use a breed profile site to start slotting potential breeds into place in the diagram according to your needs. When you finally arrive at a breed (or two or three) that fits best in the center of the diagram, you're ready to move on.

The following ten points will allow you to carefully weigh your options and choose a candidate that's well suited for you.

1. The Source

First and foremost, you must consider the ultimate source of your puppy. Will your partner be a rescue or come from a breeder? There are pros and cons for each option. Due to the sheer number of breeders and rescues available, this first item of contemplation can seem overwhelming. Start by asking yourself the following questions:

How long has this breeder been producing this breed or how long has this rescue facility been in service?

A breeder who has been working with Labradors for thirty-five years has much more experience than one who has only been breeding for two years. While a new breeder or rescue shouldn't automatically be excluded, taking this into consideration is a precautionary measure of discernment in the selection process. Knowledge comes from a variety of sources and can be amassed quickly, but experience comes only with time and practice.

Does this source have return clients?

It's commonly said that word-of-mouth references are the best form of advertising. The best indicator of success, though, lies with return customers. Anyone can have a positive experience once. It's those who come back time and time again that offer the best indication of good service.

If a breeder's or rescue's name keeps popping up among your friends or contacts in the service dog world, it's a good rule of thumb to at least add them to your list so that you can do some more research on the side.

Do you like this person?

Many people say that you don't have to like a person in order to do business with them. In many cases, that's correct. When it comes to choosing your puppy's source, though, nothing could be further from the truth. You are, in essence, picking your puppy's godparent—pick carefully! This is the person who has the most experience with your puppy's line, genetics, and potential. You need and want them to be an invaluable resource, much like a mentor, and not a person that you dread communicating with. It cannot be overstated: set yourself and your partner up for success.

Do you agree with the source's philosophy?

The best potential service dog puppies come from sources who socialize extensively and expose the puppies to a wide range of experiences long before they ever go home. Does your source use early learning or bioconditioning with their puppies? Do you agree with the source's beliefs on training, raising, and loving dogs?

2. The Parents

"The apple doesn't fall far from the tree." When it comes to puppies, this quote is very sound. Quite simply, you cannot create what you do not have to begin with. You cannot create something from nothing. If there's something about the parents that you just don't like, don't assume that your puppy won't inherit that characteristic. While the way you raise your puppy has much to do with how they turn out, your puppy's parents have even more influence. Insist on meeting at least the puppy's mother. If you wouldn't want to own her yourself, don't put a deposit on one of her puppies.

3. The Parent's Genetics

Make certain that your puppy's parents have been tested for all genetic diseases common in your breed of choice. You have too much at stake with your new team member to pour thousands of hours of training, love, and socialization into them only to lose your friend and partner to a genetic mismatch.

4. The Parents' Joints

There's been a lot of debate concerning hip and elbow dysplasia and whether these diseases are genetic or not. Regardless, if your puppy's parents have good hips and elbows, it's likely that your puppy will as well. Adult dogs can't have their hips or elbows certified until they are two years of age. Common hip and elbow certification and registry agencies include the Orthopedic Foundation for Animals (OFA) and PennHIP. If a puppy's parents have their hips certified, that information will be visible on the puppy's pedigree and registration certificate. Additionally, the breeder will have certificates to show you for each parent.

If you're picking a service dog candidate from a rescue, it's all but impossible to be certain of the puppy's genetics or joint health. It's a huge gamble, but if you look for basic structural soundness in mom and babies and have preliminary X-rays done early to check joint health, you'll have a better chance of success. As a professional recommendation, regardless of whether your partner will be doing brace and mobility support work, it is strongly advised to get the preliminary X-rays.

5. The Parents'/Relatives' Success

The phrase "history repeats itself" also rings true in the performance dog, working dog, and service dog world. If you want a top-notch service dog, you need to select a puppy from parents who are known for producing top-notch service dogs. While many excellent service dogs have come from parents who have never produced service dogs and from unproven lines, you increase your team's chances of success exponentially by carefully examining your potential puppy's performance history.

Look for repeat service dog status, multiple therapy dogs, and a wide range of performance indicators, like basic obedience certifications (CGC or C.L.A.S.S.), temperament testing (ATTS), sports titles (like obedience, rally, or agility) and other signs that the line produces dogs with stable temperaments and that are able to succeed in a wide range of work, particularly the type of work that requires handler focus, high degrees of specialized skill or training, and a calm, stable demeanor. Though sports titles don't necessarily indicate qualities you'd want for a service dog, it indicates that a breeder produces their puppies purposefully and can provide guidance.

6. The Puppy's Temperament

Temperament is, quite simply, your puppy's nature. It's the demeanor your puppy was born with and the tendencies your puppy will have the rest of their life. The best tip to remember as it relates to temperament testing is "What you see is what you get." Your puppy will not "grow out of" anything you see at an early age, including, but not limited to, aggression, timidity, aloofness, overstimulation, or asserting dominance.

Familiarize yourself with some basic puppy temperament tests and then select one or two to use with candidates. The test should measure temperament, drives, and potential, and give you a base idea of what you're looking at. They're not always 100 percent accurate, but they provide a starting point. You want the puppy who is firmly in the middle of the road—not dominant, but not submissive. Again, find that happy medium. The dog should not be cocky to the point of stupidity, but also not cautious and wary about everything; not clingy but not aloof. Strive to find the happy medium.

7. The Puppy's Attitude

The puppy's attitude can be most closely equated with their personality. Some puppies are extremely happy and others stoic. Some puppies are goofy and others poised. A puppy's temperament may be perfect for your needs, but their attitude and approach to life may not mesh with yours. Make sure that you spend some time with your puppy before you take them home so that you can ensure you like your puppy's personality. Good compatibility lends to long-term success.

8. The Puppy's Drives

A puppy's drives motivate a puppy to work. Some puppies have an extremely strong play drive; others have a strong prey or food drive. Before testing a puppy's drive, you must first determine what type of training you use most frequently. Many service dog handlers and programs favor clicker training and positive reinforcement. That being said, balanced methods are also common, especially when working on distraction proofing and advanced skills.

You do not want a puppy who is insanely driven to chase the toys or who seems positively desperate to get the food no matter what. Those puppies can have a difficult time focusing while learning and working if rewards are present. They're also a nightmare to distraction proof! To the contrary, though, you don't want an aloof puppy without interest. Never assume that you can "build" a puppy's drive—they either have it or they don't.

Select the puppy who happily chases a ball and follows a food lure without a frantic, agitated air. You want the puppy who doesn't quit, but not the puppy that will push past the point of exhaustion to win.

9. The Puppy's Health

A healthy dog starts out as a healthy puppy. Always remember that a sound structure is built on a sound foundation. If your puppy starts out unhealthy, you can oftentimes fix it. You cannot, however, fix the foundational damage that might have been done. A healthy puppy is active, has bright eyes free of discharge, and has a soft, shiny coat free from bald patches, scabs, scales, dandruff, or sores. Make sure that the entire litter looks healthy and then spend extra time examining the puppies you are considering bringing home. It is always advisable to enlist the help of an animal medical professional for assistance in specialized areas such as a thorough health examination.

10. Your Gut Feeling

Last but not least, don't ignore your gut feeling. If something is right, it will feel right. Even if there's not an instant spark or connection, you'll feel in your core if you're making a good choice. If something in you says that your choice isn't quite right, listen to it!

When you've done all the research, carefully weighed your options, checked the health and personality of the parents and other puppies, and you're not quite sure what to do next, listen to your heart and of course the professionals whose help you have enlisted. Pick the puppy who resonates with you the deepest and begin the long, arduous journey to success with your best potential service dog by your side.

Evaluating Candidates at the Shelter

There are thousands of service dogs in the United States. Many of those service dogs graduated from programs or organizations, some were owner-trained, and still others trained and placed via other methods. For many owner trainers and programs, rescue dogs are selected to complete service dog training, and have varying degrees of success. Very few dogs are capable of enjoying and succeeding at service dog work. Even in service dog and guide dog programs that use well-established breeding programs, the rate of failure can be high. It truly takes a unique and special temperament to flourish as a partner to a person with a disability, and while temperament is most important, there are lots of other factors that matter, too.

Breed, gender, and color aren't as important as good health, genetics, and structure. If a dog isn't bred for service dog work, and it has an unknown history or backstory, it can be very difficult to decide whether or not that dog should be considered for service dog training. When it comes to evaluating rescue dogs or dogs at a shelter for service dog work, you must first keep in mind what disqualifies a dog from becoming a service dog in training. If a dog exhibits any fear, timidity, reactivity, or aggression, or showcases any kind of health or structural flaw and/or behavioral concerns, then that dog is *not* a candidate, all other factors aside. Again, it is highly encouraged to seek a professional's opinion when in doubt, as well as for a second opinion.

Never select a dog for service dog work with the belief that you can "fix" an inherent temperament flaw or issue. Generally speaking, if you have to fix a dog's problems, then the dog isn't a service dog candidate. There are exceptions, of course, as with anything, but they're few and far between. That being said, you've also got to remember that training and temperament are two very different things. If a behavior a dog is exhibiting is a natural behavior all dogs do (like pulling on the leash when excited or jumping up to greet), then it can be rectified with training. A happy, social dog with low touch sensitivity and an amazing willingness to interact who pulls on a leash might still be a candidate for service dog work—but a dog who scrambles away from strangers to cower at the end of the leash is not. One requires training to fix, and the other is a temperament issue, whether inherent or learned.

When evaluating any trait or tendency a dog has, ask yourself if puppies do it. Do puppies mouth? Yes. Do they typically snap, snarl, or bite? No. Do puppies jump? Absolutely. Do they typically climb fences and walls? No (Malinois puppies exempted). Do puppies take treats roughly? Bet your last dollar they do. Do they growl and snarl and protect food from anything approaching? Not usually. If a balanced, normal puppy would showcase a behavior or tendency or trait, then it's possibly something that can be fixed with training.

Adult dogs aren't automatically perfect because they're adults. Puppies mouth, pull on leashes, jump, tangle up in people's legs, grab food out of hands, and many other things because they're untrained. Adult dogs who have never been trained will also exhibit these behaviors. Your job is to look at the dog's core temperament, not their instincts or base behaviors, and work to evaluate a dog's suitability based on who they are, not what they do.

Here are five things you can look for when evaluating shelter dogs or rescue dogs for service dog work. This is not a fail-safe list; it's just a general guide on things to keep your eye out for. Only perhaps one out of every one hundred dogs is suitable as a service dog candidate, so just because a dog meets every one of these points doesn't automatically mean they'll successfully complete training. However, if a dog does meet these points of criteria, it means that there's a higher probability of success, and they should be evaluated further and with more depth.

1. Age

When you're evaluating a dog from a shelter or rescue organization, it's very important to carefully consider the age of the dog. Evaluating puppies is an entirely different ballgame, so we're only going to talk about adolescent and adult dogs here. It's preferable that a rescue dog being evaluated for service dog suitability is a bit older. You want to be able to see their structure and temperament clearly, without the possibility that puberty or growing up will change things. As such, you should consider dogs within a few months of a year to two-and-a-half years old. You don't want a dog who is too old, because training takes a long time (months to years), and the working life of the dog is shortened significantly if they begin training too late in life.

2. Health and Structure

The dog you're looking at shouldn't have any apparent health issues or concerns. This can be difficult to determine in a shelter environment, due to the dogs' close proximity, varying health care standards and diets, or other factors. However, the dog in question shouldn't have weepy eyes, gunky ears, sores, or coat issues. Heavy shedding occurs often in shelters due to diet and stress levels, but the coat shouldn't have bald spots, and there shouldn't be lumps, bumps, or growths. Skeletal or muscular injuries disqualify a dog from service dog work, and a dog shouldn't be overweight.

You need to see the dog move and run. You need to see the dog's natural gait and movement style, and how they look when just being themselves. There should be absolutely no lameness, limping, or oddities in gait. The back should be straight, and there should be good angulation in the shoulders so that there's no limitations on how the legs move. The dog's rear end should be well-muscled and appear to "drive" the dog forward when it runs.

Dogs with flatter skulls (boxers, bulldogs, lots of toy breeds) should typically not receive first consideration—there's too much tendency toward breathing issues or fragile physiology. Once again, if you are uncertain about any of the traits you are looking at or looking for, consult a professional for guidance. The road to success is yours to navigate, but don't feel you need to do so alone.

3. Noise and Cleanliness

These are two of the very first things you should check when you first walk past a dog's kennel. A dog who keeps a naturally clean space and who tends to be quiet is a huge plus. Service dogs are supposed to be somewhat invisible while out working—they shouldn't make noise of any kind, unless it's trained for their task work and it's performed on cue. When you first walk into a shelter kennel room, the barking is usually overwhelming. If you quietly walk through, though, you can sometimes find one or two dogs who aren't joining in the noise, and who are quietly relaxing in their kennel. That's a dog who is able to relax despite chaos and confusion, who has a high threshold for distractions, and who is naturally able to settle.

It's vital to determine, though, once you find a quiet, relaxed dog, whether or not the dog is quiet because they're naturally that way, or because they're depressed. How willing is the dog to interact with you? Any tail thumping? Or are they exhibiting relaxed body language, such as tail and ears in loose natural positions, calm gaze, cool and collected demeanor, etc.? If the dog is relaxed and readily comes forward to interact with the evaluator, definitely ask to spend some one-on-one time with said dog.

Next, look to see if a dog's space is clean. In a shelter environment, even house-trained dogs may struggle to not toilet in their kennel, especially if there's no dog walker program or exercise time. However, there's a huge difference between a dog who potties in a corner of the cage and then makes an active effort to avoid it, and a dog who ends up walking through it, tracking it onto their bed/blanket, etc. Check to see if there's food thrown all over—messy eaters tend to be messy in other areas, too, and again it showcases a tendency toward not keeping a clean space.

4. Important Traits

This is the most important piece of determining whether or not a dog will make a service dog candidate. Dogs who complete service dog training successfully typically have the following traits (not at all a comprehensive list):

- No timidity, aggression, reactivity, or fear issues during interactions, introductions to new environments, etc.
- Not extremely submissive and not extremely strong-willed, as seen in their socializations, their demeanor, or interactive behaviors, etc.
- Very balanced, easygoing, calm nature
- Enjoys interaction with humans
- Social, but not over the top; note their energy levels and excitability during social interactions as well as the kinds of behaviors they exhibit toward other animals as well as people; gauge whether their behavior is acceptable and appropriate for the given situation and environment
- Able to focus on people, even if there are distractions
- Willingness to learn
- Low touch sensitivity; the dog is accepting of being touched, jostled, moved, bumped, etc. and is responsive but not reactive to the touch.
- High frustration threshold; the dog does not lose poise or calm demeanor when experiencing a frustrating

situation. An example of low frustration threshold would be a dog that does not want to be tethered might start whining, fussing, pulling, or crying, versus a dog being tethered and expressing its discontent with calm, quiet patience instead. The latter dog has a high frustration threshold.

- Not excessively excited about toys or treats
- Appropriately interacts with other dogs (no hackling, overstimulation, extremely pushy play, etc.)
- No issues with other animals, including cats, birds, or small animals
- Ability to quietly relax in all environments
- Travels readily and responds to new places, people, and things with few signs of stress
- Accepts guidance and containment and boundaries willingly and readily; is quiet and relaxed while tethered, doesn't express frustration (barking, whining, scratching, etc.) when contained.

That's quite a number of things, and it's by no means a complete list. Here's what to look for once you take a (hopefully quiet, healthy) dog out of their (hopefully clean) kennel.

First, make sure the dog wants to be with people. Lots of dogs are aloof and independent—they couldn't care less whether or not a person is there. Take the dog out on a leash to the designated meet-and-greet area, and let them get their sniffing out of the way, and then sit down in a chair (or on the ground, if you're comfortable with the dog), and see what happens. A dog who enjoys the company of people will want to check in with you. They may not stay right by your side, but they'll run out to sniff or play, and then return, or they'll try to engage you, or they'll get all up in your business wagging and being happy. In a nutshell, you want a dog who is more interested in *you*, the evaluator, than in things going on around them.

Second, test the dog's response to treats and toys. You want a dog who readily takes food from your hand, who is willing to follow a lure, and who isn't so happy to see food that they can't contain themselves.

The same applies with toys—being willing to play with toys is fine, but you absolutely do not want a dog who locks on to the fact that a toy is present and who can't think about or do anything else except try to play with the toy.

Try luring the dog into sits or downs—do they readily follow the lure, or at least try to? How many times will the dog lure? You want a dog who is willing to continue to engage and who is able to stay on task, or who is at least willing to continue to try.

Third, make absolutely certain this dog doesn't have issues with resource-guarding, other dogs (including small ones), or small animals.

Fourth, put the dog on a leash and anchor the end. Step on it, loop it around a chair leg, or simply hold it. Don't say anything. Don't try to direct the dog. Just stand quietly and wait. How long does it take for the dog to recognize it can't go anywhere, to stop trying, and to just stand or sit quietly or lie down? You want a dog who accepts boundaries readily and who doesn't get easily frustrated. In a quiet location, with little going on, a dog who is on leash and who has a natural tendency to be a calm, relaxed sort of dog, will readily chill or settle.

Fifth, check the dog for touch sensitivity. Pet the dog all over their head, body, belly, legs, and tail. Touch the ears. Lift them. Look at the teeth. Gently rub the dog's muzzle. Handle the dog's feet. Gently pinch the skin between the toes. You need a dog who is comfortable with being touched all over, with a good pain tolerance, and isn't reactive to touch.

5. Final Considerations

In a nutshell, service dogs have to be stable, steady, and calm in all situations and environments, readily able to learn, willing to interact with people for hours upon hours a day, possess the independence to perform task work without being guided through every single step, and have the intelligence to learn complicated behaviors. They have to be willing to do the same thing, day in and day out, and respond readily to guidance and cues.

Good service dogs start as good service dogs in training. You can't build a solid base of training on a poor temperament or structural foundation. If you have doubts, the dog probably isn't right for service dog work.

Trust your gut and heed the advice and guidance of the professional opinions you inquire about. Don't think you can "fix" something; you shouldn't have to. Look for a canine candidate who is quiet, relaxed, gentle, social, responsive, and balanced. If you're not sure, have a second evaluator take a look. Ask the behaviorist on site. Talk to any foster homes. Never listen to the enthusiastic, "Oh, yeah, this dog would be a great service dog; she's so sweet!" There's so much more required than just being sweet.

Don't settle for a dog that's "almost" what you want, because it's very likely that dog will "almost" complete training. Be picky and patient—the perfect dog is out there. Prepare for success at every turn.

Programs

Service dog organizations provide programs that specialize in selecting, evaluating, training, and placing fully trained service dogs with individuals with disabilities. Some programs breed their own dogs so that they can select for certain traits, such as coat type or size, whereas others receive donated puppies from breeders or partner with local rescues. Partnering with a service dog organization, in a perfect world, offers several benefits, including professional treatment, highly polished training, strong support and aftercare, healthy dogs, and a wealth of knowledge.

However, not all service dog organizations and programs are created equal. In the United States, there are no required certifications, licenses, permits, or education requisites for service dog (or even dog training) programs. Anyone can say they're a service dog trainer, and, unfortunately, there are dozens of fraudulent or extremely low-quality organizations and trainers out there.

Through careful research and asking lots of questions, though, you can find a quality organization that's reputable and that meets your needs. The first thing many people do when they decide to begin researching the process of receiving a service dog is Googling some variation of "Service dogs + (their state)." While that may be an excellent place to begin the search, it's very important to remember that proximity should not be the only consideration. In fact, it should rate pretty low on the list of important things to look for when selecting an organization.

More important factors include the affiliation and status of the program, if any; the type of training methodology used; the program's experience in training service dogs (and their experience with your disability); and the program's expectations, requirements, offered support, and success rate. Every program operates differently, and it's vital to carefully screen any programs you're potentially interested in partnering with. It can be difficult knowing what to ask, so here's a list of questions to help service dog handlers, owners, and trainers find a program that best suits their needs.

PROGRAM QUESTIONS

1. Is this program a member of any professional service dog organizations? Which? For how long?
2. Is this program a member in good standing with Assistance Dog International or the International Guide Dog Federation? If not, why not? Are they planning to seek ADI accreditation?
3. If the program is not an ADI program, do they uphold ADI standards for behavior, training, partnership, and their trainers? Why or why not?
4. Where is the program based? Do they accept out-of-state applicants?
5. What training and/or certifications do staff undergo/hold regarding service dog training? What about working with people with disabilities? Does the program require staff and trainers to undergo continuing education?
6. How long has the program been operational? How many teams have graduated through the program?
7. How many teams have recertified through the program? What's the success rate for candidates? Can I see some of your dogs? What about your facility?

8. What type of service dogs does the program place? Are trainers required to undergo specialty training or certifications for the various kinds?
9. What's the application process? Is there a step-by-step guide? Is an interview required? If yes, can it be done via telephone or video conference if I'm not local?
10. Can I see a copy of the contract graduates must sign? Do you require NDAs? What about noncompetes?
11. Is the program a nonprofit? If so, can I see the 501(c)3 documentation? What about the annual financial statements for the last three to five years? If the program isn't a nonprofit, why not?
12. Is there a fee to receive a dog? If so, how much? Am I purchasing the dog or providing a donation to the program? Are payments allowed? Will the program assist with fund-raising? What kind of guarantees are provided? Are receipts provided for all payments?
13. What's the minimum age for applicants? Maximum? If you place with children, how do you determine if a child is mature enough to work effectively with a service dog?
14. Is there a waiting period before I receive a dog? How long? Do you do rush contracts? If yes, is a rush fee required?
15. Are dogs chosen specifically for each applicant or do applicants receive dogs as they're ready, regardless of compatibility? How are dogs matched to potential handlers? Do I have any input regarding my dog? Can I help pick breeds?

TRAINING QUESTIONS

1. What's the program's training methodology? Do they use traditional training methods, positive reinforcement/motivational, blended methods, etc.?
2. What will cause a dog to be career changed? Does the program try to "fix" serious issues like severe reactivity

or timidity late in the training process? What temperaments or characteristics does the program look for?

3. What skills do all dogs in your program learn? Do you custom train dogs for unique needs? Do you dual- or multi-train dogs for multiple disabilities?
4. Do you train for adults with autism? What about young children? Do you tether train autism dogs? Do you train triad teams?
5. What kind of training or skills must I have before applying? Do I need O&M training? What books do you recommend I read to prepare for service dog handling?
6. How many commands do your dogs learn? What behaviors do all dogs know without a cue—house manners, potty training, vehicle manners, etc.?
7. What kind of equipment do you use during training? What equipment is a dog placed with? Does the program provide equipment after graduation or do I need to purchase it?
8. Is there required team training so my dog and I can graduate? Is it done at the program or on-site at my location?
9. How long is team training? Do I do team training by myself with just a trainer and my dog or will I graduate as part of a group of multiple handlers and dogs?
10. Is there a schedule of events for team training? Can I see it? Will there be a graduation ceremony?
11. Can I bring someone with me to team training?
12. If team training is done at the program location, how is lodging handled? Are accommodations available on-site? If not, what hotels are close by? Are discounts available?
13. Does the program provide transportation during team training or must I handle my own transport? What about to and from team training?
14. What will be required of both me and my dog to graduate from the program successfully? What if one of us requires additional training? How is that handled?

15. Is training support and troubleshooting provided by the program after graduation? Is there a set bonding protocol provided?
16. Can I continue my dog's training in obedience, task work, or performance events? If no, why?
17. What kind of follow-up or recertification is required? Will I need to return to the program for any reason after graduation?
18. Will my dog protect me? (The answer to this should always be no.)

DOG QUESTIONS

1. What breeds of dogs do you use in your program?
2. Where are the dogs sourced? Are they rescue dogs, purchased from breeders, bred in-house?
3. What health and genetic testing do you require for your candidates? What temperament tests do you use?
4. Do you offer a health guarantee? If so, can I see it? How long does it last?
5. Do you maintain ownership of my service dog? If so, why? For how long? Under what circumstances would my dog be removed from my care?
6. Can I have pets in addition to my service dog? What kinds? Are they required to have any additional training? Are there health requirements, like spaying or neutering? What about breed restrictions?
7. When my service dog retires, what happens? Do I get to keep them?
8. If my service dog doesn't work out or we're having problems, what happens? Will I receive a replacement dog? What about a refund?
9. Are dogs raised by puppy raisers? Are they kept in a kennel environment? If so, for how long?

Once you've asked all the questions you'd like to ask and you've had your concerns addressed, consider if you've seen any red flags or things that make you uncomfortable or uncertain about the program. A program that's a good fit will make you feel certain about your decision, without qualms, and excited about moving forward.

If something feels "off," you should dig a little deeper to make sure everything is okay and as it seems. Keep an eye out for red flags. Ethical programs don't place puppies as fully trained dogs. They don't make extraordinary claims regarding skill or capability. They don't make claims about training that contradict science. They don't use aversive equipment on puppies.

They openly share information about their policies, contracts, and procedures. They provide support for their teams. They adhere to industry standards. They source dogs reliably and health test them. They have health records on hand for all dogs and provide them during placement.

Some of the larger, nationally known programs, such as Guiding Eyes or Canine Companions for Independence, have multiyear waiting lists. Other programs, like 4 Paws For Ability, focus only on serving children with autism or sensory processing disorders. Still others offer extremely flexible financial arrangements and placement options. The uniqueness of each program means that somewhere out there, there's a program to fit your needs. Once you've found the one, good luck with your journey moving forward.

Pros of working with a program:

- Professional training and support
- Healthy, vetted, highly suitable dogs
- Knowledgeable staff, trainers, and volunteers
- Proven success
- Lasting support and community inclusion
- Exact procedures and process

Cons of working with a program:

- Difficult to discover the correct program
- Little owner input regarding type, breed, or specific dog

- Bound to program requirements and expectations
- Can be expensive

Started Dogs

Started dogs are young or adolescent dogs who have been extensively socialized, house trained, crate trained, and "started" in basic obedience and public access skills. Started Dogs have been carefully evaluated for service dog aptitude. Oftentimes, owner-trainers or even programs will seek "started" dogs so that they can immediately begin advanced public access work and task training.

Owner-Trainer

Under US federal law, there are no requirements for a service dog to come from a program or organization. It's perfectly legal, and quite common, for someone to "owner train" their own service dog. Typically, this is done because of the cost, but in the long run, owner training can cost significantly more as a result of failed candidates, health issues, or dogs being unable to complete training due to behavioral, genetic, or health issues.

On the Psych Dog Partners organizational website, they offer the following price comparison and notations:

> *Costs can vary widely for owner service dog training, but they tend to be much less than the cost of a program-trained dog. Here are the costs for two service dogs owner-trained by Dr. Veronica Morris.*
>
> *Dog A, rescued adult from animal shelter, 2 years training time:*
> *$100 purchase price*
> *$2,000 vet bills (inherited dental issues caused increased costs)*
> *$2,000 training expenses (emotional baggage caused increased costs)*
> *$100 service gear*
> *<u>$1,000 food/treats/toys</u>*
> *$5,200 total*

Dog B, purchased puppy from service dog breeder, 2 years training time:
$2,250 purchase price
$750 vet bills
$1,100 training expenses
$100 Service gear
$1,000 food/treats/toys
$5,200 total

Dr. Morris's experience has been that the purchase price of Dog B is offset by Dog A's increased medical and training costs due to her being a rescue with some emotional baggage and inherited medical issues. In the end, it cost Dr. Morris about the same to obtain and train a dog from an expensive breeder as it did to train a shelter dog.

Dog A went on to require $3,000 in vet bills for joint and other medical issues that may have some genetic basis. Additionally, her working life span was cut short by inherited medical conditions.

Remember that above all you are trying to find a dog that will succeed in being trained as your service dog. Save money for a few more months or fund-raise to get the dog that is right for you. Don't settle for a dog that is not your first choice. Make your decision based on what will be best for you, which type of dog will be most likely to succeed with your abilities and lifestyle.

Proper owner training requires a great dog, support from an amazing trainer or a background in training dogs, and lots of time, patience, and accepting that things may not turn out the way you want them to. Keep in mind, it is as important to know the dog's limitations, needs, and abilities as it is to acknowledge your own as the handler and/or trainer. Should you feel you are not able to perform the necessary training yourself, or have some limiting factors preventing you from providing the best possible training for your dog, it is advisable to seek help from your support group or professional resources.

It can take two or more years to train a service dog, and the time dedication is upward of twenty to thirty hours a week—properly training a service dog is like taking on a part-time job! It can also require that you spend a great deal of time in public, with strangers, doing new things, and going new places, so that your dog gets the proper amount and type of training and practice. Many types of disabilities make this kind of public access training very difficult.

It's important to weigh the cost-benefit analysis of training your own dog against fund-raising for a dog or waiting for one through a program. Remember to weigh all options and establish the best course of action based on your situation, limiting factors, and situational restrictions. The investment is big for handler and dog alike.

SERVICE DOG BREEDS

Labrador Retriever

In the working and service dog world, the stocky, social, sweet-natured Labrador retriever is iconic. They're well-known not only for their prowess as a search and rescue K-9, detector dog, and service dog, but also for their die-hard loyalty and friendship to all. The "Lab" is a top choice in service dog programs around the world and is suitable for nearly any service dog task unless the work tasks the dog must perform are better suited to a smaller breed.

Bred in Newfoundland from a stock of thick-furred, heavy-boned water dogs, the Labrador retriever originated early in the nineteenth century as a sporting, hunting, and working dog. The Lab we know and love today began taking shape in the early 1900s as the breed caught the eye of fanciers and they began breeding to a working and conformation standard. The Labrador retriever is a sturdy, solid dog bred for one thing and one thing only: to pick things up, carry them around, and bring them back to their handler. While retrieving may be what the Lab is bred for, this fleet-footed, muscular dog excels at nearly all tasks set to it. Extremely intelligent and trainable, the Labrador is quick-witted and a problem solver.

Per the American Kennel Club breed standard, Labs should possess a "stable temperament," weigh "55 to 75 pounds," and be an "outgoing and devoted companion." Those qualities combine with a short, sleek, water-resistant coat, superb handler focus, and the grit to keep working even when it's tough, to create a breed perfectly suited to assistance dog work.

It's important to remember that every well-trained service dog begins life like any other dog: as a puppy. Lab babies can be high energy, which lands them in some not-so-good situations with inexperienced owners. The Labrador's calm demeanor and unshakable obedience are often touted, but what's left out is the two-year kangaroo phase where they seem to have springs attached to their paws and chainsaws bent on destruction in their mouths.

Labrador puppies chew. They mouth. They carry. They steal. They're exceptionally happy, wiggly dogs who wish to share their joy at having *anything*, no matter how stinky or big, in their mouths with anyone who happens to be near them. They're exceptionally friendly and social dogs, which if not carefully managed, can grow into behaviors that will exclude them from service work. While the Labrador retriever puppy phase takes careful work to overcome, the resultant animal is a friend, partner, and confidant for life. A well-trained and socialized Labrador is a calm, steady, and reliable presence in the face of any of life's obstacles.

Labs are large dogs and they shed year-round. They come in three colors: black, chocolate, and yellow. Each color has varying shades. It's been proven via decades of field trials that black-coated dogs tend to be better field dogs, chocolate dogs have a calmer demeanor but often suffer from skin issues, and yellow-coated dogs fall somewhere in between. The jury is still out on whether that's the case because black Labs are worked more in the field and chocolate Labs have been relegated to the job of "house pet" or if there are actual genetic ties between coat color and working ability. Because they tend to be seen as "friendlier" in the eyes of the public, yellow Labs tend to be favored as service dogs, but you'll see a smattering of other colors as well.

Labs have a thick, dense, almost waterproof coat. They also possess a strong love of water. Throw a stick in a pond for your Lab to go after, and they'll be the happiest dog around. They're tireless workers, especially when it comes to retrieving. Labrador retrievers excel at flyball, dock diving, tracking, search and rescue, field trials and hunting, assistance dog work, and obedience. They're stellar hiking partners. Fortunately for most service dog handlers, Labrador retrievers are quite adaptable. Once out of the puppy phase, they're flexible with their needs. If you need a day to simply relax and lounge, they're happy to keep you company. Once you're ready to face the world, they'll always be by your side, shoring you up, no matter what you're doing or where you're going.

Unfortunately, due to the popularity of the breed, backyard breeders have introduced a number of health concerns into the Labrador retriever gene pool. Hip and elbow dysplasia are of a particular concern, and any service dog candidate should have parents who possess OFA or PennHIP certifications.

When selecting a Labrador puppy for service dog work, above all else, consider the temperament of the mother. It's been shown over and over again that puppies are likely to inherit the demeanor of their momma. Ideally, Mom (and Dad) would have ATTS temperament certifications or possess other titles/degrees that showcase that the puppy is trainable, solid in distracting environments, and sweet-natured.

The Labrador retriever is an all-around good dog who, with proper puppyhood education and upbringing, will excel at any job. They have a decades-long history in the working dog arena, and for most service dog programs, are a top breed of choice. With a properly bred and trained Lab by your side, you can expect reliable performance, lots of laughs, a steady temperament, tons of shedding, and a friend for life.

Golden Retriever

Golden retrievers are hardworking, soft-mouthed dogs bred for steady nerves, handler focus, predictable responses, and the endurance to work all day in substandard conditions. Their name is derived from their long double coat that comes in varying shades of "gold" that range from the lightest cream, almost white, to a deep, dark, coppery red.

They're sensitive, docile critters who thrive on human companionship and learning new things. They've been bred for decades as working dogs, and it's no surprise that they're one of the most common breeds used for service and assistance dog work. In fact, Dr. Bonita Bergin, the woman behind the modern concept of the "service dog" and the founder of the Assistance Dog Institute and Bergin University, cites Golden retrievers as the best breed for service dog work, because of their calm disposition, size, and structure. These big, beautiful dogs possess superb handler focus and easy trainability. They love nothing more than to be with their human, doing whatever job they've been assigned. They aren't known for their independence, though, and they're generally quite soft. If someone is harsh or heavy-handed with them, they're prone to just shutting down. They want to please and can be sensitive souls. They're extremely gentle, although they can be quite exuberant until they learn some manners!

They flourish with positive training, and they're almost always happy, wiggly, and willing to share a smile. Goldens are notorious for grabbing the closest item and wiggle wagging around with it when excited, which, for the first couple of years, can be all of the time! They remain puppies at heart for most of their lives, and they've got a heart that is as golden as their coat. Golden retrievers are amiable animals, and they almost never meet a stranger—everyone they meet is a friend. Sometimes, they can even be a bit too social, given how calm and focused a service dog must be.

Since these guys are a large breed, it's very important, particularly for service dog candidates, to learn manners very early. "Four on the floor" should be reinforced from the very beginning, and one of the first lessons learned should be to sit politely for greetings. Males mature at sixty to seventy-five pounds and average twenty-three to twenty-four inches at the shoulder. Females are a bit smaller at fifty to sixty pounds and twenty to twenty-two inches at the shoulder, and they're usually slightly less heavier-boned with a less magnificent coat.

Lab-Golden Cross

Lab-golden crosses (sometimes referred to as goldadors, golden Labs, or goldador retrievers) are widely used by several US-based, mainstream service and guide dog organizations. Breeding a Labrador retriever to a golden retriever commonly results in the best of both breeds—solid size, easy-to-care-for coat, calm demeanor without a soft temperament, incredible trainability, and beautiful structure. They're loving, devoted, and extremely good-natured. These sweet critters have the sensitivity of a golden retriever paired with the sturdy resilience of the Labrador retriever, and the resulting hybrid is almost perfectly suited to service, guide, and assistance dog work.

The Lab-golden mix is eager to please, with a high food drive, low to average toy drive, and intense handler/trainer focus. They're always happy to learn and work, and they have enough independence without any trace of aloofness to thrive while performing complex task work. They're a sturdy and hardy dog, with solid bone structure and relatively predictable size—they tend to be sixty to eighty-five pounds, and twenty-two to twenty-five inches at the shoulder. They usually don't have the lean and leggy look of the golden, nor the broad, barrel look of an English Labrador, but they instead rest in the middle of those extremes.

They're almost always gold or yellow in color, although it is a lottery on their appearance—some look like Labradors, some look like goldens, and some are clearly a blend of the two. Occasionally, because black is genetically dominant in Labradors, a black pup can crop up every now and again. Coat length can vary from short and dense (like a Labrador) to long, flowing, and feathered (like a golden) to anything in between.

Lab-golden crosses are playful, outgoing, cheerful dogs who can generally be found, when not working, carrying something and wagging their tail like they'll never get a chance to do so again. They're almost always happy and upbeat, and they're always good for a smile or two. They make wonderful companions, but they excel as working dogs. They're usually accepting of strangers, children, and animals of all kinds, and when well socialized, few dogs are as unshakeable as this mix.

Unfortunately, both Labrador retrievers and golden retrievers are prone to many of the same health conditions, with the most common being joint issues, diseases of the thyroid, and eye problems. Golden-crosses should always be screened for hip and elbow health, and any dog used as breeding stock should have OFA or PennHIP certifications. Additionally, any reputable breeder will have their dogs' eye health certified through the Canine Eye Registry Foundation (CERF). Thyroid and heart health can also be certified.

These friendly canines live, on average, ten to twelve years, and they remain youthful throughout their life. Starting them on a joint supplement (like Nature's Farmacy's PhytoFlex) early on can help prevent joint deterioration and stiffness later in life. PhytoFlex is inexpensive (at the time of printing, it's $24.99 for two pounds), lasts a long time, and has incredible results. Many service dog organizations start their puppies on it very early and keep them on it throughout their working lives, with great results.

Golden-Lab mixes are active dogs, although dogs bred for assistance dog work will usually be lower in drive and activity levels. Regardless, though, in order to keep them happy and healthy, they'll require some exercise every day, preferably with a human partner, because they are quite social. Fetch, swimming, walking, jogging, running, tug, and mental games are all possibilities.

Doodles

A "doodle" is any mixed breed that results from the mating of a poodle of any size (miniature, toy, standard) to a purebred or pure-typed dog. A Labradoodle is a Labrador retriever/poodle cross, a golden doodle is a golden retriever/poodle cross, and a shepadoodle is a German shepherd/poodle cross. There are dozens of "doodle" breeds/types, although they aren't breeds in the truest sense of the word—they are still crosses, and traits aren't always predictable.

The mixed heritage of the doodle types results in a wide range of physical characteristics—some doodles have long, soft, shedding coats, and some have tightly curled, non-shedding coats. Some are tiny; some are massive. Colors can be just about anything, including merle and brindle, although the most common doodle colors are varying shades of fawn, chocolate, and black, sometimes mixed with patches of white.

Doodles can be separated into three size ranges—mini, medium, and standard—and the categories are usually determined by the size of the poodle parent. Standard doodles will generally grow to be forty-five pounds or larger, with dogs up to one hundred pounds possible, medium doodles are thirty to forty-five pounds, and mini doodles are predicted to be fifteen to thirty pounds at maturity. The height of a doodle is very difficult to predict, as the doodles are often taller than either of their parents!

Well-bred doodles are generally laid-back, sweet-natured dogs with exceptional trainability, solid handler focus, good retrieve drives, and a biddable, social temperament. In fact, the original doodle was bred in Australia specifically for guide dog work. Starting in the 1990s, breeders began trying to create a breed that was capable of doing guide work for visually impaired individuals who were allergic to dogs.

Doodles are "designer breeds," meaning that they're produced as a direct cross between two (sometimes three) purebred dogs, and that they don't "breed true"—meaning that you can't cross a doodle to a doodle and get predictable results. So, the trait profile of any doodle is a direct consequence of the cross itself. Goldendoodles, for example, are usually super friendly, goofy creatures with high intelligence, and shepadoodles are often playful with family and aloof with strangers, with a keen mind and sharp response to the environment.

When doodles are used for service dog work, it's crucial to select one from a quality breeder. Otherwise, you risk poor temperament, health concerns, or other issues that would exclude a dog from successfully completing service dog training, such as too high of an energy level, too much drive, or excessive distractibility. Parents used in a doodle breeding program should be health tested, with wonderful temperaments. If bred for service potential or other work, they should have proven working aptitude, as showcased via temperament testing, performance titles, and/or come from a line proven to produce service, therapy, or other working dogs.

Doodles are prone to the issues and diseases common in the base breeds, which means that there's generally a propensity for hip/elbow dysplasia, seizure or other neurological issues, and cardiac issues. Parents should be tested for and cleared of joint problems and genetic diseases common in their breed, and they should demonstrate excellent health overall. Poodles, Labs, and goldens can all carry the genes for number of inheritable eye diseases, and so breeding stock should be cleared through CERF eye exams.

It's commonly touted that doodles receive the benefit of "hybrid vigor," or the positive results of crossing two unrelated purebred dogs from two totally different gene pools. Doodles of all kinds are generally active, hardy dogs. Poodles are sporting dogs through and through, and when crossed with retrievers or shepherds, the resulting dog is usually ready to go anywhere, do anything, and love anyone.

Their coats usually require haircuts or trimming, whether or not they have a shedding coat. Very few doodles are truly hypoallergenic, and almost none of the first- or second-generation crosses (one breed to another, or a doodle back to a poodle) will be hypoallergenic. That being said, even doodles that do shed generally shed less than would be expected. The less a doodle sheds, the more grooming is generally required to keep their coat in top shape.

These friendly, social, hardworking dogs often live to fifteen and beyond, and they tend to retain their sweet nature their entire life, with very little slowdown until close to the end. They're obedient, responsive, and quick to learn.

Labradane

The "Labradane" is a cross resulting from a Labrador Retriever and a Great Dane. They're large, sometimes bordering on extra-large, with solid bone structure, a short, smooth, typically single, coat. They're usually black, although other colors are entirely possible. Labradors, of course, make excellent service dogs, although they can be too small for brace and mobility support work. Great Danes, with their large size, gentle temperament, and general silliness, can make great service dogs, although they do have a couple of downfalls. As a giant breed, Danes don't live very long, and they can also be a bit lazy and aloof. By crossing a Great Dane with a Lab, you get a dog that (hopefully) has the best features of both breeds.

Buddy, the first official Guide Dog, leads her partner, Morris Frank, in 1928. Buddy, originally named "Kiss," was one of two potential female German Shepherds offered to Mr. Frank by the trainer.

Demo Dog Karma is performing a "vault," which is a common performance and trick dog stunt that involves the dog rebounding off part of the trainer's body.

xel is a Labrador Retriever who orked as a Brace and Mobility upport Dog. He provided bracing, ounterbalancing, retrieving, and any other tasks.

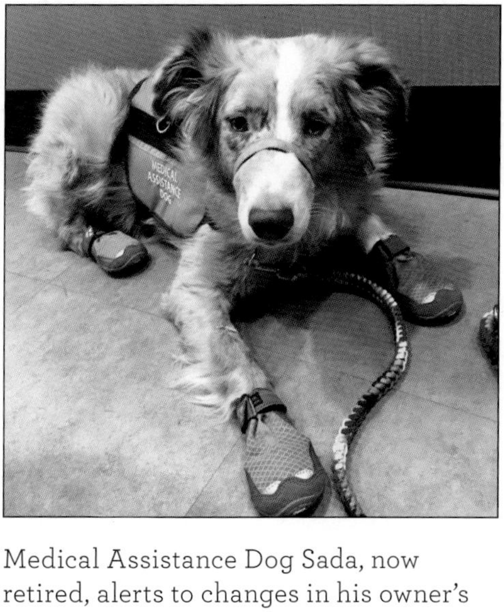

Medical Assistance Dog Sada, now retired, alerts to changes in his owner's metabolic state, primarily the presence of a rare acid in the blood. He wears boots as part of his uniform due to the temperatures common in Phoenix, Arizona.

This Standard Poodle is providing mobility support to his handler by helping him balance and transition weight safely while descending stairs.

Dobby, pictured here with his puppy raiser, was trained and placed as a Medical Assistance Dog post-graduation.

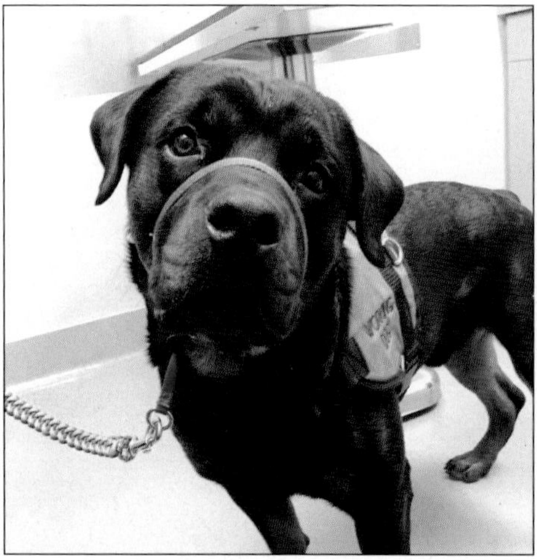

Aero, pictured here as an adolescent, works as a multi-functional Medical Assistance Dog.

Wellie, a yellow Labrador Retriever, works as a Hearing Dog for their handler. Many Hearing Dogs wear orange vests and utilize orange leashes Some states even mandate orange gear for hearing and signal dogs.

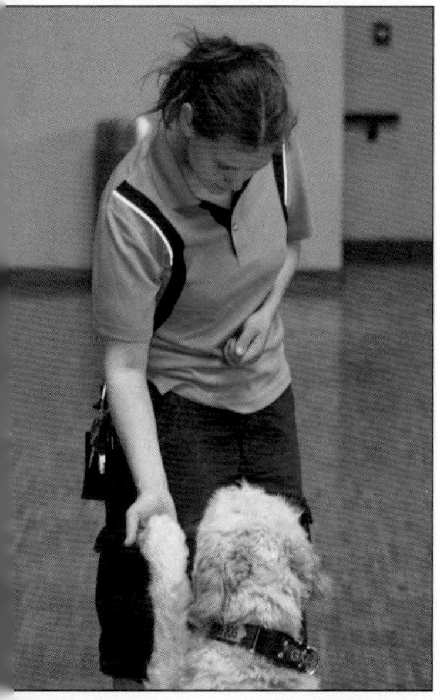

ervice Dog in Training (SDiT) raham offers his paw during paw targeting training ession. Paw targeting forms the undation for many service dog sks, including closing doors, tting handicap buttons, using K9 emergency phone, and rning on touch lights.

This young black Labrador Retriever is working on skills related to their retrieve, tug, and hold.

rvice dog Axel uses a tug to en the fridge so he can retrieve everage for his handler.

Service dog Boomer uses nose targeting to push a drawer closed.

SDiT Dobby practices his impulse control skills during a training session for "Leave It," which teaches dogs to ignore items, people, food, or distractions on command.

Once your service dog learns the basic retrieve, you'll be able to expand and teach them to retrieve all types of items!

Autism Support Dog Snipe serves as a point of support and as a sensory anchor for his young partner.

Autism Assistance Dogs can help reduce sensory overload by providing deep pressure stimulation and tactile grounding.

;ervice Dogs may be allowed to accompany
heir handlers during hospital admissions.

In addition to providing their routine task work, service dogs can also offer comfort and a sense of stability during hospital admissions.

.urora is a Siberian Husky who performs
ıany different tasks and services for her
andler.

German Shepherds, due to their intelligence, trainability, and intuitive nature, often make excellent service dogs.

When choosing a service dog puppy, be sure to look for a lack of timidity, lots of curiosity, a social nature, and mid to high food drive.

This is a Labradane (Labrador and Great Dane mix) puppy. Labradanes can make excellent mobility support dogs. They're often taller than Labradors and live longer than Great Danes.

Golden Retriever puppies are warm-hearted, wiggly, sweet-natured critters who learn easily and quickly. Make sure you keep plenty of toys around for them to carry when excited!

Labrador Retriever puppies are know for their happy, social nature. Labs tend to excel as service dogs and are one of the most widely utilized bree

While some individual herding dogs can make excellent service dogs, as a whole, Border Collies and Australian Shepherds often aren't suitable for the role.

Great Danes are most commonly trained as brace and mobility support dogs. However, their short life-span can limit their active working time.

Spartan's blue Gentle Leader signals to ɿim that he's working—it's part of his ɹniform. The Gentle Leader also allows ɿis trainer to easily guide his focus.

Service dogs need time off to recover and recoup.

Labrador Retrievers come in three colors. Coat color has little to no effect on temperament, though members of the public often interact more with yellow Labs than darker coated Labs.

Golden Retrievers are soft, gentle, highly responsive dogs who typically excel at a wide variety of service dog roles. Goldens and Golden/Labrador crosses are the second most commonly seen breed used by major training organizations.

This is a Bernese Mountain Dog. While similar in temperament to a Golden Retriever, they're much larger.

Doberman Pinschers are easily trainable and highly intuitive. Keep in mind that Dobermans with natural (floppy) ears, as pictured here, are often better received by members of the public and by emergency services.

apillions are a toy breed that excel as
earing dogs.

This young SDiT is working on handler focus during a public access outing.

ppies under the age of four months
ı no longer fly as service dogs on most
jor airlines.

Service dogs who are going to travel via plane should have low noise sensitivity, excellent public access skills, and maneuver well in tight spaces.

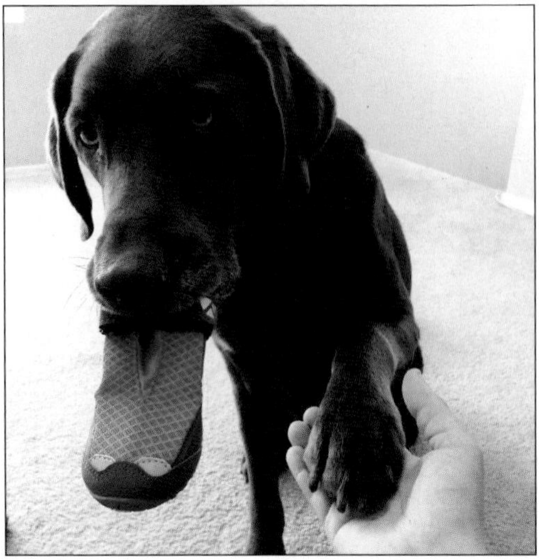

Boots offer foot protection for service dogs working in hot, cold, or specialized environments.

The best boots for working dogs are specifically sized for your dog and aren't just a "general" size like medium or extra large.

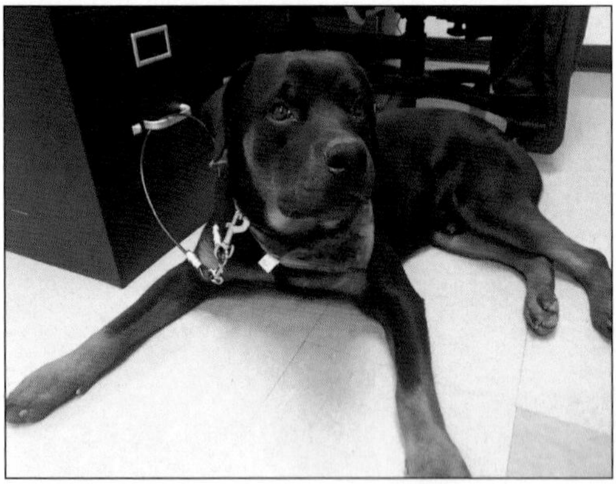

Here is an example of tethering. Aero, a young Rottweiler, is calmly observing the classroom where members of his puppy raising program attend school.

This doodle puppy, Cassius, is goi through TSA. See page 162 for mo information on airplane travel wit your service dog!

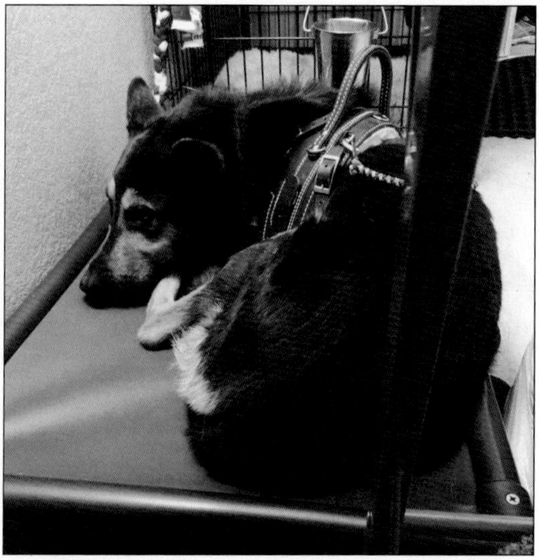

Tergio, a German Shepherd service dog candidate, wears a mobility harness while on a bed in his trainer's office.

Training your service dog to get on and off an escalator is possible, though it can be quite difficult and may require professional training help—some service dog teams prefer to avoid this altogether.

Retrieves should be trained with a wide variety of objects and materials.

Transitioning your dog from a nose touch to your hand to a nose touch to an object (like this sticky note) allows you to begin working on foundation skills for closing doors and other common service dog tasks.

Targeting can be done with the nose or a paw. Drawers and doors are often more easily closed with nose targeting but touch lamps might be easier with paw targeting.

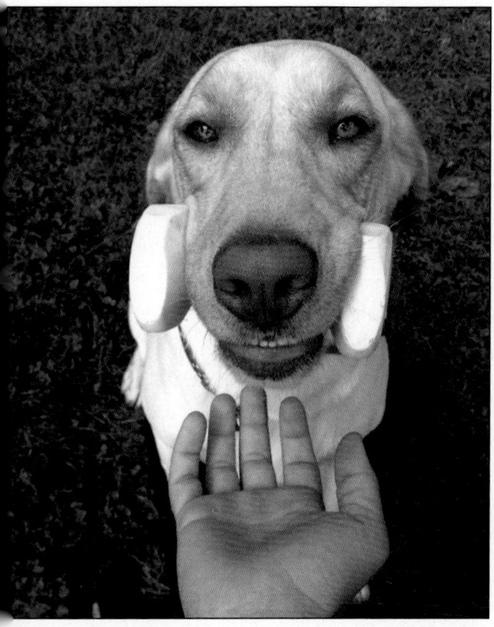

The hold portion of a formal retrieve equires patience and excellent timing rom the handler.

Carrying items is part of the formal retrieve task work.

Carrying objects can be especially useful in stressful environments like the airport.

Leashes come in a wide variety of materials. Leather leashes are a favorite of many handlers and trainers, although biothane and nylon are regularly encountered as well!

Autumn, pictured here with yellow Labrador Meta, served as a puppy raiser (along with her mother) for many young Service Dogs in Training. Young SDiTs should meet children of a variety of ages so the dogs become well-rounded adults.

ngus, an Australian Cattle Dog, lies under
e table at a university library.

This dog's vest explains that she isn't yet a fully trained service dog.

Axel served many roles throughout his life—service dog, demo dog, performance dog, and friend. He is pictured here with young trainer Alyx Tuttle.

Mobility Support Dog Intel wears a Bold Lead Design bracework harness. Intel's handler has Ehlers-Danlos and POTS and routinely needs assistance with walkin and after fainting spells.

These are regular dog tags that can be attached to a child's backpack or harness. In the event of an emergency, the tags tell responders not to separate the dog an child. They also announce that additional information or instructions can be fou in the service dog's pouch.

While the characteristics and temperament of Labradanes can vary widely, most are exuberant, friendly, affectionate, gentle souls who adore everyone and anything. They usually excel at learning and will happily follow their handlers anywhere. They tend to be "Velcro dogs," meaning they'll stick to your side no matter what! However, that does mean they're prone to separation anxiety, so it's very important to build independent and alone time into your training schedule for these guys.

They're quite low maintenance, with a sleek, glossy, short coat and low to medium energy levels. They do, of course, require some exercise and mental stimulation every day, but overall, they're easy to care for and even easier to love. They've got a goofy, silly side, and they're always worth several laughs a day.

Both parent breeds are prone to joint issues, so it's vital to choose a Labradane from a source that offers health testing. If that's not possible, your candidate should be x-rayed as early in the training process as is possible so as to rule out joint or structural problems. These guys can still be growing well until their second year. If a Labradane is going to be doing brace and mobility work, you'll need to confirm via X-ray that their growth plates have fully closed before starting them on any weight-bearing tasks. All in all, these gentle giants are healthy and hardy, and they can live to be ten to twelve years old, on average.

Labradanes can come in many colors, including black, fawn, blue, and brindle, and any of the above mixed with white. Their eyes are usually brown, although, very rarely, blue or green may occur. They can reach ninety pounds at maturity, and they average twenty-five to twenty-seven inches at the shoulder, although thirty inches is not unheard of.

Standard Poodle

Everyone seems to think standard poodles are froufrou dogs, but the truth of the matter is that these critters are hardworking dogs bred for stamina, intelligence, hardiness, and handler responsiveness. Far from being just a fashion accessory, poodles are one of the most intelligent breeds, coming in just behind border collies. They're excellent problem solvers with a strong ability to work independently. They thrive when presented with complex tasks and they require lots of mental stimulation in order to be happy.

They're a proud and dignified breed, and when properly groomed, they're quite striking. Their coats do require specialized care, but they have the benefit of being the most hypoallergenic breed of all the coated breeds. They do not shed, but they do require careful grooming, brushing, and clipping. There are lots of cuts available for poodles, ranging from the easy-to-care-for, short, sleek puppy cut all the way to the more intricate designs that are usually reserved for the show ring. They come in all solid colors, and while "parti" poodles, or poodles who have white splotches mixed into their coat, do crop up, they're not allowed by the breed standard.

This highly active breed loves to work, and well-bred poodles make excellent service dog candidates. They're cheerful, graceful, and a pleasure to be around, and while they can be quite social, their temperaments can range from friendly to politely aloof. They're quite sensitive, sometimes even hypersensitive, and some lines are prone to being high-strung, neurotic, and anxious, all of which are traits that can prevent a dog from successfully completing service dog training.

Standard poodle males are forty-five to seventy pounds, with females weighing in at forty-five to sixty pounds, and in order to be classified as standards, poodles must be more than fifteen inches tall at the shoulder.

Bernese Mountain Dog

Per the Bernese Mountain Dog Club of America, the Berner, as they're affectionately known by those who love them, is a "highly versatile working companion." As one of the four Swiss working breeds, Bernese mountain dogs have a long-standing history of helping humans. Few breeds can match their striking appearance, with their long, satiny black coat accented by gorgeous, deep shades of rust and white. Berners are all-around stunning, and their quiet, solid work ethic and easygoing temperament makes them a reliable, calm working candidate.

These guys are a sturdy, well-built breed designed for heavy work, including drafting, herding, and other farm dog chores. They are not, however, workaholics and they're just as happy to relax as they are to work. Berners aren't massive, but they are quite large, averaging twenty-five to twenty-seven inches in height for males, and twenty-four to twenty-six inches for females, which makes them an ideal mobility support candidate. Males weigh between 80 and 115 pounds, with females smaller, at from sixty to ninety pounds.

Their temperament stands out just as much as their stunning appearance. They're people-loving, affectionate, gentle souls, and their responsiveness and keen intelligence make them a joy to work with and train. Some can tend toward aloofness, but overall, they're social, sweet critters who want nothing more than to work and be worked with.

The downside to Bernese mountain dogs is their tendency toward health problems, including joint issues, neurological conditions, autoimmune diseases, cancers, bloat, and other diseases, and their short life span. Berners, on average, live seven to nine years, although many enjoy longer life spans. With such a short life span, though, and such a long time required to fully train a working service dog, the result can be a working time frame of five years or less in the field, on average.

Doberman Pinscher

The Doberman pinscher is a powerhouse of loyalty, strength, alertness, and potential. Cited as a breed who can "truly do it all," the Doberman of today has come a long way from the vicious, intense, hard-to-handle breed it used to be. Now suitable for almost any job, the Doberman pinscher makes an excellent service dog candidate.

Originally bred as a guard dog, the Doberman pinscher is medium- to large-sized, dark, and exceptionally powerful. Typically sixty to ninety pounds of solid muscle, a Doberman is physically capable of besting a full-grown man as a guard dog. Dobies stand twenty-four to twenty-eight inches high at the withers (all great heights for brace work or mobility support) with females smaller than males. The breed possesses exceptional endurance, speed, and intelligence.

Dobermans have two genes for coat color. There is a gene for a black coat and then a diluted coat. Depending on how these genes are combined, four different colors of Dobies are possible. There are black, fawn, blue, and red Dobermans. Each color of Doberman usually has tan, rust, or cream-colored accent markings that matches their base coat color. In the international breed ring, fawn and blue Dobermans are not allowed to be shown and can be disqualified as breeding stock. They also have been proven to suffer from skin issues. While there are white Dobermans, such dogs aren't allowed in the show ring and are forbidden by the breed standard. In addition, white Dobies often have extensive health and temperament issues due to inbreeding. Many breeders will cull a white puppy at birth or will place the puppy with limited or no registration and a spay/neuter contract.

The Doberman pinscher coat is extremely sleek, smooth, and shiny. Dobies shed very little, which makes caring for their coat a breeze. To keep a Doberman's fur in optimum condition, run a grooming glove or bristle brush over their body once or twice a week to redistribute the body's natural oils and to loosen dead hair. With just a couple minutes of brushing a week, Dobies glow.

In the United States, Doberman pinscher puppies are commonly "cropped and docked" at birth. The breed standard states that the tail should be docked at the second joint. There are two different types of cropped ears, a shorter military crop and a longer show crop. With both types of cropped ears, aftercare is extensive and can take months. For a Dobie who's going to be a service dog, many trainers and breeders recommend leaving the ears natural to give the dog a softer, more approachable look, especially if you have frequent dealings with emergency medical services (EMS). Be aware that some EMS teams may be apprehensive and refuse to approach a person accompanied by an intimidating-looking dog—and in a medical emergency, time can be of the essence.

Doberman pinschers possess an alert, calm, and loyal temperament. They're often called "Velcro" dogs because they bond very tightly with their handler. Dobies are known for following their person from room to room and insisting on being close at all times. As a service dog, this behavior can be exceptionally helpful, but it needs to be watched so it doesn't develop into separation anxiety. As a guardian breed, Dobermans require careful and extensive socialization from an early age so they can learn to discern threats from mere day-to-day life.

The Doberman pinscher ranks among one of the most highly trainable breeds and it possesses an innate joy when working with and for its handler. Capable of learning any complexity of task, Dobies are a pleasure to work with. That same ease of trainability, though, can get a Doberman in trouble if it's not receiving enough mental or physical stimulation. Dobies have no qualms about creatively "entertaining" themselves at your expense. The wily Doberman is not a dog for every handler. They work best for experienced handlers who know how to harness their intelligence and working ability and maximize their potential.

Because of the Doberman's history as a guardian breed and because of the stigma still associated with the breed, Dobies are best partnered with adult handlers. Finally, when picking a Doberman as a service dog candidate, be certain to select a breeder who has extensively socialized her puppies, who has certified the parents' elbows and hips, and who does genetic testing for the most common genetic illnesses in Dobermans, including cervical vertebral instability/spondylomyelopathy (wobbler syndrome) and von Willebrand disease, a blood disorder. Ideally, the puppy's parents should possess temperament certifications (the American Temperament Test Society offers mainstream certification popular with breeders) and working or performance titles.

American Pit Bull Terrier and Other Bully Breeds

When it comes to the American pit bull terrier (and other bully breeds), there is no question that many of this group are gentle, happy, social, easygoing, highly trainable, sweet-natured, amiable critters who would excel as service dogs. In fact, the Animal Farm Foundation, based in New York, uses only bully breeds in their service dog program!

Whether it's deserved or not, bully breeds do not have a good reputation, and it's very important to consider the repercussions of that reputation. In many areas, owning a bully breed comes with increased insurance costs and special regulations, or is forbidden altogether. EMTs or first responders may be hesitant to approach. Access challenges may skyrocket. There are breed bans in many states and countries. People will react to your partner differently, merely because of their breed. Even if a particular bully breed dog tests beautifully for service dog candidacy, carefully consider day-to-day life with one of these beautiful, stocky, bighearted dogs, and whether or not it's something you could embrace.

Papillon

When comes to toy dogs, few breeds can match the papillon in stamina, intelligence, and whimsy. These dainty little dogs are full of enthusiasm, energy, and passion, and while they're pint sized, they are every bit a worker. Bred down from spaniels and named for their beautiful, flowing ears (*papillon* means "butterfly" in French), they have retained their big dog spirit, even though it's housed in a little dog body.

While not overly social, papillons are polite and accepting of strangers, although they may not always be so quick to make friends with strange dogs, and they are notorious for chasing small animals. They're extremely easy to train, and their sharp wit and intelligence is matched by only one other toy breed, the miniature poodle. Papillons are responsive and quick, and their awareness of the environment and high energy levels makes them ready candidates for hearing dog work or diabetic alert training.

Paps, as they're referred to by those who love them, are very sporty in nature. They love to run, jump, and play, which is why many people do competitive obedience, rally, agility, or tricks work with them. However, these little guys are quite dainty and fragile, and they're easily injured. If not trained and socialized from the very beginning, they can become wary and pick up a habit of alarm barking.

Their coat requires grooming, especially around the ears, as they have long, flowing fur cascading down that mats easily. They will need regular brushing to stay in tip-top shape. They're generally quite healthy, and they weigh seven to ten pounds, with females slightly smaller than males. A sixteen-year life span is not at all uncommon for these hardy little dogs.

Mixed Breeds

Whether you call them Heinz 57s, all-American Dogs, mutts, or something else, there's not a question in the world that mixed breeds can make incredible service dogs. It's the temperament that matters, and possessing the proper size and structure to do whatever work needs to be done. The actual breed and appearance of the dog is totally secondary.

Using a mixed breed, however, means you might not know important factors, like full grown size, health or genetics, personality or temperament traits, or other important considerations. Keep that in mind when evaluating and selecting puppies, and always remember that your puppy could grow up totally different than expected.

4

SERVICE DOG GEAR OVERVIEW

GEAR OVERVIEW

When it comes to service dogs, there are as many gear options as there are stars in the sky. Here's a basic rundown of available options for service dog gear, equipment, and supplies.

Keep in mind that every team is unique. Every service dog and their human partner have different needs, face varying circumstances, and are individuals. What works for one team may not work for another, and you may find your dog's needs change throughout the partnership. Not everything on this list will be (nor should it necessarily be) needed for each team, and at the end of the day, you should strive to have a safe, working partnership with your pup—everything else is just details.

Head Collar

Head collars are a training tool used to teach loose-leash walking and handler focus. There are various designs available, and most come in both neutral and bright colors. Many service dogs wear head collars as part of their working uniform, even if they're not technically necessary any longer due to the high degree of training. Three recommended brands due to superior fit and design are:

NewTrix: Uniquely designed head collar originally intended for use in a Canadian service dog program.
Gentle Leader: Industry standard favorite and readily available in all sizes and numerous colors.
The Perfect Pace™: A simple, minimalistic head collar originally designed as an all-in-one leash/head collar combo for service dog teams.

MUZZLE

Every dog should be conditioned to wear a muzzle as a matter of everyday training. As an example of why this is important, if a service dog were to be injured and brought to a veterinarian, a muzzle may be placed on the dog. It is very common for even the best-behaved dogs to nip when hurt. That is not the time to introduce the added stress of wearing a muzzle.

There are two different kinds of muzzles: basket and soft muzzles. Soft muzzles are a great addition to an emergency or first aid kit, and they should only be used for short periods of time. Basket muzzles are extremely comfortable, come in sizes for all breeds, and are available in many different styles. Every dog should have one of their own and be comfortable wearing it. Top brands include:

Jafco: These lightweight vinyl basket-type muzzles are used across the working dog and veterinary industry for their superior fit, sizing, safety, and comfort. They're easy to store, sanitize, fit, and use.
Baskerville: Baskerville muzzles are a great choice for good fit, comfort, training, and casual, everyday use. They're readily available at major chain pet stores and they're inexpensive!
Leerburg Wire: This style offers outstanding airflow and near-custom fit. They're a great choice for a hard-to-fit breed or a breed with a smaller, bigger, or wider skull than average.

Face Wipes

While not "gear" per se, face wipes are a delightful addition to your service dog's personal items. Keeping your partner's face, muzzle, eyes, and ears clean is made far easier with face wipes. The earthbath brand is a great resource for anything related to grooming.

Collar

Every service dog needs a collar of some kind with tags attached. Your partner's only link to you, should they become lost, are their tags. Even if your partner is microchipped, they should wear a tag—not everyone will take a dog in to be scanned. Even if the tag just says, "I'm microchipped!" your partner needs a tag.

A great deal of debate exists about which types of collars are acceptable or not. For everyday, routine use and regular walking, a flat collar (also called a buckle collar) or martingale can't be beat. "Limited slips" are a martingale variation that also work well for most dogs and handlers. For your dog's safety, collars should only be worn when the dog is attended and never while alone outside, in a crate or kennel, or while playing with other dogs. If taking a collar on or off isn't feasible, breakaway or "play safe" collars offer some peace of mind.

Training-only collars include pinch, choke, and remote collars. Should you elect to use these, they should only be worn for training sessions or while the handler is supervising the dog while working. This type of training gear requires proper instruction on safe and effective use.

ID Tag Holder

An alternative to a collar if you need something minimalistic, free of frills, and functional, is an ID tag holder. While these are often constructed well enough to take some pressure, they're not built for walking and are instead designed to carry just the essentials: an ID tag optimally placed to be seen. They easily slip on and off over your dog's head.

Bandanas are always a fun, flashy means of adding some color or additional ID to your partner!

Harness

There are all kinds of harnesses available, ranging from training harnesses like the Ruffwear Web Master™ and PetSafe® Easy Walk to wheelchair pull harnesses like the Alpine Outfitters harness and brace mobility support harnesses. There are also regular body harnesses in a variety of styles, as well as vehicle safety harnesses.

Vest

Most working dog teams use a vest or a jacket while out in public. You aren't required by federal law to "dress" your service dog, but having identifying gear is usually seen as a courtesy to the public. If you live in Canada, rules regarding vests vary from province to province. Ontario requires vests, for example.

Regardless of the actual law in place, dressing your service dog in a vest or identifying clothing is a courtesy to those around you. There are many styles, fits, functions, and colors available, so you can be sure there's something for everyone! However, you should avoid purchasing vests or other identifying equipment from one of the many "service dog registry" organizations that purport to offer letters or other identification certifying your dog. These contribute to the problem of service dog fraud, and it's best to avoid funding them.

Coat

When the going gets chilly, even the tough might need a coat. If your partner will be wearing a coat with their working gear, look for one that offers full coverage for their belly with a streamlined, close fit so their vest can go over it and still look professional. Ruffwear and Hurtta coats or sweaters work beautifully for this.

Boots

Boots often come in handy for service dogs who routinely work in slick environments (like on tiled floors) or service dogs in cold areas. Even if you think your partner's feet don't get cold, it's important to protect them from the chemicals and salts found on sidewalks and streets during winter months.

Nail Caps

Nail caps can be handy for service dogs who perform paws-up tasks on walls, cabinets, fridges, vehicles, or people. The caps help prevent scratches.

Other

Other gear that your partner doesn't wear but that come in handy (or are all but required, like a leash) include a bed, crate, bowls, a tether, and toys.

VESTS, JACKETS, AND HARNESSES

While federal law doesn't mandate that service dogs wear any kind of gear or identification, most service dogs have some kind of vest, jacket, or harness. If you live outside the United States it is important to determine what the laws in your local community legislate.

Sometimes the gear is for identification only and at other times, like in the case of a brace dog or a service dog who carries medical equipment, the gear is used during the dog's work. There are too many types of service dog harnesses and vests to mention them all, but here are five of the most common items.

Cape Vests

Cape vests are very common and can be worn by any size or type of service dog. Service dog capes consist of fabric that drapes across the dog's shoulders and back, and they usually have straps that go around the dog's chest and belly to hold the cape in place. Capes are often introduced to very young service dogs in training, and while you may need different sizes throughout your partner's life, they can be used in any situation. Even service dogs who work in a brace or mobility support harness often have a cape vest lying around somewhere!

This versatile piece of gear comes in all kinds of fabric choices for all seasons (mesh, cotton, nylon, corduroy, canvas, etc.), comes in every size imaginable, and is relatively inexpensive. They're great to add patches and embroidery to, and many have pockets, extra rings, or other fun/useful features.

Cape Harness

The cape harness is similar to the cape vest, but it's usually a little more sturdily built and may or may not have a handle. Many cape harnesses have D-rings at the sides, which makes the addition of a pull strap very easy.

These harnesses are ergonomic and typically well-made, although they can sit a little funny on some breeds of dogs. There's usually ample space to add patches, and these come in multiple sizes to fit the average-sized working dog. There's no limit to color choices, and if you look on Etsy, you can even find fabric choices like tie-dye, bohemian, or other nontraditional patterns.

Pulling Harness

Pulling harnesses are worn by service dogs who need to pull wheelchairs, wagons, or move/open heavy things. While there are many different types of pulling harnesses, most service dogs wear a harness with Y-straps that come over the shoulders and between the front legs, and then the harness has a girth strap around the dog's belly. Pulling harnesses are typically padded for comfort, and they should only be worn by dogs large enough to perform the physical task work.

Brace and Mobility Support Harnesses

Used by service dogs who need to assist their human partner with walking, balancing, or ambulatory task work, brace and mobility support harnesses are designed to be extremely ergonomic for the dog and the handler, and typically have either a rigid handle or a sturdy pull strap attached.

It is extremely important to use a properly fitted harness for you and your dog's safety, and to only use a dog for brace or mobility support once they have finished growing and their joints have been checked by a vet for soundness.

ALL ABOUT BOOTS

There are lots of reasons a service dog might wear boots, most of which revolve around the dog's safety and comfort. While boots and shoes look curious on dogs, for lots of working and service dog teams, they're the only way for the team to work comfortably and safely. If you and your service dog routinely encounter any of the following scenarios, you may want to think about getting your partner a pair of boots:

- Your service dog walks on pavement, asphalt, stone, sand, or metal (such as bus steps or outdoor ramps) when the temperature is routinely 90°F or hotter. It takes only a few seconds to blister and burn the pads completely off a dog's feet when they're on surfaces that are too hot, and in some areas of the United States, the ground gets baked in the summer sun and can cause burns on contact. Similarly, hot road tar can become sticky and cause burns to vulnerable paws.
- Your short-haired service dog is routinely out walking in snow, slush, or ice.
- Your service dog walks on city sidewalks or in urban neighborhoods after it has snowed, sleeted, or iced, and your community uses salt and chemical trucks.
- Your partner is ever asked to traverse rugged terrain.
- Your partner works indoors on tile, stone, or laminate floors and needs the extra traction.
- Your service dog works in a health-care facility or at a laboratory where shoe changes are required of humans before being allowed to enter the area.

All those reasons and more are perfectly valid occasions for service dogs wearing boots. Now that you've determined whether or not your partner needs boots, though, the next questions are "What kind?" and "How do I help my service dog adjust to their boots?"

There are dozens of different brands available for boots. Two of our favorites are Ruffwear and Muttluks. Both companies make solid, durable, ergonomic boots that fit well and are very durable. Ruffwear has boots for warm environments, cold/snowy environments, and city environments, and Muttluks also has several options for various uses and environments. Ruffwear has a special program for service dogs, so you should contact their customer service people for more info.

Regardless of what kind of boot you get, for everyday and working wear, the boot needs to be sized specifically to your dog. It needs to fit well and not cause any compression, soreness, or hot spots. It needs to fully cover the foot and be easy to put on and take off. Make sure you get boots made for the environments your service dog will be working in.

Most dog boots fasten with wraparound Velcro straps, but a few brands require manipulation of snaps or friction slides. Someone with limited dexterity may want to consider boots that just slide on so they're easier to put on and take off.

Teaching Your Dog to Adjust to Boots

Now for the fun part—how to get your service dog to like their boots. First and foremost, it's important to have two skills already in place—a "settle" or "relax" position where your dog lays on their side or back, and a "shake" that's solid enough that your dog will leave their paw in your hand and allow you to touch their feet and fiddle with them.

In order to use the method below, you'll need to be on the same level as your dog. Some trainers can kneel or sit next to their dog on the ground. Others may be more comfortable remaining seated and putting their dog on a raised training platform, bench, or table. Any surface you use for training should be sturdy, stable, safe, and easy to reach while you're sitting or standing in your preferred position.

There are lots of guidelines to teaching your dog how to "shake" online, but not so many for "settle." To begin working on "settle," lure your dog into a down position, and then carefully lure your dog over onto their side. Click and treat, or simply reward. Continue this training until you can lure your dog all the way over on their side or back comfortably, and then work on extending the duration.

Alternately, you can simply flip your dog over between your legs and rub their belly and offer cookies. The important thing is that your dog be comfortable and not stressed by this position. How you get there is really up to you and your service dog. Spend a minute or two playing with all your dog's feet, treating often. You're treating not just for your dog allowing you to mess with their feet, but also for remaining calm and relaxed while on their back or side.

Next, grab the first boot and slide it onto one of your dog's front feet. Give plenty of cookies while you're doing this, and tighten the strap on the boot. You need to make sure it's secure and will stay in place. Give cookies, cookies, cookies throughout this process. Repeat with the other front foot, and then spend a couple minutes rubbing your dog's belly. Continue treating and softly praising your dog. Don't get too excited, or your service dog will want to get up.

For some dogs, two boots to start with is more than enough. For others, they can handle all four. It's up to you, and how your partner reacts. If they're comfortable, continue. If not, skip the next few parts until they're comfortable with the two paws being booted.

The easiest way to put the boots on your service dog's back feet is to hold the boot in the hand opposite the foot (so if you're putting the boot on the left side, hold the boot in your right hand) and reach across your dog's body while holding the foot stable with the same-side hand.

Finally, put the last boot on in the same way you did the first back foot—reach across your dog's body, secure the leg, slide the boot on, tighten the straps.

Now you've got a fully booted dog! Keep your dog on their back or side between your legs, still offering cookies and belly rubs. Talk gently to them, and once you're certain your dog is relaxed, release your service dog. Expect some hilarity—your dog is going to forget how their feet work, and they may act like their legs are broken. Toss a handful of kibble or treats around the area so they can run around sniffing and picking it up, and thus relearn how their legs work.

This might take a couple of rounds, but once your dog is moving confidently and without issues, call them back to you and begin working on some basic obedience or tricks that your service dog knows really well. Both activities help your dog figure out how to move with the boots on and help them to understand that there's really nothing scary going on here.

Continue working with your dog until you're both comfortable, and then remove the boots. Place the boots on during your dog's meals for the next several weeks, and during particularly fun events, and before you know it, they'll be wearing boots like a pro!

One final thing—if your boot "flips over," the boot is either too big, or you didn't tighten it enough. This is especially common on back feet, because, strangely enough, dogs often have different-sized back and front feet. Always measure all four of your dog's feet before buying their boots.

Personal Protective Equipment (PPE)

Just as human rescuers or technicians must wear PPE when dealing with possible biohazards or dangerous substances, so must service dogs. Service dogs who work in sterile, medical, or other specialized environments may need boots, eye protection, hearing protection, bodysuits, or other safety items.

Just as you must wear your PPE in every circumstance dictated by your work environment each and every time you perform a given task, so too your service dog partner must wear their PPE consistently in all circumstances where they are called for.

5

SERVICE DOG TRAINING

BASICS OF TRAINING

THE THREE DS

There are only three aspects to teaching and proofing any behavior: duration, distance, and distraction. Called the "Three Ds," those components form the basis for increasing your dog's understanding and performance of any given behavior, command, or cue in any situation.

You should only increase one variable or "D" at a time. If you're working on increasing duration, reduce distraction and distance. If you're working on adding distance or performing a behavior from a distance, cut down on duration and distraction. If your service dog suddenly starts failing at something they were reliably performing before, examine the three Ds—you've likely increased duration, distance, or distraction too quickly or you're trying to increase two at once. While methods of obtaining a behavior can vary, the variables themselves never do.

THINGS TO REMEMBER

Dog trainers are professionals, and service dog trainers are no exception. When it comes to working with dogs, trainers are amazing, but sometimes, their people skills can leave a little to be desired. It is possible your service dog trainer might not discuss issues that make them feel awkward, or if they do, might convey them in far more tactful terms. You are responsible for your dog's training and growth.

"My dog just won't focus on me in public."

"My partner refuses to pick up items, even though they'll do it while we're at class."

"My dog does __________" or "doesn't do __________."

Service dog trainers hear all of the above on a regular basis. They've heard it all, and there's always an accompanying excuse. "He's a herding dog." "She's a rescue." "I didn't have high enough value treats." "There were children around."

The fact remains, though, that those are excuses. If you're not controlling your partner's environment, there's something about your training approach you need to correct. It is your responsibility to know if your partner isn't ready for what you're doing. You are responsible for selecting your service dog. You are responsible for making adequate training time—and your trainer will know if you aren't doing it. Don't create reasons your dog does something or doesn't do something; instead start finding solutions.

When you choose a trainer to work with, you are selecting them as a professional you are comfortable with and respect. This means it is important to listen to the advice and guidance given by the trainer—you should not be telling the professional what should, would, or could work. You picked this trainer for a reason—trust that decision, and trust your trainer. It is important to be able to listen and to be able to recognize when something about your approach is not working. Remember that once a dog has been socialized badly, the trainer cannot always undo this undesirable training.

Tips

Keep practice sessions short, upbeat, and positive, with consistent treat rewards for optimum learning. Don't let sessions run so long that either of you end up frustrated. Take breaks as necessary.

Several very short (60- to 90-second) sessions multiple times a day work far better for some training (like the retrieve) than one or even two several-minute long sessions.

Multiple "micro-training" sessions a day lead to significantly faster progress, too. Intermix a few pieces of your service dog's all-time favorite reward into your normal training treat blend to keep interest and motivation high. Spend as much time on each step/stage as is necessary for consistent, reliable performance.

Logs and Documentation

It's well known that logging your performance is one of the keys to continual growth and progress in any discipline. Whether it's a fitness program, painting, academic classes, or dog training, you can't figure out where you're going if you don't know where you've been. When it comes to service dogs, though, a training log is even more vital so you can track progress, plans, goals, and troubleshooting opportunities.

Anything Pawsable, an online magazine dedicated to service dog community education, states "Our mantra is document, document, document. We highly suggest keeping a notebook or a blog as a log or record of your training dates and accomplishments. It will not only serve to help you during the training process but will also serve as a useful paper trail for your service or assistance dog."

Your service dog is your lifeline, your independence, your partner, your friend. You know they work hard to help you live life to the fullest and that they make all the difference in the world. If you live in the United States, then you know they have access to places of public accommodation and can accompany you almost anywhere you'd like to go. Not everyone knows what you do concerning your partner and unfortunately, some encounters with the public can leave you stunned, furious, and seeking legal assistance. While federal service dog law dictates businesses may only ask two questions concerning the legitimacy of your canine assistant, case law has proven the same is not true in a court of law. If called upon legally by a judge to prove your partner's status as a service dog, you have two avenues available: a letter or documentation from a reputable service dog organization or careful written documentation (logs) of your partner's training.

For many service dog teams, the second is the only avenue available. Additionally, documenting service dog training is not only legally useful, but it's a good plan regardless. It allows you to make, track, and meet goals and prevents your training from becoming stagnant. It allows you to document and log trends in behaviors, what works and what doesn't, and the learning cycles your canine partner goes through. Beyond that, it's an excellent scrapbook and journal of your partner's life and will allow you to learn much about yourself, about your service dog, and about training in general. Should you go on to train a second service dog, your previous partner's training log will prove an invaluable resource and a wonderful collection of memories, milestones, and precious moments.

Every reputable service dog organization requires careful written training logs for all their dogs. Standards and the information to be included varies group to group, but written details on behavior, training, socialization, and public access outings are typically required in the log. Many organizations (including ADI, IAADP, and IDGF) require minimum training hours for service dogs, and maintaining a log is an easy way to see where a dog falls on the spectrum and whether or not they meet the minimal behavioral/training standards set by larger organizations. Even if your service dog isn't a program dog, you should strive to meet and exceed standards of excellence.

At any time in your service dog's career, should you decide to partner with a professional trainer or compete in dog sports, your dog's training log will help your trainer see exactly where you stand, how you and your partner learn, what works and doesn't work, and how to best proceed. It prevents covering ground twice, demonstrates that you and your partner know what you're doing and that you approach your service dog's education with intent and professionalism. It also saves time, which saves money.

An oft-quoted nugget of wisdom is, "The best time to plant a tree was two years ago. The second-best time is now." If you have been keeping a training log, good job! Keep it up! If you haven't, though, don't fret. Just start now and once you get into the habit you'll wonder how you ever lived without it!

1. Look through examples of training logs currently in use by various service dog programs.

2. Determine what information you'd like your service dog's training log to cover. At a bare minimum, it needs to include the date, what you did, and how long you spent on it. You may want sections for types of rewards, distractions, checklists, additional notes, responses, or other types of information. No one has to like or approve of your log but you, but it needs to be a system that's easy, understandable, and that you're comfortable using daily.

3. Pick a place to keep your log. You may decide to use an Excel workbook, a Google document, Evernote, a good ol' fashioned notebook, or a beautifully designed journal made specifically for logging your dog's training sessions and milestones. It needs to be easy to use, easy to access anywhere, and readily available. Regardless of whether you keep your log via an electronic or physical medium, you need to keep a hard copy of it at all times. If you need quick access to it, need to turn it over to a lawyer, judge, or trainer, or something happens to your computer, you'll be mighty grateful for your organized, up-to-date offline copy! Consider including plastic document sleeves for copies of training class certificates, veterinary records, registry/pedigree documentation, or any other important paperwork.

4. Create your log. Whether that's designing an Excel spreadsheet template or drawing sections in a notebook, nail down your training log's design, sections, terminology, and layout. Play with it until you arrive at something you like. Make a hard copy and place it in your service dog binder.

5. Set an alarm or reminder to go off at some point every day, ideally toward the end of the day when both you and your partner are winding down and activities are over. For many teams, a few minutes

before bed works well. When your alarm goes off, update your training log for the day if you haven't already done so. Don't skip a day, ever, and promise yourself you'll "catch up." You won't, and you'll forget important details. Additionally, the further behind you get, the harder it is to get started again.

For many teams, jotting down a quick note in their phone or recording a voice memo just after training/socialization outings and then transferring the info to their log at the end of the day works well. You'll develop an ongoing system that works for you with time, and the reality is that nothing about the formatting matters except getting it done.

Log your service dog's training, learning, progress, socialization, and milestones. Logging training can be a chore, but the benefits are huge. You may never need it but if you do, you'll *really* need it.

Titles, Paperwork, and Certifications

While it's very common for service dog teams to be asked for "paperwork," there is, in fact, no paperwork legally required. As we've seen, any dog that is partnered with a person with a disability that is trained to perform specific tasks to mitigate that disability is a service dog, and thus has the right to go everywhere in public their handler can go, with only a few exceptions.

Federal law does not mandate that teams have any kind of credentials whatsoever, nor that they be partnered with an organization.

"Certifications" may or may not mean anything. By law, there are no certifications required in order for a dog to be a service dog, and yet, many programs offer them as a way to show a particular dog meets their requirements and standards. A certification is only as good as the program behind it, though, and so careful research is required when selecting certifications to apply for.

Outside of service dog certifications, there are lots of certificates a team can earn, such as the American Temperament Test Society's Temperament Test certification, any of three levels of the AKC's Canine Good Citizen testing, and Canine Life and Social Skills (C.L.A.S.S.) certifications.

Many teams love documenting their training through obtaining certifications together, although it is completely optional. Be careful, though—don't pay for a "service dog certification" through some kind of registry, as these are companies that perpetuate the service dog fraud issue, and shouldn't be supported.

Lots of service dog teams relish the opportunity to polish and show off their teamwork and skill by earning titles through organized dog sports or performance events, like obedience, rally, freestyle, agility, or tricks work.

PUPPY TRAINING

Puppy Basics

While your puppy is cute and loveable, they are with you primarily for socialization and training. While training, always treat your puppy with honor and respect. There is to be *no* rough handling or mistreatment of your puppy in any way, shape, or form.

If you're working with an organization or trainer, training is to be done under the guidance of your program's training director. Do not progress too quickly through exercises, and do not progress without the approval of your team leader. Check in frequently, especially when you feel your puppy is ready to progress.

Keep a log of your puppy's training. This can be as simple as the date, the exercise, and the amount of time. It can also be as elaborate as you wish. We suggest obtaining a binder that can be filled with printouts and your puppy's weekly progress reports. Your puppy's training log will prove invaluable to you when the puppy starts advanced training.

Do not provide your puppy with a "crutch." Fade the use of treats as quickly as possible. Do not let your puppy become reliant on a "lure." For example, many people tap the ground to cue their puppy to down. Do not do this. Fade the "lure" for all commands as quickly as possible.

Your puppy should not be crated for long periods of time during the day. Your puppy should not be tethered on any collar but their flat buckle collar. When your puppy receives their working collar, your puppy should only be tethered on the "dead" ring. Your puppy should *not* be tethered when you're not with them.

Socialization

When it comes to training a service dog, very little comes close in importance to socializing your service dog in training. Socialization and exposure to the world is the foundation upon which all other training rests, and a service dog who hasn't gained real-world experience via systematic socialization is not ready for public access. With this list of oft-missed opportunities, you'll be able to ensure you're hitting all the bases while socializing service dogs in training (SDiT).

As difficult as training a service dog can be, the knowledge that you have taken a blank slate, a tiny ball of uneducated fuzz, and provided it with the foundation necessary to begin training for assistance dog work is payment in and of itself. There is nothing like the feeling of pride, satisfaction, and delight that comes when an SDiT graduates from its puppy raiser's care and returns for advanced training.

Unfortunately, though, not all SDiTs are able to continue their career as an assistance dog. While many are dropped from service dog programs or "career changed" due to inherent temperament flaws or not having the right personality to succeed as an assistance dog, more puppies are released from training programs across the country for socialization concerns than any other reason.

Important Considerations Before Beginning

Before bringing your SDiT home, you need to have a defined plan for socializing them. While many people decide to simply take the puppy with them and introduce them to everything and anything they can, using that approach results in missed experiences and an uneven education. Protect your partnership by not only picking a puppy from a source that began socialization and stimulation at birth, but by also continuing socialization and exposure throughout your puppy's training.

Use the checklist below or prepare one of your own that includes everything your partner may encounter as both a puppy in training and as a working adult service dog. By keeping track of your service dog in training's education, you'll better be able to spot and fill in holes before they become an issue.

The most important rule of socializing service dogs in training is to never, ever, for any reason, force an SDiT to approach, interact with, touch, or be on/near/with something that appears to frighten them. Forcing a puppy in training to engage when afraid ensures he'll never form positive associations with the object, person, place, surface, equipment, or situation. Instead of forcing your SDiT, always keep high-value treats with you and use them to encourage a suspicious puppy to explore a situation of their own accord. If you lay a solid foundation of socialization that rewards a puppy in new situations, you'll create a confident learner who thoroughly enjoys circumstances he's never encountered.

Finally, your service dog in training needs to encounter a situation more than once before you can ensure they'll always be comfortable with it. It's best that your puppy/SDiT have at least three instances of positive exposure with a given person or situation before assuming the dog is comfortable with it.

Why Items Were Included in the List

This list is the brainchild of several service dog and working dog trainers. Trainers were asked to think back over their experiences, consult with their puppy raisers and teams in the field, and consider what they do differently now that they didn't in the beginning of their programs concerning socialization. Those answers were integrated into this list to give you a sense of what new situations might take some extra effort to become accustomed to.

Surfaces

- Dirt
- Grass
- Gravel, loose and packed
- Sand
- Tile
- Concrete
- Granite/marble
- Slippery surfaces
- Puddles/water/fountains
- Carpet
- Metal

- Grates (where the dog can see through and may be fearful of falling)

Animals

- Small animals
- Birds
- Cats
- Cows
- Horses
- Reptiles
- Large dogs
- Little dogs

People

- Babies
- Toddlers
- Preteens
- Teens
- Young adults
- Men of all sizes
- Women of all sizes
- People of all races
- People wearing hats/coats/hoodies
- Police officers
- EMTs/paramedics
- Firefighters
- People with odd gait
- People in wheelchair
- People with medical equipment
- People with varying disabilities
- People with varying hair lengths
- People with head scarves/face covering/helmets
- People in costumes

Equipment

- Collar
- Leash
- Crate (wire, metal, plastic)
- Harness
- Vest
- Boots
- Cooling coat
- Sweater
- Head halter
- Basket muzzle

Smells

- Pizza
- BBQ/grilling
- Food courts
- Exhaust (bus/truck/car)
- Gas fumes
- Paint
- Rubbing alcohol
- Dog food besides your own
- Something rotting
- Scents commonly encountered at job

Events

- Bouncy houses/ blow-up displays
- Sporting events
- Birthday parties
- Holiday celebrations
- Place of worship get-togethers
- School events
- Seminars
- Street fairs
- County fairs/rodeo

Places

- Grooming appointments
- Physical exams
- Car rides
- Dog shows
- Veterinary office
- Zoo
- Bowling alley
- Skating rink
- Movie theater
- Farms
- Woods
- Boats
- Buses

Sounds

- Thunder
- Fireworks (only via CD or video)
- Gunshots (only via CD or video)
- Barking dogs
- Diesel engines
- Music
- Burning wood
- Crying babies
- Engines starting
- Hunting calls
- Banging on pots/ pans

Miscellaneous

- Full-length mirrors
- Nerf/water guns
- Vacuum
- Stairs
- Balloons
- Umbrellas
- Hula hoops
- PT/gym equipment
- Soda/vending machine (money in, heavy item falling)

It can be difficult to find safe situations to take your SDiT to for socialization concerning sounds. Prerecorded sound effects during training are a good option to provide the best, safest, and easiest route to ensure your SDiT develops a thick skin regarding all types of noise. You can find noise desensitization CDs for dog shows, agility trial, and performance events; for babies, city sounds, natural sounds, and hunting sounds; for thunder, storms, rain, and fireworks, and pretty much anything else you could hope to expose your working dog or future service dog to. Clean Run provides sound socialization CDs, as does iCalmPet. You can certainly record your own recordings, and YouTube now has many audio recordings of varying sounds and backgrounds as well.

Science

If you were to replace the word "human" with the word "dog," the Merriam-Webster definition of socialization would be, "the process by which a dog, beginning at infancy, acquires the habits, beliefs, and accumulated knowledge of society through education and training for adult status."

While that's a great technical definition, socialization can be more simply defined as the process of exposing a puppy in training to varying people, places, animals, things, and concepts so it is comfortable in all situations and under all circumstances. When it comes to training a service dog, absolutely nothing is more important than exhaustive socialization. Socialization while being exposed to the world is the foundation upon which all other training rests, and an SDiT who hasn't gained real-world experience via systematic socialization will not succeed as an assistance dog.

For dogs, socialization begins at birth. Puppies have a highly developed nervous system and even before they can see or hear; they're gathering information about their world via touch and smell. Once their eyes and ears open, it's game on. At five weeks of age, a puppy possesses the same ability and aptitude for learning as an adult dog but lacks the attention span.

Proper socialization begins in the whelping box, with the breeder. The optimal time to socialize a puppy is from birth to 16 weeks. Many service dog breeders use early conditioning programs like the Rule of 7, the military's "Super Dog" bio-conditioning program, or Puppy Prodigies' "Early Learning Program" to introduce puppies to various sounds, people, stimuli, textures, surfaces, and ideas long before they leave the litter.

A service dog in training's education ideally begins with the breeder and builds from there. Because dogs do not generalize as easily as humans do, or apply one situation or concept to another, a service dog in training must be exposed to every situation on an individual basis. As an example, just because an SDiT is familiar with small, female children with blond hair does not automatically mean it'll be comfortable with small, female children with dark hair or a small, blond-haired male child. Each circumstance has to be specifically and individually addressed to ensure there are no gaps in an SDiT's education.

Theory

Your puppy thinks very simply. It will repeat behavior that is rewarded and it will eliminate behavior that is corrected. Your puppy is a pack-driven creature. They thrive on knowing their place in your family pack and will be comfortable only with a strong human leader in charge. Remember that your puppy is instinctively programmed to take charge if the position of "pack leader" is empty or weak.

Be a strong leader. Express confidence and assurance. Always remember that you are in charge and that you must act as though you are at all times. Do not give in to challenges, and expect unwavering obedience from your puppy. Ensure that your puppy obeys all commands the first time they're given. Establish firm rules with high expectations and do not change them for any reason.

Make sure you reward all behaviors that you want and desire. Be consistent and maintain your criteria at all times. Do not allow or tolerate sloppy work. Make sure you're keeping logs and notes of what you do and where you go with your puppy, as we have discussed.

Most service dog organizations offer guidelines and support for their puppy raisers, and the puppy raising team leader at your organization will be a valuable and trusted resource. Always defer to the policies set by your organization. Many programs require puppy raisers to keep detailed socialization and training logs, and for a good reason. Hands down, socialization and training logs are the best way to track your SDiT's education and ensure your puppy doesn't miss out on any vital experiences or knowledge.

Additionally, the training and socialization logs provide you (or your team leader) with a way to track and revel in your puppy's progress. Without logs, it's easy to slide into a training rut of doing the same thing or to progress too quickly. It's also fun to look back through logs simply for the memories.

When you're socializing your service dog in training, always remember the ultimate goal of socialization: to create a well-rounded, unshakeable, stable, solid, confident service dog in all situations. It's only through systematic exposure that makes obtaining that goal possible, but it's easy to become overwhelmed by the sheer volume of available socialization opportunities and circumstances.

Don't get bogged down in the details. Start with your fundamental training and branch out to give your SDiT a wide variety of social experiences, and use the lists here and your training log to help you keep track of what you've accomplished and what tasks remain to achieve.

Housetraining

Lack of housetraining is one of the few things that a business or place of public accommodation can exclude your service dog for, so it's vital that service dogs in training master proper bathroom habits quickly and early. Here are some tips and tricks on how to housetrain your service dog in training (or any young puppy).

Set Up a Schedule

What comes in, must come out. Feed and water your SDiT on a set schedule so you can (reasonably) predict when your puppy will most need to go out. Feed your puppy in the morning, and for very young puppies, again in the afternoon, and pick up water by about 6:00 to 8:00 p.m. so that your puppy will be able to comfortably sleep through the night without accidents. For puppies younger than about 12 weeks of age, you will need to wake up sometime during the night to take them outside.

Keep treats to a minimum until you know your puppy's elimination habits. Use meals for training, and train during mealtimes so that you don't have to worry about your puppy needing to "go" multiple times due to scattered food intake throughout the day.

Keep Eyes on Your Puppy

Watch your puppy. This can't be stressed enough. It's your responsibility if your puppy has an accident and isn't ill. Always, always keep eyes on your puppy. Puppies who are sniffing excessively, holding their tail funny, circling, or otherwise acting "off" need to be scooped up and immediately taken outside.

If you cannot keep your eyes on your puppy, then your puppy should be crated or tethered. There are no exceptions. This includes puppies who are in the same room with you when you're busy doing something else.

Use Management Tools

Management tools include a properly sized kennel, a tether, leashes, exercise pens, or other tools that allow you to keep a close eye on your puppy and manage their movement and space. Puppies naturally like to keep their area clean, which is why crating and tethering are vital to house training.

Lots of service dog programs use bell training. Bell training is one method of training in which a dog is trained to sound a dangling bell when they need to go out. A popular brand is PoochieBells®. Bell training allows your puppy to communicate with you when they need to go out, and thus they can earn a bit more freedom more rapidly.

Take Your Puppy Out on Leash

Puppies who are just let out into the yard often will begin playing and forget what they went out for, and then, once brought back in, they have an accident. Take your puppy out on leash to do business, and then remove the leash (if you're in a safe, enclosed environment) for playtime.

Pottying should always be done on leash for two reasons: it keeps your puppy focused on what they should be doing when they first go out, and it allows you to teach a "go potty" command, which is vital for service dogs.

Offer Ample Opportunities for Success

In the very beginning, take your puppy out every hour or two, no matter what. Set an alarm on your phone so you don't forget. Puppies need to go out before they're crated, after they wake up or come out of their crate, while switching activities (for example, after playing and before snuggle time, a puppy needs to go out), after eating or drinking, and whenever it's convenient for you to take them out, whether it's on schedule or not.

Time between outside trips can be gradually increased as your puppy gets older and is able to "hold it," and mature puppies can often go several hours between trips.

Special Notes Concerning SDiTs

When it comes to public access training opportunities for very young puppies, it's vital to keep outings very short, with opportunities offered to potty outside just before beginning the outing, every few minutes during the outing, and at the end of the outing before going home. Always set your puppy up for success and keep outings safe. Don't frequent places other dogs visit regularly, since young puppies usually haven't finished all their vaccinations.

Tether Training

A "tether" is a short, two- to four-foot-long piece of coated cable with a snap on each end. The coated cable prevents the puppy from chewing the tether and escaping. When it comes to training a service dog in training (SDiT), few tools are as helpful as the tether. Read on to find out why tether training works, what it does, and how to do it!

Tether Training Teaches Manners

Everyone knows that every service dog started out as a puppy, and puppies are kind of crazy. They jump, they run, they bite, and they chew. They're excitable, and don't really know how to be civil members of society. In short, they're puppies, and they're masters of chaos. It's part of why we love them, but in order to be a good service dog and in order to start working in public, they have to do . . . none of the above.

Enter the tether. When introduced at a young age, tether training helps teach and reinforce manners. Its short length prevents jumping, running around, and chewing on inappropriate items, and it allows the handler/trainer to reward the puppy for lying quietly and relaxing. Tethering helps your puppy gain public access earlier than they otherwise would, since they learn very quickly that when they're tethered, their only option is really to relax quietly and watch the world go by.

Tether Training Assists with House Training

Tethering is so helpful with house training that it should be considered a hack. Puppies like to be clean. They don't like to go potty in their immediate space, which is why crate training works. However, for service dog candidates and puppies, being crated means they're no longer in close contact with their trainer/handler and learning active service dog skills, like relaxing quietly in all environments.

Tethering allows you to control your SDiT's immediate surroundings, while allowing your puppy to remain with you. Due to the tether's short length, your puppy can stand up, walk around a bit, lie down, sit, and relax, but there's not enough space for them to potty in one area and sleep in another.

When used as a house-training tool, the tether lets you keep your puppy on a potty schedule, while also allowing you to work on other vital skills at the same time.

Tether Training Helps with Impulse Control

Puppies are social. Puppies get excited. Puppies steal things and run around like wild fiends. Puppies . . . well, they do puppy things.

It's important for service dogs and service dogs in training to learn to do things calmly and to possess some measure of self-control. For very young SDiTs, though, it's all about practice, rewarding calm and proper behavior, and managing the environment so your puppy can be set up for success.

Tethering limits your puppy's behavioral options. When tethering is introduced early, your SDiT learns that fighting the tether achieves exactly nothing, and that being calm, quiet, and settled earns pets, treats, interaction, and the right to engage with the environment in an appropriate way, if the handler/trainer allows.

A tether-trained SDiT can be taken out in public, even in extremely high-distraction environments, and they remain calm and relaxed because the tether sets up expectations for behavior and prevents unwanted activities.

Tethers are Inexpensive

Almost all of us have lost shoes, socks, cords, chargers, leashes, and many other items to an exploring puppy. Tethers are extremely inexpensive, can't be chewed through, are lightweight, and when compared to the cost of replacing puppy-destroyed items, pay for themselves many times over.

Training and behavioral benefits aside, tethers cost next to nothing to make (all materials to make them are readily available at Home Depot or Lowes), or they can be purchased online. Our favorite place to get them is from Guide Dogs for the Blind, which is one program among dozens that extensively use tether training for raising top-tier service dogs and guide dogs.

Tether Training is Easy

Tethering is extremely straightforward. Snap one end of the tether onto your puppy's nonslip collar or harness, and clip the other end around a sturdy piece of furniture or a ring drilled into your baseboard. Give your puppy an activity, like a peanut butter–filled KONG or a bone, and leave them be.

Quietly wait for your puppy to settle and lie down, and then toss them a treat. Practice in short increments, increasing time and distraction levels as your SDiT becomes more experienced. Once your puppy can lie quietly and relax for the length of an average movie (90 to 120 minutes), you're ready to take the show on the road and introduce tethering in public.

Important! Tethers should *never* be used on an unsupervised puppy or dog, regardless of level of training or experience. Never leave a puppy or dog alone while they're tethered, especially if they're wearing a collar.

For young service dogs in training and other working dogs with public access, "place" training is an invaluable tool that teaches rock-solid impulse and self-control, along with laying the foundation for "stays." Here's a brief story outline of how "place" training works:

> *The whine of the engines reached his ears long before they reached mine. I gave the 25-pound puppy curled at my feet a bemused look and a quiet reminder to "settle" as his shifting began. The sound was nothing he'd ever heard before in his life and the vibrations reverberated through his body. He was uncertain of what was going on even though he dutifully held his place. I slipped him a peanut butter–filled KONG and he happily settled back onto his mat, reassured by the familiar routine of place training.*
>
> *I gave a soft grin as the puppy, a young Doberman Pinscher, responded exactly as I knew he would—with confidence and poise. For this handsome little man, it was his first of many cross-country flights.*

The puppy above was a young search-and-rescue dog in training. State law and the airline we're flying with afford him the same rights as a service dog and, as such, he gets to fly free of charge in the cabin with me, his trainer. Many people look in awe at the very young puppy and exclaim, "He's so well behaved! I wish my dog would behave like that! How do you train them to stay like that?"

The answer is twofold: foundation and location. As the old adage goes, "Location, location, location." From a very young age (six weeks), these puppies are all "place" trained. Quite simply, they know that when they see a familiar object (typically a soft bed that self-compresses into a stuff sack, like Ruffwear's Highlands™ bed), they are to settle attentively onto their mat.

Place Training

The "place" is the foundation and the literal location. Work that foundation every single day for two or three hours a day.

While we're working on paperwork or in class, the puppy is tethered. If we settle down in a meeting, the puppy is tethered. Within a couple of weeks, the rambunctious puppies who cried and pitched unholy conniption fits quickly settle and self-soothe. Typically, they work on their provided activity and then they fall asleep. As quickly as possible, though, we want to take the puppy off the tether. It's a very useful tool but it's just that—a tool. We don't want it becoming a crutch.

It's at this point that positive reinforcement and the "stay" games begin. We tether the puppy as normal and begin handing them very small (pea-sized) treats. Every couple seconds, the puppy receives another taste. Sometime in the middle of the treat giving, we casually reach down and untether the puppy.

The puppy will have one of two responses: they will either sit there, waiting for the next treat, or they will run. If the puppy runs, the "stay game" ends completely. The puppy is scooped up and deposited in a crate and all treats/fun/interactions ends for a few minutes. Once three to five minutes have passed and the puppy is quiet and calm, they may be returned to their mat to continue.

If the puppy stayed on the mat, congratulations! You've got a "focus hound" on your hands. Continue giving the puppy small nibbles of treats every couple seconds until the puppy decides to move, which will happen at some point. Your response with this puppy is slightly different than if you were teaching a "stay"—the game merely ends. No more treats, no more interaction with you. Game over. Return to the game after a while and begin anew.

Your goal is to increase the amount of time between treats. Two seconds turns to five, then ten, thirty, up to one minute—then five minutes, ten, up to half an hour. Literally, second by second, minute by minute, the puppy learns a rock-solid stay that's connected to their "place." Eventually, the mat itself becomes so high-value during these games the puppy happily assumes their place when directed. The puppy will wait there all day on the off-chance that a treat or fun activity will be delivered—and it's a waiting game they love to play.

This pup rather enjoyed his first flight. His place provided a secure spot of safety and familiarity, no matter the conditions around him. Long into his working life, his place would provide the same portable sense of safety and confidence. For dogs and puppies in uniform, their portable location, consistent standards of behavior, and solid foundation give the skills to succeed in unknown and sometimes chaotic situations.

We do place training as a conditioned response with a tether. The best tethers are eighteen to twenty-four inches long with a snap on each end. When the puppy is placed on the bed, they are tethered as well. As such, the puppy can either lay quietly on their bed or they can self-correct themselves by fighting the tether.

While on "place" training we provide a much-loved activity—stuffed KONG, a raw knuckle bone, or some other fun, attention-grabbing activity. The puppy quickly learns to settle in place and enjoy the provided task because they are not going anywhere soon.

BASIC TRAINING FOR SERVICE DOGS

First Five Things to Teach

When you first bring home a new service dog candidate, it's easy to become overwhelmed at the sheer volume of "stuff" that needs to be mastered. While every service dog's end job may vary, there are foundational behaviors and concepts every working dog should know, no matter their specialty. Teams should be adept at skills in addition to the ones presented below, but these are, without a doubt, the first five skills you should teach any service dog in training.

Opinions will no doubt vary widely as to the "best" foundational, or fundamental, behaviors to begin teaching a service dog in training, but this list was developed with input from several nationally recognized service dog trainers to focus on the skills necessary to enjoy your service dog in training's company, communicate easily with them, and begin additional, vital socialization and training as quickly as possible, both in and out of public. In light of this organized compilation of fundamental tasks, the SDiT basic commands list should be tailored to meet the core needs of the team in which they are a part. Order of basic command teaching priority may vary. For example, if the SDiT is being trained to be a brace and mobility support partner, it would make more sense to teach the "brace" command as a core skill perhaps sooner than something like the "sit" command.

Name

One of the first things your new service dog in training must learn is their name. If your new (potential) partner doesn't know their name, you can't communicate with them, get their attention, or reorient their focus to you easily.

The quickest and easiest way to teach your SDiT their name is to link their name with something highly reinforcing. Grab a bowl of food (the same amount you'll feed in a meal) and with your service dog candidate on a leash, sit or stand close to them. Simply say their name and immediately offer a very small handful of food. Repeat five to ten times in a row, then just wait patiently for them to start to look around or to move away. Say their name, click when they look at you, and offer another handful of kibble. Repeat until your new service dog in training immediately reorients to you the instant they hear their name.

Do this exercise daily for two or three days, and then begin using their name while on walks or just while hanging out. Always be ready to offer a quick reward for the correct response, which is to immediately look at, focus on, and move to you.

Hand-feeding your potential partner offers great benefits like quick bonding, creating strong handler focus, and presenting a ready-made opportunity for training sessions without the need for additional treats. Consider hand-feeding your partner at least one meal a day for several weeks while they're working on mastering the basics or any time you need to gently reorient their focus, attention, and drive to you.

If you measure out your service dog in training's daily allotment of food into a bowl or baggie and carry it around with you, you can use it throughout the day for training, impromptu reinforcement of attention or good manners, and for bonding.

Clicker Conditioning

Using a clicker will make communicating with your service dog in training much easier. While not a requirement for training, clicker training introduces a level of precision into obedience training and skills performance that otherwise couldn't be achieved.

The click takes 1/10th of a second to complete and it marks the *exact* instant you want repeated. In essence, it takes a "snapshot" of the behavior and freezes an exact instant in time so your service dog in training knows exactly what to do again. As such, there is little room for error. Timing, of course, is crucial—if you click a "stand" as your bouncy puppy rolls from a stand to a down, then you've rewarded the wrong thing!

Before teaching your new service dog in training anything, you need to condition the clicker so it has meaning to your SDiT. Simply click and hand your SDiT a free treat, twenty times in a row (use pieces of kibble for this). For the twenty-first time, click and see if they look for the treat. If your SDiT does, congratulations; they equate the click with the treat. If not, click and treat twenty more times.

Always follow a click with a treat; there are no exceptions. If you click, then treat.

Settling Quietly for Long Periods

Laying quietly and minding one's own business for long periods is a necessary and vital skill for every working dog, and one of the most important foundation behaviors an SDiT will need to master. Beginning the day your new service dog in training comes home, you should start tether training them. By tether training your (future) partner, you allow them to discover for themself what works and is the most comfortable (laying quietly) without your having to be the "bad guy" continuously asking for or forcing a down or a stay long before they're ready or able to offer those types of behaviors.

A tether-trained dog always knows what's expected when they are presented with a mat and a tether (or leash/other restraint) and will settle beautifully for however long it's required of them to do so. Tether-trained SDiTs are a dream to teach formal "stays" to, they possess excellent impulse control, self-control, and manners, and they're never presented with the opportunity to get themselves into trouble. The tether is a useful tool to teach your puppy to calmly accept boundaries and how to settle in one area. The tether also assists in teaching your puppy how to maintain control of themself and to maintain decorum when presented with tough situations, such as riding on public transportation, when guests come over, or sitting through a class or seminar.

However, you can't just hook your puppy up and expect everything to go well. Tether training takes time and patience and is accomplished much the same way as crate training. Always tether your puppy with a fun activity, such as a raw bone or a stuffed KONG. For the first couple of weeks, your puppy will just have to throw the fit and wear themself out. The end goal of tether training is that your puppy learns to accept boundaries gracefully and to quietly entertain themself in one spot without a lot of movement. This skill is crucial to your puppy's success as a dog with public access.

Work on tether training daily. Your puppy may never be left alone on a tether. You must be in the room while your puppy is tethered. Your puppy could potentially hang themself, and it is too dangerous for your puppy to be tethered alone.

Sit

Sit is the easiest obedience command for your service dog in training to master and, as such, it should be taught first. Having a command you know your SDiT will respond to under any circumstance provides you with the ability to easily secure and keep their attention by giving them a job to focus on, and "sit" provides you with a reference point and foundation to teach other positional commands like down, stand, laying on side, and sitting pretty/begging.

Use a treat to lure your SDiT into position and click when their bottom is firmly on the ground. Give the puppy the treat after the click. When your puppy responds quickly and consistently to the lure, add the cue "sit" to the behavior. Use a drawn-out "s" ("Ssssssit") in order to distinguish the command from any other command. Once your SDiT responds consistently to the cue, start by holding the lure in your other hand so they aren't being lured into position.

Once your pup performs reliably at that level, place the treats in a bowl on a table so that you have to reach into the bowl in order to treat your SDiT. Once you've reached this stage, treat your puppy randomly. Ensure that you always offer verbal and physical praise for a job well done.

Leash Walking

If your service dog in training doesn't walk nicely on a leash (as a young puppy, most of the time, or as an older/more experienced trainee, all the time), then they shouldn't be in public, period. As such, they need to master leash manners quickly. Keep in mind, leash training is a necessary foundational skill that will affect future skills training. While some types of service dogs (e.g., guide dogs or mobility dogs) may use specialized harnesses and specific positioning that can deviate from basic heel position, this basic skill is a necessary learning block and milestone for any SDiT to master.

Your SDiT should stay by your side, stop when you stop, start when you start, and not wander. Keep in mind that distractions are a learning opportunity and while they may be interested, you need to be far enough away that you can easily redirect, reward, and keep their attention.

Start by taking a nice walk indoors with your puppy on a leash attached to their collar. When your puppy reaches the end of the leash, simply turn and go the other way. Click and treat when your puppy comes back to your side. Continue this drill until you notice your puppy watching you. Always praise your SDiT exuberantly and slip them a treat after clicking for them being in proper position.

Gradually migrate this activity outdoors. Always respond to your service dog in training ending up at the end of the leash in the same way: turn and walk the other way. Encourage your SDiT to catch up with you with an excited "hurry, hurry." Once they're back by your side in proper position, always greet them with praise, a click, treats, and lovies. Even if you are in public and your trainee's focus wavers, turn and walk the other way until your service dog in training reorients and moves back to your side. Your SDiT will very quickly learn there are no exceptions to this rule and they only get to go places when they walk nicely.

Gradually add distractions into the loose-leash walking, always being sure to reward proper position and to turn and walk a different direction if the SDiT moves out of place.

Applications

Once your service dog in training has mastered the first five skills, it's easy to apply them to other behaviors and expectations for service dogs, like sitting politely for greetings. If your pup will sit and immediately focus on you when their name is said, you have, in essence, laid the foundation for "leave it" and sitting nicely.

If your SDiT always moves to you and looks for direction when you call their name, there's your "come" foundation. You can apply these first five skills in so many ways we can't even begin to list them here, but you'll find yourself using them and falling back on them time and time again. "Sit" and "come" commands must be among your "go-to" tools.

Have fun with your new potential partner and remember, this is only the starting point—there's always something new to learn, master, and delve into, so enjoy the journey!

Next Steps

Once you've covered the first five things to teach, it's time to move on to actual obedience and the foundations of public access training. It's best to find a trainer locally to help, as the socialization and distraction-proofing aspects of a group class are invaluable for young service dogs in training. Here are some of the skills your puppy (or older SDiT) will need to master in basic training:

- Sit
- Down
- Come
- Stand
- Heel: A generalized term to establish a kind of position or attention reset to the task at hand. A common use example of this it to recall the dog to a standing position to the left of the handler, in line with the handler facing the same direction as the handler. This is one example and the only singular default scenario for this command. It is used in a number of different contexts.
- Side: Heel position on the right-hand side of the handler.

- Load up: A common use of this command is to instruct the dog into a vehicle.
- Kennel: Command to get into a kennel.
- Wait: A cue to refrain from doing a task; however, it is not synonymous with "stay." Examples: *Wait* to exit the vehicle, or enter a building, or take an object. This is a reminder command more than an action command.
- Release cue (okay, break, free, etc.): This is a follow up cue for "wait" to let the dog know they may do the given action. Example: *Okay* to come out of the kennel, etc.
- Sit stays
- Stand stays
- Down stays with long duration under high distraction
- Finishes: Moving to heel position; orienting to handler.
- Turns while in heel position
- Pivots/hind end awareness: The dog is instructed to turn in place by sidestepping.
- Under: Instructing the dog to go under something (e.g., table, chair, legs, etc).
- Tail tuck

Some additional skills that are very helpful form the foundations for later task training, including paw targeting, nose targeting, and foundational retrieve work.

PUBLIC ACCESS TRAINING

Vital Public Access Skills

One of the most commonly asked questions is, "when is my service dog in training ready for public access?" While that's a question only you or your dog's trainer can answer completely, here are five vital public access skills every service dog or service dog in training needs to know before beginning work in public.

House Training

This public access skill is nonnegotiable. Your service dog must be house trained, and your service dog in training, if young, must be housebroken to a schedule with regular opportunities to go outside so good habits are built. Your partner needs to be accident free and offer a clear indication that you, the handler or trainer, can read when they need to go outside.

House training is one of the few directly stated points in federal service dog law that can allow a business to remove your service dog from the premises, so make sure your partner is ready for an outing before beginning it.

Down-Stay

A rock-solid down-stay is the mainstay of many service dogs' work in public. While there may be brief interludes of task work, many service dogs are expected to relax quietly near their handler, under a desk, or on a bed until they're expressly needed. A service dog needs the ability to quietly relax in any environment without being intrusive, and a down-stay is usually the default method for most handlers and trainers.

Service dogs aren't robots, and some shifting is to be expected, especially if your service dog or SDiT is place trained to a mat or bed. That being said, most service dogs need to be able to quietly rest for two or more hours at a time, which is the length of an average movie, college class, or time spent working without a break.

Down-stay training begins early, with reinforcement for calm, quiet behavior. Formal "stays" can be taught via many methods, but many people have success with gradually lengthening and rewarding the amount of time their dog spends in one place.

Under

"Under" and "down-stay" often blend to the point of being indistinguishable. "Under" is a behavior that consists of your service dog or service dog in training moving fully under a table, bench, or chair on cue, with their body full tucked beneath the object or your legs as much as if feasibly possible, size depending. The purpose of this public access skill is to prevent your service dog from being an obstruction, to facilitate or ease travel (such as on a bus, plane, or train) and to help your canine assistant be unobtrusive while in public. One of the biggest compliments a service dog handler or trainer can receive is, "I didn't even know a dog was there!"

To begin teaching "under," it's helpful to use a low table, like a coffee or end table. Lure your service dog in training or service dog candidate under the table, from one side to the other, and tell them to down. "Down" should be built into your partner's "under," and your partner should remain "under" until released, just like a stay.

Leave It

"Leave it" means "disregard entirely and do not engage in any way, shape, or form." It's a vital command not only for your partner's safety, but also for basic public access manners. "Leave it" can be used to discourage inappropriate sniffing, being overly social with another person or dog, picking up food off the floor, or engaging with distractions.

It's important that "leave it" be properly practiced and reinforced with a plethora of distractions before trying to use the command in new places, as dogs don't generalize behaviors or concepts well. There are many methods of teaching leave it, but one way to begin involves offering your dog praise and a treat for redirecting from a distraction to you. When you notice your service dog or service dog in training starting to automatically offer eye contact when faced with a distraction, you can add a verbal cue.

Heeling or Loose-Leash Walking

Regardless of what you call it, the ability for your service dog in training or service dog to be in public without dragging you, straining at the leash, coughing, choking, trying to get to distractions, etc. is vital. No dog is perfect, and like any skill, loose-leash walking is perfected via practice.

This part of public access actually involves many pieces: ignoring distractions, being focused on the handler, impulse control, being responsive to direction changes, etc. Service dogs need to be able to walk for several minutes at a time, focused on their handler or trainer, able to ignore distractions, before starting work in public. Introduce public access skills in small doses, and always reinforce handler focus!

Note that even meticulous training doesn't mean your canine partner will be perfect. Rather it means they have the basic skills necessary to redirect to the handler in the face of distraction, even if it requires verbal cueing, luring with a treat, an assistive training device, or other method of securing your partner's attention and focus, like backing away from the distraction until your partner is again able to focus on you and move with you.

The point of this public access skill is that you shouldn't have to fight for your partner's attention. Before working in public, you and your SDiT/service dog need to have already figured out how to proof distractions, redirect focus, and reward sustained focus. With time, this focus exercise turns into effortless loose leash walking, but everyone starts somewhere.

Final Considerations

Many people will ask, "How can I prepare my dog for public access without working them in public?"

What's important to realize is that your partner needs basic obedience skills before working in public, so that you guys can focus on the public-specific behaviors, manners, and training without worrying about basic manners and skills. The skills above form the foundation of public access training, and they can be practiced at home and polished so that when you get in public, you already have the competence and confidence to not have to worry about fighting over food, basic distractions, or stays.

Do SDiTs need to be perfect? No. Even very young puppies can go on short, ten- to fifteen-minute outings where they work on age-specific exercises, such as remaining sitting with the handler when someone walks by. Training an SDiT well requires proper foundation and reinforcing, but it's best to work out the basics before emerging into the public eye.

Being Prepared to Answer Questions in Public

Even though you know that your state allows SDiTs and you're doing everything correctly, answering questions about service dogs in public may not be your favorite thing in the world—or, maybe you do enjoy connecting through your dog! When the manager approaches, you smile graciously, informing the manager that this is your service dog in training, and SDiTs are allowed public access for training purposes under your state's law. He apologizes for bothering you, shakes your hand, and goes on his way.

You breathe a sigh of relief, knowing it could have gone very, very differently. Unfortunately, not all business owners or employees are fluent with the law as it pertains to service dogs. While it can be uncomfortable at times, you have to be prepared to be an advocate for yourself and your service dog on some level. When working your service dog or SDiT in public, be certain to keep the following points in mind, especially if your service dog works "naked," without any gear. Consider that identifying gear like a vest, while not required by law, may make your life easier and will be better diplomacy for the service dog community.

Service Dog Status

Service dogs in training are not service dogs. While service dogs are protected by federal law and may accompany their disabled handlers anywhere the general public is allowed to be, service dogs in training are not. It is up to each individual state to determine whether or not SDiTs are afforded the same public access rights as service dogs.

Always be honest concerning the status of your partner, and never fudge the facts. Know the laws in your state as well as in any areas to which you frequently travel, particularly if your partner is in training. Consider keeping a copy of the laws or the ADA Business Brief: Service Animals in your service dog's vest. Assistance Dogs International offers a valuable resource (ADI Guide to Assistance Dog Laws) for service dog handlers, organizations, and trainers that outlines important service/working dog laws for each state, including whether or not service dogs in training have public access.

Service Dog Gear

Federal law does not require a service dog to wear gear of any kind. Your service dog does not have to wear a vest, harness, tag, ID card, collar, or any other working equipment identifying your partner as a service dog or service dog in training. This is because anyone who uses a service dog is disabled—a fact some disabled handlers choose to be discreet about.

However, the simple fact remains that the public is conditioned to recognize service dogs and service dogs in training only when they're vested or wearing identification. Teams without gear should expect more resistance than teams who work while fully dressed. If your service dog performs a job that requires minimal gear for service dog or handler safety/comfort, such as frequent movements around sensitive medical equipment, full-body deep pressure stimulation, or simple sensory interruption using grooming or touch, then consider working your partner in a bandana or leash that identifies them as a service dog.

You may wish to dress your SDiT or service dog in a vest or identifying clothing simply to avoid some of the more intrusive questions you might encounter, even if local laws do not require it.

Service Dog Access Questions

When you work a service dog in public, you quickly get used to questions like, "What's your dog for?" and "Why do you have a dog?" Most service dog handlers know that according to federal law, businesses may only ask two questions:

Is that a service dog?
What tasks or work does your dog perform for you?

You're not required to disclose information on your disability, the exact function your partner serves for you, or any other information concerning your service dog. However, if a business asks you, in any way, "Is that a service dog?" be prepared to politely answer.

If your dog isn't wearing any gear at the moment and you're informed that there's a "No Pets" policy, diplomatically let the access challenger know that federal law allows your partner to work "naked" and that this is your service dog and they are working for you. Always be polite—be certain not to respond defensively or belligerently—it rarely works out to your advantage because it only encourages the questioner to respond in a similar fashion. Before working your partner in public, be sure you're familiar with the types of questions people may ask, particularly business owners, and consider practicing your responses so you're comfortable and confident with your answers.

Just as your service dog is not a robot and cannot react perfectly, no human being, service dog partner or not, can be perfect or react robotically, and you shouldn't have to. Do your best to be a "service dog diplomat" but recognize that everyone has bad days, including you.

Escalator Safety

Escalators and moving sidewalks are everywhere in today's convenience driven-world. Today's service dog teams are likely to regularly encounter them, especially teams that travel, work in a large or multistory office building, or those that enjoy frequenting the mall. For humans, getting on an escalator or moving sidewalk is simple: step on. For service dogs, though, there are some additional considerations for safety.

Escalators are pretty simple. They work great for most people who simply want an easy ride to or from one floor of a building to another, but for service dog teams, escalators are a blessing and a curse.

There are many concerns in the service dog world about escalator usage. One of the biggest revolves around the moving parts on an escalator. At the top and bottom of an escalator, the steps flatten out horizontally, and then they feed back into the "loop" that cycles behind the scenes to keep the escalator moving. For service dog teams, a huge fear is that small paws or longer fur will get caught in the link mechanism or at the end of the escalator during that split second of time there's a gap. Another issue is that without proper training and socialization, service dogs can be fearful of the escalator or moving sidewalk. It has an odd texture (grooved and ridged metal), the grate surrounding the entrance and exit is off-putting, and there's a low mechanical hum. Additionally, people often hurry or rush and they're typically carrying large items, like luggage or lots of shopping bags. Space is tight, and anything less than a relaxed and calm service dog could cause major disturbance and stress, not only for the handler, but also for those around the team.

Many service dog teams opt out—the great thing about modern urban society are the plethora of escalator alternatives. If you don't want to ride that contraption, you don't have to. You can take the stairs or hop on an elevator, and the problem is solved.

Many service dog teams simply do not take escalators or moving sidewalks, and they don't train for the possibility. They simply resolve to always use the stairs or take the elevator, and that's just fine. There's nothing that says your service dog must be able to navigate an escalator and teaching a service dog to do so is completely up to the discretion of the training program or handler. If a handler or trainer isn't comfortable with escalator or moving sidewalk usage, then there are always other options.

We would not advise someone try to train a dog to ride an escalator without professional assistance for various safety reasons.

Required Skills for Flying

For some people, air travel is a regular occurrence and others may only fly very occasionally. Whether you fly several times a week or only once every few years or anything in between, integrating a service dog into your trip doesn't need to be stressful or a hassle. With some preparation and forethought, the process can be simple and painless. Preparing means considering each step of the journey, from start to finish.

Book your flight however you normally would. Many service dog handlers gravitate toward flying with Southwest Airlines, and Alaska Airlines recognizes and allows service dogs in training to fly in cabin with their handler. Still, don't worry about your carrier too much—all major US airlines are required to follow the same rules of access for service dogs, which means that a dog that is task-trained to mitigate their handler's disability gets to fly in-cabin, at their handler's feet, free of charge.

International airlines likely have different rules concerning flying with your service dog, so make sure to check. Many airlines allow you to add your dog to your reservation as a special accommodation when you purchase your ticket. If they don't, call your airline and let them know you'll be flying with a trained service animal. This smooths the check-in process and can help reduce delays once you arrive at the airport.

Some airlines may ask you for your partner's weight. If asked for your partner's weight, an estimate is just fine. If you want to sit in bulkhead seating, you should definitely call ahead to request it.

Before you fly with your service dog, make sure they possess the skills and training required for a smooth and stress-free flight. Both of you will be happier if the flight isn't a struggle. Checking in for your flight online can streamline the process. While it's not mandatory for domestic flights or flights to Canada, consider including a copy of your partner's rabies certification in addition to your regular flight documentation (picture ID, boarding pass, etc.). It's better to have it and not need it than need it and not have it.

Pack lightly. Juggling multiple heavy bags and a service dog by yourself is difficult and unwieldy. Try for one checked bag, if you must, and one carry-on. There are lots of resources to learn how to pack lightly and you can learn how to fit more in smaller spaces by using some folding/organizing hacks.

Consider fasting your service dog the day before you fly, or only feeding them a small meal in the morning. Give fasting your partner extra consideration if this is your service dog's first flight, or if they tend to have a nervous stomach. Depending on the length of the flight (and definitely if it is international or more than eight hours), pack a pee pad in case the only option is to toilet your dog in the plane—this can be done in the bathroom. Keep in mind that once you are airside (through the security checkpoint), you will not be able to leave the airport to take your partner for a restroom break without going back landside (the other side of security), and then having to come back through the screening process. Some, but not all, airports offer indoor relief areas for service dog teams. Check this in advance of arriving at the airport.

The day of your flight, offer your partner a small drink of water in the morning. Don't overload their system, especially if your flight is going to be a long one or you have a long layover. They can eat and drink to their fill once you arrive at your destination. Make sure to pack a calorie-dense, but healthy, treat, such as canine-specific Wellness Protein Bars or Zuke's® Power Bones, so that you can offer them to your partner throughout the day to help keep their blood sugar levels steady and stave off rumbly tummies. You should offer them one of the bars (or a similar treat) every three to four hours throughout your travel time. If your partner has an especially sensitive stomach, then offer them a small handful of their regular kibble/food.

When you arrive at the airport, get your luggage and bags out, and then unload your partner. Place your partner in a down-stay on the sidewalk or between parked vehicles in a parking garage so they're safely out of the way and not moving. Get your goodbyes out of the way, release your partner, and head into the airport.

If you haven't checked in yet, need your boarding passes, or need to drop off bags for cargo shipment, then head to the proper ticket counter for your airline and get in line. When you get to the counter, place your partner in a down-stay and work with the agent to complete the check-in process. Even though your partner could easily remain standing, placing them in a down-stay demonstrates they clearly have training, and can help you bypass a lot of questions of a dubious nature. Sometimes, an agent will ask you for "paperwork" for your service dog. Be friendly, but firmly inform them that federal law does not require paperwork for trained service dogs to fly. The presence of harness, vest, or working gear, plus the credible verbal assurance of the passenger, suffices as proof of the dog's service dog status. Oftentimes, they'll ask you what tasks your partner performs, or what kind of assistance your partner offers you. Just answer their questions and be patient. Ensure that your partner is relaxed and displaying excellent manners and behavior throughout this process.

After you're fully checked in, with boarding passes in hand, proceed to the security checkpoint. Current regulations say passengers must remove their belt, outerwear, scarves, and shoes. However, individuals with a disability are not required to remove their shoes. If you can remove your shoes, it's often easier to just do so, as not removing them means you'll be subjected to secondary screening, which includes visual or physical inspection of your shoes, and a possible hand test for trace explosives. You do not have to undress your partner.

Since you have a service dog, you will walk through a metal detector. You will not have to go through the full body scanner. When the security officer waves you forward, place your dog in a sit, down, or stand-stay a couple of steps from the metal detector, and walk through as usual. You will then be asked to call your partner through. Occasionally, TSA agents might say the dog's equipment needs to be removed and run through the metal detector. This is not correct—you can remove vest, collar, etc. but the dog should always stay attached to a leash. If you are asked to take the dog totally off leash, a supervisor should be called over who is better informed.

Depending on your service dog's gear, they may or may not set the alarm off. If they do not, then you'll typically be released to leave the security checkpoint. If they do, then the officer will ask if they may touch your dog and your dog's equipment. Answer this question with "yes." The officer will put on gloves and, without removing any of your dog's gear, run their hands under your service dog's collar, vest/harness, and lightly examine their leash. Once that's complete, you'll be able to pick up your partner's leash, and you'll likely be asked to hold your hands out to be quickly swabbed for a trace explosives test.

Once you're released, retrieve your items from the bin, and go to the benches provided on the edge of the checkpoint. Place your partner in a stay, and then redress yourself, put your items back in your bag, and head to your assigned gate.

Feel free to grab a bite to eat or a drink if you like. Once you get to the gate, pick a seat, or take a spot on the floor against a wall, if you're so inclined. Your only job now is to hang out with your dog and wait for boarding to begin. When the gate agent begins the boarding process, they'll ask for anyone who'd like to preboard to come to the gate. That's your cue to gather your things and go line up. Since you are accompanied by a service dog, you may board early to get settled.

The gate agent will scan your boarding pass and direct you to the proper door. Most of the time, you'll be walking down a spacious hallway to the plane, but sometimes, you may have to take a bus shuttle, or walk out on the tarmac to climb steps into the plane. If you're in a wheelchair or require other assistance, the airline will have someone accompany you to the aircraft. You'll be transferred to another chair, and your chair gate checked (you'll pick it up at the end of the jetway once you arrive).

You will board the plane and make your way to, or be helped to, your seat. Direct your partner into the proper row so they're out of the aisle, and then remove reading materials or work you'll need, headphones, and anything else you'll need for the flight. Zip your bag up securely and place it in an overhead bin. Then, cue your dog to either "under" or back into the appropriate seat area.

Remember that your partner cannot encroach on another passenger's space, so until you know if there will be seats open around you, be sure your dog maintains clearly defined boundaries. If you are able, place your foot on each side of your partner while everyone else boards. Once everyone else boards, you can relax a bit, and so can they. Everyone else will board, and most people, if you aren't in bulkhead, won't even notice you have a service dog. Once boarding is complete, if there are open seats, it's possible that others sitting in your row will be given the option to move so that your partner has more space. This is dependent on the airline and staff, however.

The flight itself is fairly straightforward. Your partner should already be lying down and relaxed, and thus they should remain for the duration of the flight. You can provide a quiet toy for them to entertain themselves, if you're so inclined. If you're wearing headphones or plan on sleeping, secure your dog's leash to your ankle or wrist so you'll know if they move too far afield.

You can request a cup of water or ice from the flight attendant for your partner at any time. If your flight is more than four or five hours, you and your partner should get up and walk the aisle, and then return to your seat and settle back in.

Landing can be difficult for some dogs because when the landing gear deploys, it causes a pretty loud "thump" and vibration, and then during the landing itself can be anything from smooth as silk to absolutely horrible. Either way, give your partner reassurance, and a few treats, and don't be surprised if they sit up or want to nestle a little closer to you.

Getting off the plane is much the same as getting on. As long as you're relaxed, your partner will be. Stand up when it's close to the time for your row to leave, and as you step into the aisle, release your dog and grab your carry-on from the overhead. Head off down the jet bridge, and when you get inside the terminal, place your items back in your carry-on, if needed.

If you have another flight, then repeat the above steps until you arrive. You can seek out a relief area if the airport has one, and you should make a point of walking a bit so your partner can stretch. Otherwise, follow the signs for "Baggage Claim" and proceed to exit the airport. Gather around the carousel to wait for your baggage, if you checked a bag. Remember that an alarm will sound, and that the carousel makes a rumbling noise when it activates. Both things can startle first-time flying service dogs, so make sure to let them know all is well. Your dog should wait quietly. When you see your bag, either of you can wade through the crowd to grab it, or you can direct your dog to wait in a down-stay while you grab it and return to them. Make certain to give your partner a chance to relieve themselves as soon as possible, and feed them.

When it comes to flights, flying, airplanes, and service dogs, the law is clear: your service dog gets to ride in the cabin free of charge. Disability or the size of the service dog doesn't matter, as long as the dog in question is partnered with someone who has a disability, and the dog is task trained to help mitigate that disability.

Just because your service dog has access to the plane, though, doesn't mean they're ready to just waltz on board and go. Here are five vital skills your service dog needs before flying with you.

Excellent Leash Walking

From the time you exit your vehicle all the way through the time you exit the airport at your destination, you are going to be reliant on your partner's excellent leash walking skills. The distractions in an airport are numerous and they range from hordes of people, to food, to exceptionally loud noises, to whirring luggage, to running children or people trying to catch flights. Your hands will likely be full of carry-ons or baggage, and now is not the time to have to be focusing on ensuring your partner walks well.

Your service dog should be able to calmly walk on lead, remaining by your side, no matter the distraction, unless their task work dictates otherwise or they are directed to do something else. Additionally, your partner should know how to follow you on lead when it is required that they do so. Airplane aisles are often very narrow, and there likely won't be room for your dog to heel next to you.

Back Up

Your partner needs to know how to back up, and they need to be comfortable doing so when asked. You may need to change direction when there's no room for them to turn around (queued up in a tight security line or in an airplane aisle), or it may be better, due to your dog's size, to ask them to back into your seating area so that they can more comfortably lie down for the ride.

Don't just assume your service dog partner knows how to back up, especially if they're a larger breed. Your service dog needs to be taught this skill, as most dogs aren't used to having to independently move their back feet.

Under

As mentioned earlier, "under" is a vital service dog behavior, and it means that when asked, your partner moves "under" the designated bench, chair, table, seat, or other item. It can also direct your partner to scooch under your legs if there's not room directly under where you're sitting.

When riding in a plane, your partner will be expected to occupy the floor space in front of your seat, and the best way to do this, especially for bigger dogs, is for them to "under" the seat in front of you, almost as if they're a carry-on. Even if your dog doesn't fit all the way under the seat, having their back half under and their front out means they'll be much more comfortable during the flight.

Stay

Being in airports and on planes means there's a whole lot of waiting around for long periods of time. Your partner needs to be comfortable lying quietly for extended periods of time, even under heavy distraction. Don't expect your service dog to suddenly be able to lie down and remain there for several hours if you've never taught the skill. A great way to practice resting quietly for long times and navigating tight spaces is to attend movies or theater performances. The aisles there, as well as the length of the show or movie, allows you to practice skills you'll need for airplanes and similar outings down the road.

Your partner should also know how to stay so that they don't have a difficult time at the security checkpoint. You can either go through the scanners with your partner, or you can ask your partner to "stay" and walk through separately. The second option is usually better, as most service dogs wear gear that will alarm and going through separately means only your partner needs to go through a pat-down. During a pat-down, a TSA officer wearing gloves will gently check your partner's gear and collar. It is helpful if your partner knows how to stand for examination, or has a stand-stay.

Leave It

Food. People. Dropped items. There are all kinds of opportunities for your dog to be presented with something they shouldn't have. "Leave it" is not only important for your service dog to know because it is polite, but it can keep your partner safe. Your service dog needs solid food refusal, and they should know how to redirect their attention to you when asked.

TASK TRAINING

Task training is advanced skills training that teach the SDiT how to do the specific jobs required to mitigate their partner's disability. These tasks are not simple or easy to teach, and often take a great deal of knowledge and understanding of dog behavior and training to develop these skills in your SDiT partner. Seeking professional help from trainers, especially those who specialize in service dog training, is highly advised. Whether you have a limiting disability or not, getting quality training assistance will help set you and your SDiT partner up for success.

Target Training

When it comes to service dog training, the hundreds of available tasks can be boiled down to nine essential behaviors. One of those behaviors, targeting, is an easy foundation behavior every service dog should know. By learning how to teach a service dog to target, you'll be able to start task work with a solid base upon which to build.

Nine Task Work Foundations

- Retrieving
- Carrying
- Depositing
- Tugging
- Targeting
- Physical work
- Hearing
- Guiding
- Alerting

Targeting forms the basis for a variety of common service dog tasks, from opening doors to closing cabinets to helping the human partner in/out of bed; from nudging a fallen arm back onto an armrest to preventing crowding in public. There are too many tasks built upon a foundation of targeting to mention, but any task that requires an assistance dog to purposefully use part of their body with a nudge, shove, or push, begins with targeting. Targeting can be done with any part of a dog's body, but for most service dog tasks, targeting with the nose or paw are the most common.

These instructions can be used for nose or paw targeting, and most teams prefer to teach both. When you teach a service dog to target, you'll quickly notice most pups seem to prefer using their nose over the paw or vice versa. Make sure you keep your partner's preferences in mind while training and offer extra reinforcement when teaching the nondominant behavior. So, if your assistance dog prefers using their nose to hit a button, if you're teaching them to use their paw to complete a targeting task, make sure you reward them with something very high-value.

Pick your targeting cue before you begin training. Switching cues in the middle is confusing. Many people use "push," "touch," "hit it," "button," or "target" as their cue, but it can be anything. Pick a distinctive cue for nose targeting and a different cue for paw targeting. We'll use two cues throughout this training process, one for nose-targeting a closed fist and the other for targeting at a distance.

Targeting your fist is a very useful behavior for teaching focus, proximity, heeling, and position work, which is why we'll put it on cue separately.

Prerequisites

Your partner should be familiar with a clicker or a verbal marker and understand that a treat always follows the click. Ideally, your partner enjoys playing the training game and is willing to hang out with you and puzzle through a new lesson.

Things You'll Need to Teach a Service Dog to Target:

- Handful of high-value treats (diced chicken, cheese, hot dogs)
- Clicker
- Blue or yellow sticky notes

Nudging Your Fist

Place your service dog or service dog in training on a leash if they won't stay close to you while you're training. Sit or stand with your partner facing you. Click and treat for eye contact two or three times to warm up and gain your service dog's focus.

Show your partner a treat, then place it in your closed fist. Offer your fist to your service dog. Click and treat for nose-nudges. Ignore mouthing, teeth contact, or anything you consider "rude." Click only for a clean, firm nuzzle or nudge to your closed fist.

Click the instant your service dog nudges your fist. Open your hand and feed the treat. Repeat several times in a row until your partner happily nudges your fist with their nose and then waits expectantly for the treat.

Offer your partner a closed fist without a treat in it. When they nose-bump your fist, click and treat. Repeat several times in a row. Begin varying the location your fist is in. Move it to the left of your partner, to the right, above your partner, between your legs—anything you can think of. Always click and treat for nose-nudges. If your service dog suddenly acts like they don't know what's going on, you need to practice more with your fist closer to them.

Move to the next phase when your service dog will move several feet in any direction to nose-bump your empty closed fist.

Cue Introduction

Begin saying the word "touch" the instant your service dog nose-bumps your closed fist. Remember to click and treat for successful nose nudges. Place your fist close to your partner initially, then begin varying the distance and placement. Move to the next phase when your service dog will reliably nose-bump your closed, empty fist on cue ("touch") no matter where you place it.

Target Introduction

Dig out your blue or yellow sticky notes. Scientific research suggests dogs are able to distinguish blue and yellow easily but have limited ability to discern other colors. If your partner will be targeting handicap door buttons for you, consider sticking with blue Post-it notes.

Stick a Post-it note to the knuckles of your closed fist. Offer your fist to your service dog and hope for the best. Click and give several treats in a row (a jackpot) when your partner happily nose-bumps you. If your partner doesn't nose-bump your fist, offer it again and give the cue "touch." Click and treat. Repeat a couple of times.

Continue practicing until your service dog readily nose-punches the sticky note on your fist. Click and treat only for direct nose contact with the sticky note. Move to the next phase when your partner is able to reliably hit the sticky note from any angle regardless of where your fist is positioned.

Increasing Distance

Pick a blank wall or sturdy object, like the back of a couch. Place a sticky note on the object. Place a second sticky note on your fist, and arrange yourself so your fist, with the sticky note, is positioned directly beside the one you've placed on the object. Cue your service dog to "touch" the sticky note on your fist. Click and treat. Repeat a couple times to warm up.

Remove the sticky note from your fist. Move it out of sight. Tap the sticky note on the wall with your hand positioned with palm toward the wall, knuckles just above the sticky note. This presentation is similar enough to the sticky note on your fist that your service dog will quickly make the connection.

Encourage your service dog to target the sticky note with their nose. Click and treat several times in a row (jackpot) when they nose-bump it. Have a party, let your dog know you're happy with this performance. Repeat a couple of times. Simply tap the sticky note. Click and treat when your service dog nose-punches it.

Next, stand super close to the sticky note looking bored. Don't give a verbal cue and don't touch the sticky note. Wait. The second your service dog nose nudges the sticky note, have another party. Pass out treats galore. Repeat a couple of times.

Move on when your partner readily touches the sticky note with their nose with no guidance from you.

Distance Cue

Introduce whatever cue you'd like to use to mean "Go touch that thing with your nose." We'll use "target" here.

Say "target" every time your service dog nose-bumps the Post-it note on the wall. Remember to click and treat.

Distance Targeting

Cue your partner to target the Post-it note with you standing right next to it a couple of times. Take a single step away from the Post-it note, preferably straight back. Cue your partner to "target." Continue increasing distance one step by tiny step at a time until your partner can reliably be sent to target the Post-it note from a variety of angles, distances, and setups.

Begin introducing distractions. Remember, if your partner fails two or three times in a row, you've increased the distance or the distraction too quickly. Move closer to the Post-It note again and lower the distraction level until your partner can succeed.

Congratulations! You can now teach a service dog to target!

The same behavior chain used to teach your service dog to target can also be used to teach your partner to open/close doors. For those with physical disabilities, training your service dog to close doors can be incredibly helpful. Whether you're not steady on your feet or even if it just takes a while for you to move across the room, training your service dog to help with basic everyday tasks can be a huge help. Closing the door is a task that's easy and straightforward to teach, so grab your partner and get ready to have some fun!

Incidentally, the same behavior chain used to teach your service dog to close a door can also be used to teach your partner to open doors using a handicap button, push elevator buttons, and close cabinets or drawers. All similar tasks are based on the "targeting" behavior.

Teaching a Service Dog to Close a Door

Prerequisites

Your service dog needs to know how to target a Post-it note or other defined target on cue and at a distance. For our purposes, either nose or paw targeting works, although you should work on your dog being able to do both.

Things you'll need:

- Clicker
- Treats
- Post-it note/target
- Door

Step by Step

1. Stick the Post-it note or other target to the door, close to the edge, at nose-height to your dog. Stand directly next to the door and show your service dog the note. Tap it a couple of times if your dog doesn't

see it. Encourage them to nose-bump the paper. When your dog touches the note, praise them enthusiastically, click, and give them a treat.

2. Practice having your service dog touch the Post-it note while it's stuck to the door. Reward your partner enthusiastically for every success. If your dog isn't quite getting it, return to foundational targeting and practice those behaviors for a bit longer.

3. Introduce the cue you're going to use to ask your service dog to close the door. Good choices include "door," "close," or "push." Stand next to the door and wait. As your dog goes to touch the note, happily state your chosen cue. Click and treat your dog. Repeat this process ten times in a row, two or three times a day, for three to five days. It's very important that your assistance dog learns to link the command you're using with the actual behavior of touching the door with their nose before moving on to the next step.

4. Open the door two to three inches. Bring your service dog over and give them your cue. They should immediately touch the Post-it note with their nose. If the door moves at all, even a little bit, praise them very enthusiastically, click, and give them a jackpot (several treats in a row). Open the door again, and practice until your dog noses the door with enough force to close it the couple inches.

If you find your dog struggles with closing the door, work with a lighter target. Cabinet doors can be easier to close than full-sized doors. Nudging a hanging target can help build reinforcement for the movement for very gentle dogs. Always be upbeat and enthusiastic.

5. Begin to gradually open the door wider and wider and practice having your service dog nose the door closed on command. Teach your service dog to take it slow and only reward your partner when the door clicks closed. That's their cue that they're done performing the behavior. Remember to have fun. If your partner stops closing the door, go back to the last point they'd do so reliably, and spend a couple days working at that level before increasing the difficulty again.

6. Take a step back from the door so you're standing a few inches away. Ask your four-legged worker to close the door for you. When they do so, give them several treats and have a party! Praise them enthusiastically, and then try again.

7. Increase the distance you're standing from the door a single step at a time. Always reward your hardworking partner for success and keep in mind that if your service dog stops performing the behavior, you've increased the distance or the difficulty too quickly. Work a little closer to the door so that your dog can succeed, and then continue adding distance when your dog is comfortable with the behavior.

Teaching a Service Dog to Retrieve

For many service dog teams, formal retrieving is one of the most important tasks. Unfortunately, it's also one of the hardest to teach. It's possible you'll need professional help for this one. In the professional dog-training world, a formal retrieve consists of picking up or taking, holding, and carrying any object pointed out to the dog until they're told to release it to the trainer's hand. While it takes patience, time, and a good sense of humor, you too can learn to teach your service dog to retrieve.

If a human would use their hands to do something, it's likely a service dog is going to use their mouth. Retrieving is the foundation for more service dog tasks than we'd care to count. Tasks like opening doors, carrying bags, picking up dropped items, fetching the phone, delivering messages, and helping a handler to dress/undress all begin with retrieving. By teaching your service dog to retrieve, you open up a whole new realm of task work possibilities.

When teaching the retrieve, it's important to remember the end goal: creating a happy, motivated worker who clearly understands what they're being asked to do. In this case, your goal is to teach your service dog to retrieve, or pick up and hold until released, any object pointed out to them. It's vital that you take things as slow as is necessary for your partner. Trying to rush will only create frustration and stress and will wreak havoc on the training process. Training a service dog to reliably retrieve takes a lot of time, patience, and understanding, but the end results are well worth it.

There are many different methods of teaching a service dog to retrieve, but I'm going to present the "motivational retrieve," or a method of teaching the service dog retrieve that relies solely on positive reinforcement and shaping.

Keep in mind that any age of dog or puppy can begin learning the foundational retrieve behaviors. Puppies as young as five to seven weeks old are capable of mastering the skills required in formal retrieval. When you're first starting with a young puppy, your job will be infinitely easier if you accustom your future service dog in training to carrying, mouthing, and playing with a variety of textures.

When your puppy is supervised, offer them short lengths of metal and PVC pipes, keys on a ring, and other "toys" with slick, cool, or otherwise "not fun" textures to play with. If your SDiT is used to a variety of textures, you won't have to struggle nearly as much when introducing the traditionally more difficult objects.

Prerequisites

Before beginning to train your service dog to retrieve, you need to understand how to mark behaviors with a clicker. Timing is vital during retrieval training, and you need to be confident in your ability to get it right before starting to teach your service dog to retrieve. You also need to thoroughly understand that retrieval training is a process and that it will take as long as it takes. Your puppy or dog needs to be clicker conditioned, able to focus on you for short periods of time, and know the basics of how to target.

Things you'll need:

- Plastic canine dumbbell or retrieving dummy (check out J & J Dog Supplies for dumbbells and K9 Lifeline® for fleece retrieving dummies)
- Clicker
- High-value treats (diced chicken, cheese, hot dogs)

Targeting

Sit in a chair with your service dog facing you. Hold the dumbbell and clicker in one hand and treats in the other. Present the dumbbell to your partner. Click and treat for nose bumps. Move the dumbbell from side to side. Continue clicking and treating for nose targeting. Ignore pawing, vocalizing, or anything except nose bumps. Continue practicing until your service dog will move a couple feet in either direction to nose-bump the dumbbell.

Mouthing

Stop clicking for nose bumps. Just wait. Don't offer any cues and don't lead or guide your partner. After a few seconds of trying to nose-bump the dumbbell without any response, your service dog is likely to open their mouth in frustration. Immediately click and treat several times in a row (jackpot). Don't worry if they didn't touch the dumbbell; simply click and treat for their mouth opening.

Continue to ignore nose bumps. Click and treat once for your service dog's mouth opening, and jackpot if they actually brush or touch the dumbbell with any part of their mouth for any reason, even if it's an accident. Work toward your service dog purposefully putting their mouth on the dumbbell, even if they spit it out instantly. Click and treat for mouth-to-dumbbell contact. Begin clicking and treating only for actual "grabs," which are mouth opens, teeth close around middle of dumbbell, no matter how briefly, and then dog lets go.

The next step in this training is extending the hold, as we have described previously.

Troubleshooting

If your partner just won't move from nose-bumping to mouthing, it's time to troubleshoot your retrieve. Try smearing just a trace of peanut butter on the backside of the dumbbell grip, the side that's facing your body that your service dog can't see.

Alternatively, if your partner won't snatch it from you, freeze a hot dog to use for the first couple of sessions. You can also position a treat just behind the dumbbell, close to the grip, so that when your partner opens their mouth to get the treat, they touch the dumbbell.

Tips

The easiest way to keep organized is to hold the clicker and the dumbbell in your left hand and the treats in your right. If your partner needs to be on-lead to keep from wandering off, then simply step on the end. Use very high-value, special treats while teaching your service dog to retrieve. The more interest and focus you can generate in the process, the quicker your partner will progress.

Warnings

The formal retrieve can be a difficult and frustrating behavior not only for your service dog to learn, but also for you to teach. Take breaks as necessary, keep the energy high, and above all, relax.

If you feel yourself getting frustrated, ask your partner to perform a couple of quick, easy, fun behaviors they know well and then end the session. Be careful not to drop the dumbbell or whatever object you're using on your feet or your service dog's paws—it hurts!

You know it takes work and practice to train a service dog to retrieve. You've managed to get your service dog to mouth at the dumbbell, but now you're stuck. No matter what you try, your service dog keeps spitting the dumbbell out immediately. Now we need to know how to easily and positively obtain the ever-so-elusive "hold" behavior.

Introduce the "Out" Cue

It seems counterintuitive, but we're going to start to train the "hold" by training the release. Once your service dog understands the release cue and the fact that an item should only be released to your hand, it's far easier to introduce the concept that they need to wait for the release cue before letting go of something. Begin with a couple rounds of clicking and treating for grabbing the dumbbell. After three to five quick reps, move to the next step. Remember, at this stage of the game, the dumbbell always stays in your hand.

Introduce the "out" cue. Offer the dumbbell to your partner. They'll reach for it and grab it. Click the grab and immediately say, "out," as they spit it back out. Treat. Do this several times in a row until you notice your service dog is beginning to pause, even if it's just for a microsecond, before spitting the dumbbell back out. They're starting to listen for that new word, the "out" cue.

Click for the pause between the grab and the instant they start to spit the dumbbell back out. Continue saying "out" as the dog lets go. You'll notice the pause building microsecond by microsecond. Jackpot (give several treats) for especially noticeable or lengthy pauses. Keep in mind the click itself marks the behavior you want to encourage, so click the *pause*, not the "out." Click the pause, say "out," and then deliver the treat that goes with the click.

Move on once you can count "one Mississippi" between the instant your service dog's teeth close on the dumbbell and they go to spit it out. Slide your hand off the dumbbell and position directly under your service dog's mouth.

Release to Hand

For this stage, it's important to keep sessions short, upbeat, and positive. This section can be extremely frustrating for both the dog and handler. The goal for the "release to hand" step is for your partner to begin to understand that they only get a reward if the dumbbell ends up in your hand.

Offer the dumbbell to your service dog. The instant their teeth close on it, let go and move your hand directly under the chin so the dumbbell falls into your palm when they let go. Click and say, "Out," at the exact same time, then treat. If they spit the dumbbell out before you manage to say "Out," move your hand and let it fall to the floor. *Do not click and treat if that happens.* Simply shrug, pick the dumbbell up, and offer it to them again. Repeat five or six times in a row.

Start the same routine, but instead of saying "out," just wait. When your dog spits the dumbbell out, shrug, say nothing, pick it up, and offer it again. This time, cue "out" and allow the dumbbell to fall in your hand. Jackpot your partner. Continue practicing. Every third to fifth time, randomly, don't cue the "out," and let your dog spit it out. Shrug, pick the dumbbell up, and offer it again. Jackpot the next grab and release on the "out" cue. Look for the first time your service dog noticeably, purposefully holds on to the dumbbell for longer than they had been during one of the "no cue" reps. Instantly cue the "out," and jackpot. Give two jackpots.

Continue practicing, always ensuring your partner succeeds far more than they fail. The more you successfully reinforce the waiting-for-"out" behavior, the more likely you are to get it.

The Guided Hold

Be gentle during this phase. Remember, we're teaching a motivational retrieve, not a forced retrieve. Position your partner beside you in a sit. If you're right-handed, they need to be on your left side; if you're left-handed, sit them on your right. If you sit your service dog in front of you, it won't be as easy to gently apply the upward stroking and keep your partner calmly sitting, but it can be done.

Offer your service dog the retrieving dummy with your dominant hand. As their teeth close around it, let go and slide your hand under their chin. Gently stroke upward from your dog's neck to the end of their chin with your dominant hand. After a second or two, stop stroking, position your hand to catch the dumbbell, click to mark the hold, cue the "out," and treat.

Position for the guided hold exercise so your SDiT is to the left side of the right-handed trainer, with their body settled lightly against the trainer's left side or the chair so they can physically, but gently, help them hold their position, and the trainer's right hand is gently stroking upward under the dog's chin.

From the initial one to two seconds, increase the duration a second at time, only adding time when your partner calmly holds the dumbbell for the current duration without struggling, moving, or trying to spit it out. If your dog manages to spit the dumbbell out, calmly replace it without fuss. Continue the soft, gentle stroking under your partner's chin for now. Slow, gentle, patient, and steady win the "hold" race.

Practice until you reach thirty seconds of comfortable, calm "hold" while you're gently stroking under your service dog's chin.

The Hold

Start the same way you do for the guided hold. Offer your service dog the dumbbell, gently stroke under their chin once or twice, and then take your hand away. After a couple seconds, click, cue the "out," treat, and calmly pet your partner. If your dog releases the dumbbell before you cue the "out," simply shrug, pick the dumbbell up, and offer it again.

Repeat the above two to three times, and then stop stroking under your service dog's chin after you hand them the dumbbell. Simply hand it to them, take your hand away, wait three to five seconds, click, cue the "out," and treat. Build time gradually, a second or two at a time, until your partner is able to hold the dumbbell for at least thirty seconds until cued to "out" to your hand with no guidance at all.

At this stage, if your partner's "hold" isn't successful for any reason, it is very likely you're missing something. There's either too much distraction or you've added too much duration at once. Go back to a point you know your service dog can succeed and work forward from there again. Keep things upbeat and set your partner up for success far more than you let them fail. As always, if your partner spits the dumbbell out before being cued, simply shrug, remain silent, pick it up, and offer it again. Keep sessions short, sweet, and to the point to ensure your dog's interest in formal retrieve training remains high.

Desensitizing Touch

By now, your service dog is used to hearing "out" and dropping the dumbbell into your waiting hand. Many assistance dogs begin to associate touch with the "out," though, and stop waiting for the verbal "out" cue. For many disabled handlers, that's an issue because they may not be ready to take an object the first time they touch it or touch their partner. Use the following steps to counteract this tendency, and remember to only deliver a reward for a dumbbell that ends up in your hand after a verbal "out" cue is given.

Position your working dog in front of you or beside you. Hand your dog the dumbbell, drop your hand, and wait for a couple of seconds. Reach up and very gently touch the edge of the dumbbell or retrieving dummy. If your dog spits it out, let it fall to the floor. Shrug, pick it up, and silently offer it again. Reinforce the verbal "out" cue a couple times, then repeat the light touch again without the cue. If your dog holds, immediately click, "out," and reward.

Hand your dog the dumbbell and gently stroke your dog's head or the top of their muzzle. Click, "out," and treat for continued holds, and ignore drops entirely. Never reward a dropped dumbbell without a verbal "out" cue, even if you're reaching for it, touching it, or touching your partner. Work until your partner reliably waits for the verbal "out" cue even if you curl your fingers around the dumbbell, pet/stroke their head, ears, or muzzle, or touch the dumbbell or your assistance dog in any way.

Proofing the Hold

Once your service dog will happily take the dumbbell from your hand and hold it for at least thirty seconds at a time until cued to "out," you know they understand the concepts of "take it" and "hold it." At this point, you can start to "proof" the hold. This means to introduce variations and distractions for the purpose of solidifying your dog's understanding.

Introduce variations in position first. Ask the dog to take the dumbbell and hold it while they're standing, sitting in front of you, positioned on the other side of you, or lying down. Next, ask them to hold the dumbbell in other circumstances. Perhaps they're standing on the ledge of the stairs and you're positioned two or three stairs down. Maybe they're sitting in the front seat of the car or are standing in their kennel. Be creative and help your service dog begin to generalize the "hold" behavior to anywhere they may (or may not!) need to use it.

The "may or may not" is part of the *Green Eggs and Ham* training philosophy—will they do it in a box, will they do it with a fox? Will they do it in a house? Will they do it with a mouse? Will they do it on a train? Will they do it in the rain?

The *Green Eggs and Ham* method of proofing dictates asking your dog for behaviors in wild, crazy, off-the-wall situations so you can test their understanding and performance in circumstances far beyond what they're likely to encounter. Have fun with *Green Eggs and Ham*, and take lots of pictures.

Movement and Positions

Introduce movement next. Begin asking your partner to change positions while holding the dumbbell—shifting from a sit to a down, a sit to a stand, or a stand to a down works nicely at first. Only ask for one position change in the beginning and reward your partner profusely for success. Build up to three to five position changes in a row before asking for the out, but be gradual about it. As always, if your assistance dog starts spitting the dumbbell out before the cue, you're asking for too much too quickly. Revert back to a point at which they are able to succeed, and move forward more gradually.

Once your partner is able to change positions fluidly while holding the retrieving dummy, start asking your dog to carry the dumbbell while heeling. Start with a single step and build gradually to thirty seconds of heeling. Always reward your partner for success and ignore them completely should they drop the dumbbell. Silently pick it up, offer it again, and work on a shorter distance you're confident they'll succeed with.

Introducing a larger or different dumbbell is an excellent way to proof the hold.

Using the Three Ds

Finally, begin to fiddle with the three Ds. Keep in mind that you've already worked on duration by building your service dog's "hold" to more than thirty seconds at a time. The next step is to begin increasing distance. Start by handing your partner the dumbbell and taking a step back. Pause for a beat, return to your dog, click, "out," treat. Increase the distance a single step at a time until your dog will happily and comfortably hold the dumbbell while you walk ten steps away, turn, and come back to release them.

At that point, you can start to increase the distraction. Perhaps work at a park or begin incorporating "hold" into your public access outings. Ask your partner to "hold" a dumbbell while you're preparing their meal or while you're working on basic obedience with another dog.

Be creative with your distractions, but always keep the three Ds in mind. Stay close to your dog and don't ask for long-duration "holds" when first introducing distractions. Be generous with your rewards and ensure your partner succeeds far more than they fail.

If they start dropping the dumbbell, reduce the distraction level until they're able to reliably succeed and then gradually begin to increase the difficulty again. The easiest way to reduce distraction levels is to simply move farther away from the stimulus, and then gradually move closer again.

Final "Hold" Steps

By now, your service dog should be able to take, hold, and carry a dumbbell or retrieving dummy in almost any situation and under almost any circumstance. Congratulations! You're finished with the hard parts of teaching a formal service dog retrieve. From here, it's smooth sailing.

Continue proofing your hold in any way you can dream up. Start combining aspects of the three Ds—walk five steps away and ask for gradually increased "hold" durations—five seconds, then ten, fifteen, then thirty seconds. Always return to your partner and reward a job well done.

The "hold" process cannot be hurried or rushed. If you try to move faster than your partner is willing or able to proceed, you'll only end up with a frustrated and stressed-out service dog. Take your time and grant your hardworking pooch as much time as they need to be comfortable with each phase of the formal retrieve training process.

If either of you begins to get frustrated or irritable, ask your service dog for a couple of fun, easy behaviors they know well, like hand-targeting, sit, or shake; click and treat each, and then end the session.

Once your partner will take a dumbbell out of your hand and hold it under a variety of circumstances, it's time to teach them to pick it up off the ground and to introduce new objects. By the end of our next step, your partner will be able to complete a formal service dog or obedience retrieve.

Remember to *always* cue the "out" verbally and only click and treat if the dumbbell is released to your hand after the verbal cue and not with a simple touch or even a grab. Start combining carrying and distractions while building ever-increasing distances. You're limited only by your creativity during the final hold proofing, and the more *Green Eggs and Ham* practice you put into it at this stage, the more smoothly the next steps will go.

Generalization

While working through the part three steps, keep in mind that dogs do not generalize behaviors as easily as humans do, and it is therefore important to deliberately work on generalization. For example, just because a service dog in training understands "down" in the kitchen doesn't mean they are able to perform the behavior in a new environment, like the living room or a store or outdoors, immediately. A behavior may need to be retaught in each new location or with each variation and re-proofed specifically for or in each variation or environment.

Similarly for the service dog retrieve, you'll need to start at the beginning when introducing a new object, at least for the first few new items, but eventually you will need fewer steps for each. You would begin again with nose targeting and then progress through the "take it" and "hold" steps detailed previously. After three to five new objects, your partner will start to quickly apply retrieve criteria (take or pick up what I present or point out to you and hold it until given a verbal cue to release) to any object required. While your partner is learning to relate formal retrieve criteria to new items and in new situations, be patient and help them learn to generalize.

Common Retrieval Seeding Kit Items:

- Metal food bowl
- Spoon
- Pen
- Heavy card stock paper
- Cardboard squares

- Strips of fleece or cloth
- Empty medicine bottle
- Phone
- Large dumbbell
- Water bottle
- Small book
- Spare keys on a ring
- Key fob
- Leash
- Vest
- Twelve-inch section of PCV/metal pipe
- Wallet
- Old credit/ID card
- Empty cans (with no sharp edges)

To teach a formal service dog or obedience retrieve, you need a retrieval seeding kit (RSK). Quite simply, an RSK is a collection of objects and items you need your partner to learn to retrieve. Items are also included in the RSK to teach dogs learning to retrieve to take and hold any object, no matter how weird, oddly textured, or unfamiliar. You can include absolutely anything your dog is physically capable of safely picking up, regardless of "like" or "dislike," in your retrieval seeding kit—but please be aware of which items could be dangerous.

The best way to store your retrieval seeding kit items so they don't get lost, scattered, or strung out all over the place is in a basket, duffel bag, tote, or plastic container with a handle. The name "seeding kit" comes from the retrieval seeding puzzles service dogs undergoing advanced training are asked to complete—ten to twenty items of varying sizes, shapes, textures, materials, and palatability are laid out and the dog is asked to formally retrieve each, one by one.

Assisted Pickup

You may need to modify the exact steps if you're unable to stand, bend over, sit on the floor, or kneel comfortably for long periods of time or if your partner is smaller than the average service dog. The point of this stage of training is to progressively get the dumbbell closer to the ground while still hanging on to it, so whatever you need to do in order to make that happen will work just fine.

If at any point during the retrieve assisted pickup stage your dog stops taking the dumbbell or retrieving dummy on cue, go back to the last height at which your dog was reliably performing and continue practicing at that point before progressing again. Take things slow and steady.

Hold the dumbbell or retrieving dummy in your hand and ask your dog to "take it." After a couple seconds of holding, "out" your dog. Repeat a couple of times. Drop your hand, while still standing, until the dumbbell is as low as you can comfortably get it while still hanging on. Ask your dog to "take it." After a couple of seconds of holding, "out" your partner. Repeat a couple of times.

Kneel or present the dumbbell to your dog at knee height and ask your dog to "take it." After a couple of seconds of holding, "out" your service dog or service dog in training. Repeat a couple of times, then drop your hand midway down your calf. Repeat again.

If you are able to, sit on the ground. Present the dumbbell to your dog at roughly (sitting) knee height and ask them to "take it." After a couple of seconds of holding, "out" your partner. Next, drop your hand close to the ground, but not touching it. Repeat again.

While sitting on the ground, lay the fingers of your dumbbell hand on the ground while still hanging on to the dumbbell or retrieving dummy. Repeat the normal retrieve sequence a couple of times. While sitting on the ground, place the far edge of the dumbbell on the ground and hang on to it with just a couple fingers. Ask your dog to "take it." After a couple of seconds of holding, "out" your pooch.

Place the dumbbell on the ground and place a single finger on the side you normally hang on to. Repeat the normal retrieve sequence. Jackpot (give several treats in a row) successful repetitions. While sitting on the ground, place the dumbbell on the ground. Keep your hand close, but don't touch it. Ask your dog to "take it" and after a couple of seconds of holding, "out" your dog. Jackpot successful repetitions.

When transitioning the retrieve from your partner taking the object from your hand to picking the object up off the floor, you need the following steps:

- Dumbbell at hip height
- Kneel with dumbbell
- Sit on ground with dumbbell
- Place dumbbell close to ground
- Place fingers on ground
- Hold with two fingers while contacting ground
- Rest on ground and touch with only one finger
- Don't touch dumbbell at all.

Shaping the Pickup

Place or drop the dumbbell at your feet. If you're not familiar with teaching targeting or with "shaping" a dog to perform a behavior, check out the instructions for training a service dog to target. Sit in a chair or on a set of stairs close to the bottom with your dog standing or sitting within touching distance in front of you. Place the dumbbell on the ground and take your hand away. Remain silent; don't give your dog a command or a cue. Simply wait. Glance meaningfully toward the dumbbell every now and again if need be.

Click and treat the instant your dog looks at or lowers their head toward the dumbbell or retrieving dummy. Continue shaping your dog to pick the dumbbell up the exact same way you did in part one of retrieve training. Click and treat for movement toward, nose nudges, and mouth contact with the dumbbell.

Remember to stay quiet. Don't give commands or cues or "help" your service dog or SDiT out. You need them to puzzle their way through this section so they're certain to know the right answer in the next stage. Instantly click, "out," and jackpot the first time your dog picks the dumbbell up off the ground, unassisted, and raises their head to look at you. Practice until you can place the dumbbell on the ground or toss it a short distance away while sitting in a chair or on steps and your dog immediately goes to it, picks it up, and raises their head to wait for the "out."

Repeat the above steps while standing. If you will need your partner to retrieve things (like a phone or medication) while you're lying on the ground or in another position, now is the time to introduce those variables. Repeat the above steps with each new position.

Proofing the Retrieve Pickup

While standing, drop or toss the dumbbell or retrieving dummy a short distance away. Tell your partner to "take it." Jackpot compliance after outing your dog. Repeat the entire retrieve sequence (dropped dumbbell, "take it," holding under a variety of circumstances, and the verbal "out") several times. Once your dog performs reliably eight out of ten times without assistance, hesitation, or do-overs, move on.

Reintroduce *Green Eggs and Ham* proofing and the three Ds. Begin practicing the entire formal retrieve sequence with the dumbbell in any situation or with any variable you can dream up. Just remember to be mindful of the three Ds—you can only change one variable (duration, distance, distraction) at a time.

Revel in the fact that your dog is now completing a formal retrieve from beginning to end, and that you achieved it using fun, motivational methods. Good job!

Introducing New Objects

If you're training the retrieve for AKC (American Kennel Club) or UKC (United Kennel Club) obedience, the bulk of your work is finished. You'll need to combine the retrieve with a formal recall and front/finish and increase distance and distraction on the retrieve itself.

If you're training a formal service dog retrieve, all of your foundational work is finished. Now, you'll need to introduce the items your partner will need to pick up for you or retrieve for you on a regular basis. When introducing new objects, start with dumbbell-like objects first, then "easier" items like pens, cardboard squares/books, and cloth/fleece/key fobs, then progress to "trouble" items like metal bowls, keys, and phones. Of course, what is seen as easy or difficult will vary depending on the individual dog.

Follow the below steps for each new item you introduce. After you've gone through the process with three to five objects, you'll notice your dog progressing through the early steps far more quickly or bypassing huge chunks of them altogether. Let your dog set the pace, but if they start skipping through the steps, go with the flow. It's okay; they're just demonstrating they understand the retrieve game.

Start every session with one or two formal retrieves with the dumbbell. Make them quick, easy, and fun. Show your service dog or SDiT the new retrieve item. Let them sniff it and explore it a bit, always ensuring to click and treat for nose nudges or contact with the item. Your goal, as always with the retrieve, is mouth contact.

Shape your dog through targeting the object to taking the object. Follow the steps for retrieve training (see page 176). Remember not to give any commands (like "take it"). You don't want to create a situation where your dog "disobeys" your command simply because he's not comfortable with a new item. Move on once your dog comfortably takes the item when it's presented.

Begin using the "out" cue. Build your partner's hold with the new item, always ensuring to reward success and ignore failures. Use the steps beginning on page 179.

Only begin using "take it" once your partner is familiar enough with and comfortable enough with the object to take it reliably and hold it in a variety of circumstances, and you're comfortable that the dog won't bail out or ignore the command. By only using the command when you're certain he'll succeed, you build success into the command. If your partner never has a chance to fail for any reason after being given the command, he'll be far more likely to respond in an unfamiliar situation.

Work through the "pickup" steps with the new item. With each new item you introduce, the "pickup" stage will go more and more quickly. Proof the new item using *Green Eggs and Ham* and the three Ds. Refer back to page 129 if you need a reminder.

Retrieval Seeding

The final steps of retrieval training involve retrieval seeding puzzles. Lay out two or three familiar objects (one of which should be the dumbbell or retrieving dummy you've done all of your dog's retrieve training with) in a roughly triangular pattern. Leave enough space between them your dog can easily step between items, but not so much it looks like they're unrelated. Group them tightly enough to leave no doubt you meant an item to be exactly where it is, but not so tightly your dog will disturb them stepping between items or picking objects up.

Approach the retrieval seeding puzzle with your dog by your side. Once there, simply say, "take it," and point toward the puzzle. Don't insist that your dog retrieve any certain object first or that they complete the puzzle in a specific order. Allow them to select and pick up the object they want, bring it to you, hold it, and then "out" on command. Give them a treat after the "out," and then repeat, "take it." Repeat with the last item.

Add one or two objects to the puzzle at a time, always ensuring you've properly introduced each item and your service dog or service dog in training is completely comfortable with it before placing the object in the puzzle. Work until your dog easily and confidently completes retrieval seeding puzzles of ten to fifteen or more items. At that point, begin *Green Eggs and Ham* proofing and working on the three Ds.

Retrieval Training Tips and Warnings

Allow your service dog as much time as necessary when introducing new objects. Understand that your partner will have preferences, favorites, and "do not likes." Some items take more patience and time than others, but with time and reinforcement, your partner will be able to formally retrieve anything you'd like them to. For particularly difficult items, use extremely high-value, smelly treats they don't get at any other time.

Don't rush your service dog or service dog in training while training the retrieve. For a solid, reliable retrieve you need a great foundation. If you rush, your dog's retrieve will never be reliable or steady under pressure.

Don't repeat "take it" over and over if your dog is refusing an item. If your dog is refusing to retrieve, take, or hold an item at this point, they're not being "disobedient." They're just not comfortable with that item yet. Work back through targeting and taking the item.

If you find yourself having to ask more than once for your dog to "take" an object, your dog isn't ready for formal takes, holds, and outs with that item yet.

Teaching a Service Dog to Retrieve a Beverage

Whether your partner assists you during a seizure, detects high or low blood sugar, pulls your wheelchair, or performs any other job, learning how to teach a service dog to retrieve a beverage from the fridge and training your partner to do so can mitigate many disabilities. The training can be difficult, but with patience, a sense of humor, and lots of really good treats, your service dog will be retrieving drinks* in no time!

The situations in which teaching your service dog to retrieve a beverage could prove useful (or even lifesaving) are so varied it would be impossible to list them all, but here are some helpful instances dozens of handlers have reported:

- Retrieve a beverage to take medication with
- Retrieve a beverage to help break a dissociative episode
- Retrieve a beverage to mitigate severe dry mouth
- Retrieve a beverage to provide alternate focus during panic attack
- Retrieve a beverage to assist a partner who isn't very mobile
- Retrieve a beverage to encourage quicker recovery from a seizure
- Retrieve a beverage to ground a handler who's having nightmares or flashbacks
- Retrieve a beverage to raise low blood sugar
- Retrieve a beverage to calm anxiety
- Retrieve a beverage to prevent dehydration

*The training steps laid out to retrieve a beverage can be used to teach your partner to retrieve any named object kept in a specific place.

The same process used to teach a service dog to retrieve a beverage can be used to teach your partner to retrieve anything that is always in a fixed location, such as medication that's kept on a low shelf in your bedroom, a phone on a low table in the hall, toilet paper stored on a low shelf in the closet, or glucose tablets in a kitchen drawer.

As long as the object you're teaching your partner to retrieve can always be found in the same place, you can teach your service dog to retrieve it on cue. The trick is to always put the item back after you've used it!

Prerequisites

Before beginning to teach your service dog how to bring you a beverage, they need a solid formal retrieve. Your service dog needs to know how to take an object, hold it without mouthing, release it into your hand on cue, and tug reliably before starting this task work. If your partner isn't yet solid with foundational retrieve behaviors, spend a little more time working with them on retrieving a beverage. Here are step-by-step instructions for training the formal service dog retrieve:

Step 1: Nose targeting the dumbbell/retrieving dummy and taking it.
Step 2: Taking the dumbbell on cue and holding it until released in all circumstances.
Step 3: Picking the dumbbell up off the ground and introducing new items.

Ideally, your partner will also know how to target. You should be familiar with the use of a clicker or verbal marker, able to deliver treats smoothly and quickly, and understand the entire process of teaching your assistance dog to retrieve a beverage before you begin.

Things you'll need to teach a service dog to retrieve a beverage:

- Clicker
- High-value treats like diced chicken, cheese, or hot dogs
- Door pull (in a pinch, a section of rope works beautifully)
- Empty beverage bottle

- Full beverage bottle

Opening the Fridge

1. Select a door pull and be sure to pick a style that meets your and your dog's needs. Choose a design with a "tug" part that is large enough for your dog to grasp comfortably and long enough for your partner to get enough leverage to pull the door open. Eight inches or longer tends to work best for the average-sized service dog. Introduce your service dog to the door pull you'll be using to teach them to open the fridge door. Allow your dog to sniff it and familiarize themself with it.

   Pick up the door pull and ask your service dog to "take it." "Out," click, and treat. Practice having your service dog "tug" the door pull, always ensuring that your partner is backing straight up. The door pull and your dog's head, shoulders, back, and hips should form a straight line. This not only helps your service dog open the door more easily, it ensures that they do so with proper form, which helps them avoid injury.

   Continue practicing until your service dog reliably takes the door pull and tugs smoothly and continuously until released.

2. Place the door pull on the refrigerator door. Check the height of the door pull and ensure your service dog can easily reach the "tug" part of the pull without difficulty. Your partner needs to be able to grab the "tug" part of the door pull without straining or needing to reach above their head, and they should have all four feet solidly on the ground.

3. Call your service dog over to the fridge door. While the door pull is still attached, pick it up close to the attachment point and hold it in your hand.

   Practice having your service dog "tug" the door pull. Assist them with opening the door, and always click, treat, and release the instant the refrigerator door opens. Continue practicing until your partner enthusiastically grabs the door pull, tugs hard with proper form, and releases when the door opens.

4. Call your partner over to the fridge door. Don't pick up the door pull this time. Ask your service dog to "take it" and "tug." By this point, they should happily tug the door open. Click and treat, release them, congratulate them, and have a party!

Give your partner several treats, and practice this behavior for three to five days. Ensure that it's solid before moving on.

5. Introduce distance gradually. Take a single step away from the fridge and ask your service dog to open the refrigerator door. Increase the distance one step at a time and only add more when your partner happily trots to the fridge and opens it reliably at the current distance. If your partner stops opening the door or responding to your request, you've increased distance too quickly. Move closer to the fridge and practice for a few more days before adding distance again.

Retrieving the Beverage

1. Decide on the type of beverage you'll ask your dog to retrieve for you. Common options include bottles of water, plastic bottles of juice or soda, and protein shakes. For your service dog's safety, pick a beverage container your partner will be able to easily pick up, and that isn't slick nor pressurized, and won't break when dropped or in your dog's mouth.

2. Designate a spot in your fridge for the beverage your service dog will retrieve for you. Pick a spot that's readily accessible by your dog, roughly head height, and not in a drawer or behind a shelf. Your dog needs to be able to open the door, see the beverage, and grab it without difficulty. You will always need to replace the beverage container in this same location so it's always there when you ask your service dog to retrieve a beverage for you.

3. Empty the beverage bottle. Make the empty beverage bottle high-value for your dog. Play with it a bit and practice a few repetitions of "take it," "hold it," and "out." Click and reward your partner with a high-value treat at each repetition to cement the formal retrieve and to prevent the bottle from becoming a chew toy.

4. Place the beverage bottle in its designated spot and call your service dog over. Open the fridge and prop it open so that it won't close on your four-legged helper. Point out the bottle and tell your service dog to "take it." Have your dog place the beverage container in your hand and "out" your dog. Jackpot your partner with multiple treats. Continue practicing until your service dog knows where the container will be and grabs the beverage container without it being pointed out.

5. Begin practicing having your partner go to the open fridge, retrieve your beverage, and bring it back to you over slowly increased distances. Take one step back from the fridge at a time and repeat the retrieval process until you can send your dog to the open fridge to get a beverage from anywhere you commonly spend time, such as your office, the couch, or your bedroom. If your partner stops responding to your requests or seems confused, decrease the distance for a while until they're comfortably and reliably able to perform.

Closing the Fridge

1. Ask your service dog to open the fridge. By this point, they should be quite familiar with the process. Once your partner has opened the fridge, have them retrieve your beverage from its designated spot.

2. Before your service dog releases the beverage to your hand, use whatever command you use to request them to target an object with their nose or paws. Use your hand or your trusty Post-it note (check out our target training instructions on page 170 to find out how to use a Post-it note to help with push-based tasks) to encourage your dog to target/push on the fridge, if necessary. The door will close.

Click to mark the targeting and door closing, then ask the dog to release the beverage to your hand, then jackpot.

3. Stand right next to the fridge and practice the entire sequence. Have your assistance dog open the fridge, retrieve the beverage, target to close the door, and release the beverage to your hand. Reward

your partner every time they successfully manage the entire chain of behaviors.

Putting It All Together

Once your service dog is very solid with opening the fridge, retrieving the beverage from its spot, closing the door, bringing the beverage to you, and releasing to your hand while you're standing right next to them, introduce the cue that's going to mean, "Service dog, retrieve a beverage"—"Drink," "Water," "Fridge," and "Slurp" are good choices. It doesn't matter what cue you pick as long as you use the same one all the time.

Stand directly next to the fridge and encourage your partner to begin the retrieval sequence. As soon as they grab the door pull to open the fridge, delightedly give your "retrieve a beverage" cue. Click and treat once the behavior chain is complete. Practice until your service dog completes the entire sequence on cue reliably while you're standing next to them.

Move one small step away from the fridge and cue your service dog to open the fridge, retrieve the beverage, close the fridge, and bring the beverage back to you. Ensure that they complete every step of the process reliably before adding more distance. Move closer to your partner and repeat the tasks in a cheerful manner if they forget any part of the sequence or stop responding. Practice each distance for at least two or three days before moving further away.

Reward your service dog profusely every time they are successful and continue practicing until they successfully bring you a drink no matter where you are in the house. Never scold or punish your dog for missing a step in the sequence or losing concentration; instead, just return to the steps that are solid and go on from there. Stabilize items in your fridge so that nothing can topple over or injure your dog. Keep food in closed containers away from the beverage area so that your dog doesn't accidentally eat something they shouldn't.

6
SERVICE DOG CARE AND KEEPING

EMERGENCY PREPARATION

How do you handle an emergency situation as a service dog handler? What can you do to make it easier on you, the service animal, and the first responders? These are all questions we should think of, but rarely actually seek the answer until it's too late and an emergency situation has already occurred. So let's consider some of these questions together. Where do we start? In case of emergencies (ICE), take the following steps:

Know and educate your local response teams.
Introduce your service dog to your local emergency response teams.

Make sure all of your local authorities, particularly the fire department and EMS teams, are notified in advance of your disability and your service dog. Firehouses usually love visitors who call ahead and particularly those who bring something yummy, like a casserole, brownies, or cookies. EMS officers and police officers may also interact with your service dog and are worth the effort of making friends with and educating. It not only helps your local response teams to be aware of your partner and know them, but it also helps your partner to acclimate to the strange sights and smells of a firefighter, paramedic, or police officer in uniform, gurneys, trucks, ambulances, and a plethora of other stimuli.

The middle of an emergency is not the time to test your partner's ability to stay calm, focused, and settled while surrounded by the hustle and bustle of oddly dressed, weird-smelling, and sometimes frantic strangers. Additionally, you're far less likely to get "pushback" from these responders if they already know your service dog. Many EMS teams vouch for a familiar working dog at the ER door and help bypass the potential hassle of getting your partner admitted to the hospital with you, particularly if you're unable to communicate as well as you could in a different situation. Your partner needs to be familiar with firefighters and paramedics in uniform long before they encounter them in an emergency.

If you have a home monitoring system, you can call them and ask them to add information in your profile that describes your service dog, their distinguishing features (breed, color, coat length, size, etc.) and their access rights, regardless of whether or not you're able to speak for them during an emergency. If an emergency occurs and emergency dispatch send first responders, dispatch are able to notify these first responders about your service dog in advance.

Finally, call and notify your local Emergency Information Management office that you have a service dog and that they are not to be separated from you in the event of an emergency. Request to be added to their disability registry. Personally notify each emergency response department (i.e., Police, Fire Department, EMS, etc.) in your community, and ask that they "tag" your address as having a service dog on-site.

Remain Calm and Be Prepared to Communicate

Stay calm. It's far easier said than done but remaining relaxed will ease your stress and that of your canine partner. Remember, whatever you're feeling travels straight down the leash to your dog.

Additionally, an untroubled demeanor will make it easier for your service dog to perform their duties well. There's plenty of chaos and tension in an emergency without you adding to it. Let the first responders do their job, and let your dog do theirs.

Make sure your service dog is clearly identified so the paramedics can move quickly without wasting time asking questions. Seconds matter in an emergency! Expect first responders to be unfamiliar with service dogs unless you've specifically reached out to your local emergency response teams and worked to educate them and get them acquainted with your partner.

Be prepared to explain everything in detail and carry written copies of the laws and an explanation of how service dogs differ from pets, their job, and their access rights, just in case you're unable to speak or are unconscious. Do not be offended if the EMT calls the police K9 unit or fire department to assist with your partner. The EMT may not be comfortable around dogs or may not have the knowledge of how to handle a service dog and is reaching out for help. Patience and remaining calm are the keys!

Plan Ahead

During an emergency situation, if you are able, try to get your service dog's gear (vest with patches, backpack, harness, or cape) on, along with their harness, collar, or head halter and leash. Have them ready to go so that all anyone needs to do is pick up their leash and walk. This readiness will allow first responders to locate and identify your partner with fewer questions asked and allow them to move as quickly as they're trained to. If your partner causes undue delays, they're fully justified in leaving them behind. If you are unable to get your dog's gear, you may inform the first responders of its location when they arrive.

Service Dog Emergency

Guiding Eyes recommends acclimating all service dogs to equipment used during an emergency as part of routine socialization and training. Keep your medical information close by so that you can inform first responders, and let them know what tasks or challenges your service dog helps mitigate for you.

For instance, if you have a service dog that is able to alert to seizures, first responders will know to watch your partner and be ready for an alert. This information about your service dog's working skills will also help first responders decide whether or not your service dog needs to ride with you in the ambulance.

Keep a service dog emergency kit ready so that first responders can grab it on their way out with you. This kit should have dog food, water, any medications the service dog requires, leash, vest/harness/backpack or cape, a bowl, cleanup bags, and vet information. This will prevent the first responders from having to dig through your home looking for supplies if needed. Check the supply kit monthly to ensure that the items packed are fresh and up to date.

Depending on the type of emergency, your service dog may be transported by the fire or police department instead of riding in the ambulance with you.

Service Dog Team Benefits

Emergencies are hard on everyone, but you can prepare for the unexpected with just a little time and effort. You'll be more at ease knowing your partner is included in your emergency response plan, and if your partner has the chance to familiarize themself with the response teams, they will be more relaxed as well. Don't just "hope" your partner will be brought along or that the EMT will understand your service dog's legal rights. Hope is not a plan, and if you fail to plan, you plan to fail.

What're you waiting for? Look up the numbers for your local fire department and start gathering supplies for your service dog emergency supply bag. You may not ever need them, but it's better to have them and not than need them and wish you'd done it. Just as disaster preparedness requires forethought and packing, consider the needs of your canine partner in a disaster, and prepare a bug-out bag for your service dog as well as yourself or family members.

HOSPITAL ACCESS RIGHTS

When it comes to hospital access rights for service dogs, US federal law permits service dogs to accompany their disabled handler into nonsterile, public areas. Cut through the chaos with this simple, straightforward explanation of the rules, exceptions, laws, requirements, and expectations for service dog hospital access.

The Basics

To make a long story really short, service dogs are allowed in hospitals, doctor's offices, patient rooms, and other health care facilities as long as their presence doesn't pose a threat or danger to standard medical practices and doesn't impede operations of fundamental services and functions. Professional offices of health care providers and hospitals are specifically mentioned in subchapter III, Section 12181 (definitions), point 7 (Public Accommodations), part F, as being a "public accommodation," and federal law goes on to state:

> Individuals with disabilities shall be permitted to be accompanied by their service animals in all areas of a place of public accommodation where members of the public, program participants, clients, customers, patrons, or invitees, as relevant, are allowed to go.

As quoted directly from the ADA and the US Code of Federal Regulations, here are other pertinent parts of federal service dog law that grants hospital access to service dog teams:

> (a) General. A public accommodation shall make reasonable modifications in policies, practices, or procedures, when the modifications are necessary to afford goods, services, facilities, privileges, advantages, or accommodations to individuals with disabilities, unless the public accommodation can demonstrate that making the modifications would fundamentally alter the nature of the goods, services, facilities, privileges, advantages, or accommodations.

> (4) Animal under handler's control. A service animal shall be under the control of its handler. A service animal shall have a harness, leash, or other tether, unless either the handler is

unable because of a disability to use a harness, leash, or other tether, or the use of a harness, leash, or other tether would interfere with the service animal's safe, effective performance of work or tasks, in which case the service animal must be otherwise under the handler's control (e.g., voice control, signals, or other effective means).

(5) Care or supervision. A public accommodation is not responsible for the care or supervision of a service animal.

Consider carrying the official ADA brief on service dog law. Sometimes this can be faster and less aggravating than a constant need for intrusive questioning.

The Problems

If a service dog handler requires admission to the hospital, there's likely something wrong, either medically or psychiatrically, that requires medical attention, intervention, or assistance. In other words, the handler is sick. When someone is sick, they're often not able to function normally, especially within the context of "hospital admission."

Many hospital admissions require the use of medical equipment (like heart monitors or an IV) that may limit the ability of the handler to move around. Federal law requires the handler to be in direct control of their service dog and further stipulates that staff, employees, or other individuals cannot be expected to care for the dog in any way. If a handler can't move around effectively or is too sick or too unaware or otherwise unable to care for their service dog (feeding, exercising, taking out, cleaning up after), then, under federal law, there's an issue.

Hospitals are highly regulated, sterile environments, and disease control is incredibly high on the priority list. It's a well-documented fact that therapy dogs have been at the root of several cases of MRSA outbreak and spread within hospitals and there have been isolated cases of other infectious disease outbreaks that have traced back to dogs on the premises. Federal law is quite clear, though: even when the health codes prevent access by pets or animals, service dog teams are allowed.

That statement is not a free-for-all. The access of a service dog team can't fundamentally alter the way a "public accommodation" does business or provides their service. In a hospital, that means the presence of the service dog can't violate standards that are in place for patient or staff safety and are medically necessary.

The Real Facts

Here's what hospital access rights for service dog teams actually look like: the service dog and handler are allowed anywhere visitors are allowed without special precautions. For example, visitors are allowed in patient rooms, the gift shop, cafeterias, some labs, and other "public" areas of the hospital. However, visitors *aren't* allowed in the maternity ward, ICU, burn units, or other areas where special footwear, masks, or specific and medically necessary precautions are taken for the safety of the individuals on that unit or in that area. Visitors *aren't* allowed in operating suites or rooms or in other biologically sterile areas, and visitors aren't allowed in trauma areas or specific triage units specializing in disease control or potentially infectious open wounds.

Depending on the attending physician and the specific emergency, visitors may or may not be allowed in certain emergency rooms or situations.

Things to Consider

There's an old saying that goes something like this: "Just because you can doesn't mean you should." Before bringing your partner with you to the hospital, especially for a lengthy stay or during an emergency, ask yourself the following questions:

1. Are you well enough or stable enough to take care of your partner?
2. If you're not, can you make arrangements for someone else (a family member or friend, never staff) to care for your partner?

3. Will your partner be safe? Consider whether you'll be aware enough to properly look out for your partner's best interests, whether or not they will be exposed to pathogens, dangerous substances, or highly charged situations with which you can't help them cope, and whether or not they have the skills and training necessary to keep themself calm, quiet, settled, and out of the way at all times.
4. Will you be safe? Consider whether your partner is familiar enough with medical procedures and equipment to not be in the way, not prevent doctors and nurses from doing their job, and not create problems that otherwise wouldn't be there, like knocking over IV poles, tearing out lines or leads, and unplugging machines.
5. Will those around you, including nurses, other patients, doctors, and visitors who don't know you, be safe? Is there a possibility your service dog's presence might be dangerous to anyone for any reason?
6. How does your partner respond to high levels of stress and uncertainty? Even the most well-trained service dog can react poorly during highly charged events, especially if they're not familiar with the circumstances. Keep in mind yourself, your partner, and those who must provide care to you. If you're unconscious, unresponsive, or your health is "crashing," and your partner displays any protective behavior (which is unsuitable behavior for service dogs, but isn't unheard of in high-stress environments), typically, your partner will be removed from the situation and collected by Animal Control as quickly as possible so medical staff can tend to you.
7. How is your partner's training? Be brutally honest with yourself. If your service dog isn't capable of lying quietly on a blanket, mat, or bed for hours on end with little interaction, stimulation, and under exceedingly high levels of distraction, whether you're present or not (consider that you may be taken out of your room to radiology or the lab or for other testing, and your partner must remain behind

for their safety), and without interfering with doctors, nurses and visitors in any way, they may not be ready for a hospital trip.

8. If your partner isn't settling in as well as you would have hoped, can you make alternate arrangements for them? Would a friend or family member be able to come pick them up and care for them until you are able to do so?
9. Do you have a plan in place in case you're transferred to a unit where your service dog wouldn't be able to accompany you?
10. Does your partner possess the training and skills required to navigate the unique environment the hospital presents? For example, if you're on a locked unit, is your partner capable of using large potty pads on command, as you won't be able to leave the unit?
11. Is your partner able to successfully move with you and work with you while you're hooked up or surrounded by unfamiliar equipment, smells, and sights?
12. Is your partner able to be a calming, healthy presence during your stay?

The Hospital's Rights

Hospitals have the right:

- To be able to operate normally with regards to the movement, care, safety, treatment, and recovery of patients and staff.
- To remain as disruption-free after your partner is on-site as they were before your partner arrived. This means they have the right to zero interruption, disruption, or harassment from your partner in any way, shape, or form, unless your partner is performing necessary task work that does not impede your treatment or infringe on the rights of others in any way.
- To not have to take care of or otherwise interact with your partner. Staff members have the right to not be

expected to "take your partner out," feed, water, or otherwise care for your service dog in any way. If you are too sick or too unstable to care for your partner or to make arrangements for someone else (a friend or family member) to care for your dog, you're probably too sick to have your partner on-site during a hospital stay.

- To be able to abide by the same safety, sanitary, and medical expectations they always operate under. Hospitals have strict protocols regarding visitor and staff expectations, dress, and access to certain areas of the building, especially in environments where highly unstable, very young or very old, immunocompromised, or severely injured patients are recovering and being treated.
- To be able to ensure the hospital environment remains, first and foremost, an environment of healing and recovery.

The Service Dog Team's Rights

You and your service dog partner have the right:

- To be able to access nonsterile and non-medically regulated patient and visitor areas.
- To be able to request "reasonable accommodation" for the canine partner.
- To have the treatment team focus on the patient, not the service dog.
- To receive the exact same treatment, care, respect, and communications someone without a service dog would receive.
- To not have their service dog distracted, interacted with, moved, or otherwise molested without permission, except in the event of an emergency.

We've heard hundreds of stories of highly successful hospital stays with a service dog. However, before arranging for your service dog to stay with you at the hospital, ensure your partner is going to be a help, not a hindrance. Your first focus while you're at the hospital needs to be getting better and recovering, not on stressing over or trying to manage your partner's behavior, training, or responses.

HEALTH

Seasonal Safety—Autumn

The leaves are starting to change, there's bit of a chill in the air, and many people are pulling out their trusty hoodies and apple cider recipes. Fall is a beautiful time of year, but it also heralds the holiday season. Here are a few autumn safety tips to keep in mind for your service dog as you both begin to enjoy this wonderful time of year.

- Cinnamon, spices, apples, candy corn, smoky fires, pumpkins, and earthy leaves—for many people, the scents of fall are their favorite part, but don't forget that not everything is safe for your partner.
- Always supervise your service dog around candles, bonfires, sweets, hot drinks, or anything else that may not be safe.
- There's a chill in the air! If it's too cold for you to be outside without a jacket, it may be too chilly for your partner, particularly if they have a thin coat or very short hair. Always dress the both of you for the weather.
- The leaves are changing—and with the gorgeous autumn color changes come falling leaves. Leaf-strewn lawns, parks, and pathways can mask potential dangers, like sharp rocks or broken glass. Always be aware of where your service dog is walking.
- Days are shorter. With dark falling at a far earlier hour, it may be prudent to get your partner a light to attach to their collar or reflective gear for safety, especially if your daily routine means you must walk or exercise your partner after the sun goes down.

- Double-check your service dog's ID tag information. With holidays right around the corner, many people's social schedules pick up, and there's a lot of coming and going. If your partner gets out or gets lost, their tag is their ticket home.
- Be selective about attending holiday or autumn functions with your service dog, particularly Halloween events. Events can be highly stressful for you and your service dog; be careful not to overload them.
- Busy schedules combined with early sunset can lead to mood changes during the fall months. Make sure you continue to give your partner physical and mental exercise—it's good for both of you.
- Keep up with your service dog's monthly heartworm treatment. Just because it's colder outside doesn't mean your partner isn't at risk.
- Consider boots for your partner, especially if you do a lot of walking outdoors and it snows in your area. Not only is snow and ice hard on your service dog's feet, but the salt cities use to control it is especially dangerous.
- Keep an eye on your service dog's weight, especially if they are a brace/mobility dog. It's easy for weight to creep upward during the fall and winter season.

Thanksgiving Considerations

It's that time of year when family and friends travel, gather together, and celebrate the holidays with big meals, special treats, and lots of festivities. While Thanksgiving can be an amazing and fun time of year, for many people, pets, and working dogs, it can be very stressful. Here are some important considerations for keeping your service dog happy during the holidays.

1. Prepare for Travel

Traveling with a service dog has been covered extensively in other sections of this book (see page 155), so make sure to review them, particularly if you're flying. If you are traveling by car, make sure your service dog travels safely by putting them in a crate or a crash-tested safety harness. Roads can be chaotic and accidents happen more frequently due to the number of drivers on the road.

Stop regularly for walks and water breaks and allow your partner to rest if they aren't actively needed for task work while in the vehicle. They may not get a chance during the chaotic holiday celebrations to come.

2. Maintain Boundaries

Decide before you get where you're going what you will expect from others regarding your service dog. There will likely be encounters with lots of children or extended family/people you don't see often, and it's important to enforce your personal expectations regarding whether or not your service dog can be petted, talked to, or played with.

It's oftentimes easier for many teams to allow a few minutes in the beginning for everyone to say hello and get it out of their system, then to follow the standard, "Please don't distract them; they're working" construct. If, however, you want to allow your partner to simply be a well-mannered houseguest and play and hang out, feel free! Whatever you're comfortable with is fine, but make sure you make your wishes known from the start to avoid tension and stress later.

3. Only Share Safe Foods

While there are many safe foods that your service dog can share during Thanksgiving, there are just as many, if not more, dangerous choices. Great options for sharing include green beans, potatoes, white meat turkey, and pumpkin. Make sure any offerings aren't loaded with sugars or fats (like cream or butter) because those can cause digestive upsets.

Avoid grapes, raisins, desserts, cooked bones, onions, garlic, gravy, chocolate, and alcohol.

Seasonal Safety—Summer

Being a service dog is a tough job, one that often encompasses odd hours, long workweeks, technical or specialized knowledge, and few breaks. A service dog's job doesn't end, though, just because it's hot. Use these tips to keep your service dog cool this summer, and still able to work comfortably.

Make Allowances

Throughout much of the continental United States, from late June through early September, temperatures can soar into the high nineties and in some areas, well past the 100-degree mark. When it's hot outside, it's impossible to perform at maximum capacity. Some sports physiologists have even suggested that people's efficiency slows as much as 25 percent for every twenty-degree jump in temperature.

While dogs work better in heat than most people, it's important to allow your service dog some leeway in performance. Not only does heat make every task seem harder, it also tends to make everyone a little waspish and irritable. Keep in mind that dogs don't sweat (except on the pads of their paws), so panting and direct heat exchange with the environment are the only ways they're able to cool themselves. Give your partner extra time to complete tasks outdoors, and don't be surprised if their obedience is a little less snappy or polished than it is when it's cooler.

Acclimate Your Partner

Believe it or not, it's not at all beneficial to keep your service dog in the air-conditioning or in a cool environment all the time, and then expect them to perform outdoors when the mercury soars. Starting in late spring, begin spending a few minutes a day working outside with your partner. Carefully and systematically exposing them to rising temperatures over the course of several weeks means their body will adapt to the heat naturally, and it won't be nearly as shocking when your service dog does encounter severe heat. As an added bonus, you'll get used to the steadily rising temperatures, too!

If you know you're going to be working outside for an extended period of time or attending an outdoor function, when you hop in the car to head that way, simply roll the windows down. The air movement will keep both of you cool but will help you adjust to the heat while you're on the way.

Stay Out of Direct Sunlight

This one may seem like a given but try to stay out of direct sunlight and off dark-colored surfaces, like asphalt or blacktop. According to the US National Library of Medicine, asphalt is hot enough to cause burns from 9:00 a.m. until 7:00 p.m. during the summer months. From 10:00 a.m. to 5:00 p.m., it's hot enough to cause second-degree burns in thirty-five seconds! Hot road tar can also be sticky, and thus hard to remove when it is burning delicate paws.

When approaching stores, try to heel your service dog along a grassy median in the parking lot or only on the sidewalk. If all else fails, walk along the white line. Consider using boots for service dogs who do a significant amount of walking. Keep in mind, though, that to keep your service dog cool and safe, the boots need to provide proper ventilation. Remember, dogs sweat via their paw pads, and if the boots don't provide ventilation and wicking, not only will your service dog be in danger of bacterial infection on their feet, but they won't cool down.

The Ruffwear Skyliner™ boots are an excellent option for urban dwellers who need a summer walking boot. Ruffwear offers a pro-purchase program for service dog handlers and trainers. Qualified members receive 50 percent off all working dog gear.

Change up Your Gear

Would you ever waltz out on a summer errand wearing a parka and snow pants? I don't think so. Why, then, should your service dog wear the same gear year-round? Consider obtaining a mesh vest for your partner, or a vest with built-in cooling pockets. Alternatively, your partner could wear a backpack with gel ice packs in the pouches. Keep in mind differences between materials, too—leather is significantly hotter and heavier than neoprene, and fleece is more uncomfortable in the heat than nylon.

Use Cooling Products

Cooling products are available in the form of everything from bandanas to full-on cooling coats to collars to beds. Most dollar stores carry $2 to $3 cooling bandanas made for people, and they work beautifully for dogs, too. Simply soak them in cool water, tie them around your service dog's neck, and away you go. When it dries, soak it again, wring it out, and retie. Cooling products typically work on the basis of heat exchange and evaporation, which is the same mechanism your service dog uses to keep cool day to day. The Ruffwear Swamp Cooler™ is light enough and sleek enough to be worn under most service dog's day-to-day gear, and cooling bandanas and collars come in a variety of styles and sizes to fit any working dog.

Heatstroke is a life-threatening condition arising from being overheated. Heatstroke must be recognized quickly and treated aggressively, as it could kill your service dog if left unmanaged.

Signs of heatstroke

- Fast breathing
- Heavy salivation
- Dry, pale gums
- Rapid pulse
- Weakness
- Confusion
- Inattention
- Erratic gait
- Vomiting
- Diarrhea
- Seizures

Consider Creative Grooming

While the jury is out on whether or not shaving dogs helps keep them cool, it's generally thought that shaving a double-coated or thick-furred dog does more harm than good. That said, we've all seen how dogs gravitate toward cooler surfaces and how they enjoy lying on cool concrete, tile, or stone. Consider shaving a thin strip down your service dog's belly so their skin can directly contact cooler surfaces. Since their belly is rarely exposed to the sun, there's no worry about the harm that can come from shaving all of them, and they'll be better able to cool themself off once they come inside and are able to lie down.

Keep Safety First

Above all else, keep safety first. There are some days that are so hot no one should be out and about. If it's too hot to be reasonably comfortable in the shade with a cool towel close at hand, it's probably too hot to be doing anything extensive outdoors.

Know the signs of canine heatstroke, and be prepared to act quickly if your service dog begins displaying dangerous symptoms. Get your service dog to a cool, shady area, douse them in cool, but not cold, water, and don't let your service dog simply lie down. It's important that they keep moving so the cooler blood at their skin's surface quickly circulates through their body. Offer small amounts of cool water and allow them plenty of time to rest and recover. And remember that heatstroke takes a while to work through. Continue rehydrating your canine partner, and consider using electrolyte replacements or supplements once the initial crisis is over.

Fourth of July Safety

In the United States, the Fourth of July is a day full of celebration. With cookouts, parades, sparklers, crowds, fireworks, noise, activity, events, and chaos galore, Independence Day can be difficult not only for pets, but also for working K9s, service dogs, and their handlers. Before joining a holiday celebration with your canine partner, here are some points to consider.

It's hard to enjoy an event if your focus has to be on your service dog. Carefully consider your service dog's current level of training and how they handle crowds, chaos, unknown noises, close proximity, heavy distractions, and circumstances beyond your control.

Training should begin before the Fourth—while a good service dog is able to handle nearly anything thrown their way, many Fourth of July events are overwhelming for even the best-trained dogs, let alone one who hasn't been properly prepared for the bombardment of stimuli and distraction. If you're simply attending an event for "distraction proofing" or "socialization," consider waiting for a less-hectic time. It's simply not worth potentially setting back your service dog's training by exposing them to circumstances they're not ready for. Prepare to spend sufficient time training with your dogs in a safe, fenced-in area before taking your dog into crowds.

Noise sensitivity to fireworks and gunshots scare most dogs and both are common around the Fourth of July. Whether you're attending battle reenactments or pyrotechnic displays, the booms, smell of smoke, and the heat can put your partner on edge. Ideally, your service dog has little to no noise sensitivity, but if that's not the case, your pooch is likely to be so stressed by fireworks and the other loud noises commonly found at Fourth of July events that they'll be unable to focus on you and their job.

iCalmPet offers some excellent noise desensitization CDs, including CDs for thunderstorms, fireworks, city sounds, and others. These kinds of resources should be used before the day of an event. ThunderShirts and Bach Rescue Remedy® also help to soothe anxious dogs.

Most importantly, if your partner is showing signs of stress, don't admonish them or force them to participate. Just leave or allow your service dog the distance and space they need to be comfortable, and begin training so that next year, you'll both be able to enjoy the event.

Assess your own comfort with the type of events you're considering attending. Even if your service dog is trained to assist you with overstimulation, anxiety, or panic, the constant degree of sensory bombardment can quickly wear both of you out. If you struggle with massive crowds, tons of visual/auditory/olfactory stimulus, and oppressive heat, consider attending a smaller event, or only partaking of the entertainment you'd really enjoy and like to see, instead of making a full day of it.

If you attend a Fourth of July celebration with your partner, be certain to not only keep your service dog's comfort and abilities in mind, but also the following safety considerations.

- Take a picture of your service dog in whatever gear they'll be wearing to the event before you go, just in case. Make two copies. Keep one with you and leave one at home.
- Check your service dog's ID tags and ensure your contact information is up-to-date. Your partner can't tell anyone who their human is, so their tag is their only chance to communicate. If you're traveling, put Scotch tape over their tag and write local contact information on it with permanent marker.

- Check your service dog's microchip registration information for up-to-date contact information.
- If your partner works off-leash, consider using a leash for the event. There will likely be thick crowds and a lot of movement, and something can happen quickly. To make a hands-free leash if necessary, simply thread the handle onto your belt.
- Keep pickup bags with you. Remember, you're a service dog community ambassador.
- It's likely going to be *hot*. Make sure you have a bowl available for your service dog's use. A gallon freezer bag can easily be frozen before the event and allowed to melt through the day, and they're thick enough to hold their form while your service dog drinks from them.
- Most importantly, don't be afraid to leave the celebration if your service dog appears uneasy or frightened. Pay attention to your dog's body language and always put your team's comfort and safety first.

WORK AND SCHOOL

Service Dogs at Work

When it comes to service dogs in the workplace, they are allowed, by law, as a "reasonable accommodation" for a person with a disability. The difficulty comes in that the employer gets to determine whether or not the dog is a "reasonable accommodation."

Service dog access rights are covered in Title III of the ADA (and discussed in chapter 3 of this book) and that's the part of the law that states that people with disabilities who are accompanied by a task-trained and well-behaved Service Animal have access to all places of public accommodation (with a couple of exceptions, like places of worship and zoos). Service dogs in the workplace are covered in Title I of the ADA, however, which merely requires that employers make "reasonable" accommodation for employees with disabilities. If an accommodation fundamentally changes the way the business operates or would preclude the employee from doing their job, then it can be cited as unreasonable.

When preparing to bring your service dog to work, it's important to know your rights and to have a plan in place so you can address your employer's concerns. Many employers are hesitant to allow a service dog in the workplace because they fear interruptions, reduced productivity, or problems with allergies. Solutions for these concerns would be to reinforce the idea that the working dog is there to work, only for their person, and is not there to socialize or be the office "pet."

Most of the time, the service dog would be lying quietly under the desk or on a mat, until needed by the employee, and thus, there wouldn't be any interruptions. Reduced productivity isn't a concern, as the handler will be solely responsible for the care of the dog, and can provide food, water, or restroom breaks during their routine breaks, so no additional time would be required away from work.

It is estimated that less than 10 percent of people have a dog allergy. Furthermore, in-person contact can be eliminated, and the actual exposure can be easily limited. If there is, in fact, someone with a dog allergy who works in the same area or during the same time slot, the handler of the dog can use dander-reducing shampoos and regularly brush their dog, while also ensuring to stay away from the employee with allergies.

Functionally, having a service dog at work (if we're talking about an office job/desk work) is like having a service dog anywhere else—the dog is quiet, calm, relaxed, and controlled, until needed for task work. Playing and exercising is done during breaks or at home, and during work hours, the dog is typically neither seen nor heard.

Lots of handlers have benefited from sending around an introduction letter or email that established expected protocol and makes etiquette quite clear. Here's an example (replace "they" with your dog's gendered pronouns if you prefer):

Dear Everyone,

My name is ___________, and I work in (department/place). As you may or may not know, I'm partnered with a service dog.

My service dog's name is ___________, and they are a (breed). They're (years old), and they have undergone hundreds of hours of specialized training to assist me. While we're at work, you may notice (dog's name) lying quietly in my workspace. That's part of their job—to be calmly settled until I need them.

Please do not talk to, distract, pet, touch, make noises at, or otherwise attempt to interact with (dog's name), as that could pull their attention away from me and their work, and injury or a medical crisis could happen. We don't mean to be rude, but safety must come first. If you absolutely must get your excitement out of the way, please come see us and ask for permission to pet (dog's name), but only once!

I'm solely responsible for (dog's name) care, so don't worry about needing to do anything extra. In fact, it's best if you just pretend (dog's name) isn't here, as it's actually quite possible you'll forget about them, as they're quite good at tucking away and being unobtrusive. (Dog's name) is very well trained and is always under control, so there's no need for concern about bad manners or interruptions.

If you have an allergy to dogs or you are afraid of dogs, please let me know via email (insert address) or phone call (insert number) so that I can take steps to ensure you are comfortable, such as taking routes that don't come near your workspace or using special shampoo to reduce dander and shedding, so there's less of a chance of your allergy being triggered.

Thanks,
(Name)

Be sure to discuss this with your head of HR first—they may prefer employees not ask for health information directly, or may even have another idea of how to handle.

If your employer can demonstrate that having the service dog at work will cause undue hardship to the company, they can propose alternate arrangements or accommodations. One of the easiest ways to overcome the reluctance of an employer is to suggest a week- to month-long trial period, at the end of which things can be reevaluated and discussed.

If your dog is a service dog in training, you may request permission to bring them to work with you, but your employer is under no obligation to allow your SDiT access to the workplace.

Service Dogs at School

Service dogs in school are a totally different story than service dogs in the workplace. The ADA changes that became effective on March 15, 2011, added a new section to the prior regulations that expressly state that Title II entities, which includes public schools and places of higher learning, "shall modify [their] policies, practices, or procedures to permit the use of a service animal by an individual with a disability."

As such, under federal law, school districts are required to allow a student or child with a disability access to their service animal during school hours and on school property. The Individuals with Disabilities Education Improvement Act (IDEIA) or Section 504 of the Rehabilitation Act of 1973 (504) may also compel school districts to allow a child to bring a service animal to school as part of their right to receive a free appropriate public education (FAPE). If the service animal is required in order for the child to be safe or to have increased independence, then the dog must be allowed to accompany the child.

However, that's not to say that the dog and child can just waltz into school. There are lots of things to consider, including the child's maturity and ability to handle their dog alone, the type and level of training the dog possesses, and many other considerations. First and foremost, it must be determined if a child needs their service dog at school via an individualized assessment with the child's IEP (Individual Education Planning) team. An IEP determines what accommodations are provided for the child at school, and to what extent these accommodations are required, as well as defining any pertinent details surrounding the accommodation.

Regarding service dogs at school, IEP notes might include things like:

- A staff or aide escort outside at the beginning of the child's lunch hour so that their dog can relieve itself, and then a walk to a garbage receptacle so the child can dispose of any waste.
- Inclusion of a "place" inside the classroom for the dog, like a raised training bed or fleece mat.
- Granting the child free rein to use their dog as needed, including the ability to sit on the floor with their dog in the classroom, or to have their dog next to their desk or workspace.
- Allowing the parents to provide a safe place for the dog on campus to relax, such as a raised bed or a crate, while the child takes part in activities where the dog is not required, such as during physical education classes, or when the child is with an aide, therapist, or in a special resources class.
- The ability for parents or a trainer to offer an educational workshop, meeting, or seminar to students, staff, or faculty about service dogs and what they do, with administrative approval.
- Slight adjustments in the layout of the classroom desks to provide enough space for the dog to remain with the child while the child is at their workspace.

The most important facet of having a service dog at school is that the child or student be able to independently work their dog. The ADA is very clear about the dog needing to be under the direct control of the handler, and that outside help or assistance cannot be required of the school or facility in order for the child to work their dog. This means that the student must be able to guide and direct their dog, give cues and commands, respond to the dog's alerts or task work, potty and feed their dog, and move from place to place with their dog without extra help, as well as having the emotional maturity to care for another living being.

A good benchmark of whether or not a child is ready to handle their dog solo is whether or not they can pass an Assistance Dogs International (ADI) standard Public Access Test. This doesn't mean the Public Access Test needs to be given by an ADI organization, although that's certainly helpful, but only that a trainer who is familiar with the ADI standards and codes of ethics administer and oversee the test, even if they themselves are not part of an ADI-affiliated organization. The child should be able to independently complete the test with no more guidance than gentle verbal direction from a parent or the trainer. Once the child can do so, they've proven their ability to work their dog independently, and they should be granted access to the school environment. On average, children generally can complete the public access test on their own during their early teens. While younger children certainly have taken and passed the test, these children show a higher degree of maturity and communication skills than is average.

Allergies and fear of dogs are not valid reasons for refusing a service dog access with their student. Classes can be rearranged so that anyone who is allergic to or afraid of the service dog doesn't need to come into contact with them. Concerns about the dog biting someone or posing an insurance risk can be allayed by the sheer volume of training and testing the dog has undergone before becoming a service dog, which is another reason your logs and journals are important. Service dogs undergo thousands of hours of socialization and training, often beginning when they are very young, and only the most stable of dogs complete the training.

The American Temperament Test Society offers a standardized Temperament Test (TT) certification that allows easy proof of the dog's mental soundness and good temperament. Other tests and certifications are available, too, like the Canine Good Citizen (CGC) and Canine Life and Social Skills (C.L.A.S.S.) certificates and degrees. Any and all paperwork you can gather for your service dog is beneficial, although it is not required and you are not required to provide proof of training, any documentation regarding service dog status, or any certifications, registrations, or "ID cards." Having a TT title or other certifications can help soothe the school board's fears about bite risks.

Functionally, having a service dog at school can vary widely team to team. In general, though, the dog and student remain together, and they move from class to class together, and they take necessary breaks during a time when the child wouldn't normally be learning, in order to avoid disrupting the regular education process. Many classrooms find it beneficial to provide a designated "place" for the dog to be, and to remind the other pupils that it's best to pretend they can't see the dog, because the dog is working.

If the parents are agreeable, the students can be taught that when the dog is wearing a brightly colored bandana, that they can then approach the handler and request permission to interact with the dog. Many teams will offer this opportunity once a month or so, which helps students satisfy their curiosity. In time, the dog will become just another classroom fixture, and will no longer seem remarkable or out of the ordinary.

Access rights to colleges and universities are granted by Title III of the ADA, which includes places of higher learning in its list of the public accommodations required to admit a person with a disability who has a service animal. Exceptions to this permission include sterile spaces, such as laboratories, or spaces in which the dog's presence could disrupt or cause a fundamental difference to the way the environment functions, like sterile rooms, medical training, or other specialized situations. Typically, though, having a service animal on campus is just like having a service animal anywhere else. It is polite to inform the administration you will be bringing a service animal on campus.

RETIREMENT

Retiring a service dog is a highly emotional and difficult step to take, particularly after years of partnership, and especially if you're contemplating retiring your first partner, and one that shouldn't be taken lightly. It's hard to know when the time is right or how to go about it, but here are some points to consider before taking the leap. There is no definitive guide, but the advice to "follow your heart" offers the surest route to success.

When is it time to retire my service dog?

"When is it time" is the most frequently asked question about retiring a service dog and the one that's the hardest to answer. The truth is that there isn't one answer for every service dog. Every dog, every team, and every situation is different, and only you can know when it is time to begin easing your canine partner out of working. Follow your gut and listen to your heart—if you're beginning to think it may be time, you're probably right.

Ryan Cambio, owner and head trainer of service dog organization Lifeline Assistance Dogs and its associated working dog gear division, Phoenix KnotWork, advises, "Keep in close contact with your program/trainer/mentor, especially as your service dog ages. Another set of eyes can help show/tell you as the time comes, since it can be hard to see as you're in daily contact with your partner." He goes on to note, "Day by day, nothing seems to change, but you look back, and everything is different. It's your responsibility as the human half of the team to know when the dog is ready to retire. They can't and won't tell you."

What are signs my service dog should be retired?

The easiest way to know when it is time to think about retiring a service dog is to watch out for some of the signs that your partner isn't working as well or isn't as able to do their job well or safely. Are they slowing down, or taking longer to complete tasks? Also be aware of any indications of pain, like arthritis. Your veterinarian will be a good resource here.

Tips for recognizing when to retire a service dog:

- Your partner just isn't happy. Their tail doesn't wag, ears don't perk up, and they don't seem to be excited about going out anymore. Of course, take your partner's historical actions into consideration. If your partner has never been a waggy, upbeat dog, don't worry. But if they have, and they're slowly becoming less so, it might be time to think about making some changes to their schedule and workload.

- Your partner is slowing down. Are they able to keep pace with you still? Can they put in a full day and bounce back as good as new after a good night's sleep? If not, try to find the reason behind it. If you can fix it, and they're happy, then hi-ho, it's off to work we go—but if not and they're requiring more and more rest throughout the day, it may be time to retire them.
- Your partner's sleep needs have drastically increased.
- Your partner is showcasing health issues. Arthritis, cataracts, hearing problems, kidney issues, joint/back pain, weight gain, cancer, diabetes, or any of the other ailments of age are cause for retirement. It's not fair to ask your partner to continue working through discomfort or malaise.
- Your partner isn't as responsive. If your partner is missing cues, isn't fully completing tasks, or requires multiple reminders, look deeper than "they're disobeying." Your partner may be experiencing memory problems, have something physical going on (like hearing loss), or may otherwise not be able to work to the best of their ability. If your partner "always listens" and their training is solid, but they're starting to seem to ignore you, then it likely isn't a behavior problem.

What are the options for my retired service dog?

Options for retiring your service dog depend on the kind of service dog you have, where they came from, and what your plans are moving forward. If your partner came from a program, you'll need to follow their standards for retirement, and each is different. Guide Dogs for the Blind, for example, allows retired Guide Dogs to remain with their human partner, whereas other programs require them to be returned if the handler wants a successor dog. Regardless of the conditions of your partnership, there are a few basic options available:

- Your partner remains with you as a pet once retired and lives out their life as a queen or king with the official title of "Living Room Princess" or "Couch Prince."
- Your partner returns to the program they came from.
- Your partner is re-homed with their puppy raiser, a trusted friend or family member, or a loving family.

Retire your service dog in stages. Only you can really know what's best for your partner. However, trainers tend to agree it is best to transition your partner out of working, instead of just one day stopping your partner from working with you.

RESOURCES

ADDITIONAL RESOURCES

It's easy to get overwhelmed at the thought of training a service dog. With so many concepts, behaviors, commands, manners, situations, and ideals for service dogs in training to master, it can be hard, as a trainer and handler, to even know where to start, let alone to establish which training resources are the most valuable. After polling several successful, well-established service dog trainers, I'm proud to present this list of the top ten best service dog training resources.

Sue Ailsby's Training Levels Program

There was no question on this one; Sue Ailsby's Training Levels Program was included on every single list as the top resource for those wishing to train a service dog. This protocol is available online, as an e-book, and in print form. In a nutshell, this is a step-by-step, proven, systematic, motivational program offering phenomenal relationship building, obedience training, socialization instructions, and manners building. Specifically designed for use with service dogs, it works beautifully to guide the trainer (and the dog!) through the process of developing rock-solid impulse control, instinctive recognition of and responses to cues and behaviors even under heavy distraction, and teaching creative, independent thinking and problem-solving skills in a fun, but highly structured, way.

This program also allows the dog and trainer to create their own system of communication and to help them bond deeply through the process of learning together. Best of all, the Training Levels are free! Start with the Sue Ailsby Training Levels Introduction, and then scoot right along to level 1.

Susan Garrett's Crate Games

Susan Garrett's Crate Games DVD popped up on almost every trainer's list for a top service dog training resource. Crate Games is an invaluable, purely motivational program for teaching unshakeable impulse and self-control, especially under heavy distraction and in public and for building a solid foundation for "stays" and recalls, even in puppies as young as seven weeks. In a matter of minutes (yes, really) after beginning Crate Games, many of the service dog trainers polled who regularly use the program can have extremely young puppies (five weeks was the youngest we heard) targeting objects fifty or more feet away and remaining on the target no matter what distractions are offered, offering extremely solid positional stays (sit, down, or stand) and/or quickly offering a variety of useful training behaviors with confidence and creativity.

Additionally, the Crate Games program teaches puppies and dogs to learn to choose to be relaxed, focused, and highly self-controlled and to make those behaviors self-rewarding. Then, of course, there's the added benefit that Crate Games dogs are extremely relaxed and comfortable in a crate (or on a bed, or a mat, or . . . imagine the implications for public access!) no matter what else is going on. Who would have guessed?

Control Unleashed and *The Puppy Program*

While trainer Leslie McDevitt wrote both her books for performance athletes, not for service dogs, they cropped up on our trainers' lists enough to solidly add them to the must-have category of service dog training resources.

The Puppy Program is designed to instill a lifelong love of learning, focus, and working aptitude while creating a dog who is handler focused, solid, and stable in any situation and able to perform reliably and confidently no matter the degree of distraction or the circumstance. It is designed to prevent issues long before they begin. *Control Unleashed* is designed to help adult dogs who struggle with impulse control, focus, or performing under distractions, but it's also valuable reading for anyone training a service dog who's past the puppy stage.

Building Blocks for Performance

The book *Building Blocks for Performance,* written by Bobbie Anderson, found its way onto three quarters of the polled trainers' lists of most valuable service dog training resources. *Building Blocks* caters to trainers looking to instill into their young performance/competition candidates working aptitude, exceptionally strong handler focus, performance under distraction, and the ability to turn excitement on and off at the flip of a switch.

All of those skills are extremely valuable lessons for any service dog in training, and *Building Blocks* carries the added advantage of being a solid relationship building program, too. It solidifies the working bond between trainer and puppy very early while also creating snappy, responsive obedience and instinctive manners.

Canine Life and Social Skills Program

The Canine Life and Social Skills (C.L.A.S.S.) program was recommended by the majority of polled trainers as one of the best resources available. C.L.A.S.S. is a comprehensive, motivational training and manners certification program that uses experienced, certified trainers and set, defined protocol in a class or group environment.

The C.L.A.S.S. program has three levels of training (BA, MA, and PhD), each of which builds on the foundation laid in the previous level. While a handler will learn how to teach their service dog basic obedience (and intermediate obedience, at the MA and PhD levels), some public access skills, and solid manners, that's not the true value of the C.L.A.S.S. program for service dog trainers. The best part of C.L.A.S.S. isn't what it teaches handlers what to do, but what it provides: group training, skills practice, distraction-proofing, and socialization in a controlled, healthy environment.

Learning Games

The *Learning Games* book, written by Kay Lawrence, offers trainers a fun, motivational way to teach independent thinking, creativity, cue recognition, and reliable performance while also providing the opportunity to bond, learn to communicate effectively, and train valuable foundations for later task work.

101 Dog Tricks by Kyra Sundance

Kyra Sundance's book *101 Dog Tricks* offers a valuable guide to training basic behaviors, positions, and skills. For a person who doesn't know how to teach basic and intermediate obedience or who is completely lost on how to begin task training, many of the behaviors covered in *101 Dog Tricks* offers a perfect launching point.

For example, while sit, down, stand, stay, and heel are covered, so are opening and closing doors, turning lights on and off, pulling on a tug (opening drawers, removing clothes, pulling an alarm), retrieving, message work, and many more valuable skills that directly translate into task work.

As a bonus, you can earn trick dog titles with your service dog or service dog in training and get awesome, bright, fun patches for their vest. What's not to love? Kyra specifically states, "Service dogs and their handlers may need to alter the trick [for trick dog titling] to work within their unique needs. This is fine."

Donna Hill YouTube Channel

If you're a visual learner (or really, any kind of learner at all, except kinetic), Donna Hill's free Assistance Dog Training channel on YouTube is an excellent service dog training resource. It simply can't be beat. She offers step-by-step directions, clear explanations, and effective techniques for teaching all kinds of service dog behaviors and task work.

Teamwork Manuals

Written by service dog trainer Lydia Kelly, the *Teamwork I* and *Teamwork II* manuals are old standbys for service dog training information. Our polled trainers varied wildly in their opinions of the *Teamwork* manuals, so be certain to check the reviews to find if they'll work for you and your service dog in training.

The *Teamwork* manuals offer training advice for teaching various tasks that's specifically catered to owner-trainers. However, they're quite vague in some places and in others, they only showcase what worked for the author. For some teams, though, *Teamwork I* and *Teamwork II* can fill gaps other service dog training resources can't.

Sound CDs

Every trainer polled included a sound CD on their list of the best service dog training resources, but no one sound CD cropped up reliably, so we grouped them all together. Sound CDs offer trainers the ability to socialize and desensitize service dogs in training to sounds that they otherwise might miss out on, whether that's due to lack of available socialization opportunities for any given set of sounds, the trainer isn't able to get out as much as he or she would like, or some other reason.

The need for a specific puppy sounds CD cropped up the most, but dog trial CDs, fireworks CDs, and babies/children CDs cropped up on almost every list. They were not the same sound desensitization CD on every list—each trainer preferred a different brand. Thunderstorm CDs also showed up regularly.

There are *so* many more excellent resources available; this list is only a starting point. Explore various avenues of training, learn as much as you can, and above all, never quit discovering new things together. Service dog teams who train together stay and succeed together.

GLOSSARY

American Temperance Testing Society (ATTS): Organization that administers, oversees, and records the results of formal, breed-specific temperament testing in the United States.

Americans with Disabilities Act (ADA): The main law in the United States allowing service dogs access to places of public accommodation when accompanied by their handler who has a disability.

Anchoring: Controversial trained task commonly performed by large-breed autism assistance dogs or sensory processing disorder dogs that consists of attaching a child to the service dog via a harness and tether. The dog then uses their body weight and positioning to prevent a child from wandering or running away.

Angulation: The angles formed by a dog's joints, specifically while the dog is standing. For service dogs, shoulder and hip angulation is most important.

Assistance dog: A dog with sound temperament, body, and mind that is specifically trained to perform tasks or work for a person with a disability.

Assistance Dogs International (ADI): Global organization that provides benchmarks, standards, and accountability to member organizations.

Brace and mobility support dog: Type of assistance dog that provides assistance to someone whose disability affects their ambulation.

Such dogs may provide counterbalance, bracing, general assistance, forward pulling momentum, or a mix thereof.

Canine Good Citizen (CGC): Very basic, entry-level obedience, manners, and temperament test administered by the American Kennel Club.

Canine Life and Social Skills (C.L.A.S.S.): Training and certification program consisting of three progressive levels of obedience, manners, and temperament.

Clicker: Mechanical device that makes a sharp, short noise when triggered. It's commonly utilized in training to "mark" or "capture" behaviors.

Drive: A dog's instinctive desire or impulse that shapes their behavior. Examples include food drive and prey drive.

Emotional Support Animal (ESA): A pet who is allowed to live in rented accommodations with their handler regardless of pet policy and who may accompany the handler on flights, provided proper documentation is provided and the pet has the training and temperament to be out in public.

Finish: A command meant to move from handler's front to either heel or side position by going around the handler or pivoting into place.

Flat/buckle collar: A basic collar that does not tighten when pressure is applied.

"Four on the floor": Having all four feet on the floor, as opposed to two on the floor, which happens while a dog is jumping, counter surfing, etc.

Front: The position and space directly in front of the handler.

Guide dog: A specific kind of assistance dog trained to lead a person with a visual impairment along known routes while avoiding obstacles and hazards and alert the handler to changes in the environment, such as the presence of curbs or stairs.

Harness: Piece of training equipment or working gear consisting of straps that cross or encircle the dog's torso, shoulders, or chest.

Heel: The position directly to the handler's left.

Housebroken: Dog can be reliably trusted not to defecate or urinate indoors (i.e., potty trained).

House training: The process of teaching a dog to reliably relieve itself outdoors.

Individual Education Planning (IEP): IEPs are specially formulated educational plans designed and written for students with disabilities so that they may succeed in the classroom environment. Part of the IEP lays out accommodations for the students, of which a service dog may be one.

International Association of Assistance Dog Partners (IAADP): An American organization dedicated to education, resources, and education within the service dog community.

Leash: Means of attaching dog to handler via a length of fabric, leather, or other flexible material.

Leash responsiveness: Dog responds readily to pressure, direction changes, and guidance given via leash.

Limited slip collar: Type of collar that tightens a set amount, typically two to three inches, when pressure is applied.

Loose-leash walking: Informal obedience skill consisting of not pulling on the leash, walking when the handler walks, and stopping when the handler stops.

Lure (noun): A piece of food, toy, target, or hand signal used to guide a dog into a particular skill.

Lure (verb): The act of using something the dog wants to get them to move or behave a certain way.

Martingale collar: A specialized type of limited slip collar consisting of two loops.

Medical alert dog: Type of service dog trained to alert to changes in the handler's physical, mental, or neurological condition and/or to changes in medical equipment function.

Medical response dog: Type of service dog trained to perform specific tasks or work in response to the handler's condition.

Mouth (verb): Common puppy behavior consisting of the puppy putting the handler's hands, clothing, or other body parts in their mouth.

Neuter: To surgically alter a male dog so they are incapable of sexual reproduction.

Nose targeting: Dog uses nose to touch, bump, or hit the handler's hand or everyday objects like doors, drawers, touch lights, and access buttons.

Overstimulation: Becoming too excited by sensory input.

Partner: Refers to either the dog or the human half of a service dog team.

Paw targeting: Dog uses paw to touch, bump, or hit the handler's hand or everyday objects like doors, drawers, touch lights, and access buttons.

Pivot: Dog turns in a circle with one set of feet, either front or rear, stationary.

Place training: Training the dog to go to or remain on a bed, platform, or mat.

Psychiatric service dog: Service dog trained to provide tasks or work for a handler who has a psychiatric disability.

Reactivity: Overreacting abnormally to certain environments, things, or situations. A common example is dog reactivity, during which a dog who sees another dog becomes timid, fearful, afraid, or overstimulated and reacts by barking, growling, lunging, or displaying other unwanted behaviors.

Recall: To call a dog to come to you.

Retrieval seeding kit (RSK): Collection of objects you need your service dog to know how to retrieve or to know how to retrieve generally.

Service dog: A dog with sound temperament, body, and mind that is specifically trained to perform tasks or work for a person with a disability.

Service dog candidate: Dog undergoing testing and/or training to potentially become a service dog.

Service dog in training (SDiT): A dog in training to become a service dog.

Service dog team: Refers to a fully trained service dog and their human partner.

Settle: A relaxed position with dog lying fully on their side.

Shake: When a dog places the requested paw in the person's hand.

Shape (verb): A method of teaching new behaviors or skills by breaking them down into small, incremental steps and then reinforcing each piece step by step until the full behavior is obtained.

Side: The position to the handler's right.

Skills: Specific, concrete behaviors the dog knows and can perform reliably upon request.

Spay: To surgically alter a female dog so they are incapable of sexual reproduction.

Started Dogs: Dogs (typically available for purchase) who have been selected, raised, and given introductory training so they can be easily started as service dog candidates with a higher probability of success.

Tail-tuck (command/position): The dog tucks their tail close to the body so it doesn't get stepped on while out in public.

Task-trained: Service dog who is trained to perform tasks or work.

Temperament test (TT): A test or evaluation designed to show and/or document a dog's temperament. Formally, the "TT" title is issued by the American Temperance Test Society (ATTS).

Tether: 1. A short piece of coated steel or other chew-proof material used in early service dog training to build skill, manners, and house train. 2. The act of attaching a child to a dog via a leash or other means.

Under: When asked, your partner moves under the designated bench, chair, table, seat, or other item. It can also direct your partner to scoot under your legs if there's not room directly under where you're sitting.

Vocalize: Whimpering, whining, barking, howling, grumbling, or otherwise making noise.

Withers: Top of a dog's shoulders.

Working dog: A dog trained to perform work.

ABOUT THE AUTHOR

Keagen J. Grace, better known as Kea, is a professional dog trainer, writer, and martial artist currently based in Phoenix, Arizona. She regularly travels across the United States and internationally for work. She has also lived in Colorado, Kentucky, Virginia, South Carolina, Canada, and Germany. With a specialty in service and assistance dogs, Kea has spent years honing her craft and combines this experience with an ongoing professional curiosity that leads her to a constant pursuit of new knowledge.

Kea trains and places service dogs on a selective basis and serves as a consultant for service dog and assistance dog training organizations and groups all over the world. She is widely published online and off, primarily in canine-related arenas, including sports, nutrition, training, legalities, and behavior.

When not training dogs, Kea can typically be found on a plane traveling to her next service dog placement, reading a book, or doing martial arts. Most of the time, there's a dog or two along for any and all of the above activities. Kea also serves with a K-9 Search and Rescue team, where she is responsible for training and handling the live find and human remains detection dogs during searches. She currently shares her heart and home with Sony, a human remains detection dog, and Soleil, the silly, goofy, hilarious, hairless Sphynx cat.

ACKNOWLEDGMENTS

This book wouldn't have been possible without the support, love, instruction, and guidance of a large group of people. There are too many to list, but to all who have helped me on this journey, I thank you. Here are a few who deserve an individual callout:

To Jesse "Yishai" Beckow, thank you for your editing and organizational skills. You definitely saved the day!

To Kelli Darland, Christina Root, and Ellie Martinez—thanks for sticking with me through the years, no matter what. This book made me more than a little crazy, and you guys all just rolled with it. You're the best.

To all those who I've crossed hands, sticks, and blades with while on the journey of martial arts, I thank you from the bottom of my heart. Martial arts keeps me sane(r), and it is through martial arts I have garnered and gathered the strength of an entire tribe of passionate, skilled, and supportive people. This book would not have been possible without my tribe and training. I have learned from every person I've lined up with, but special thanks to those who gave me a wealth of knowledge, support, and love, whether you knew it or not—Shane Del Bianco, who is the person responsible for starting me on the martial path, Lakan Guro Ernie Lake and Tuhon Ray Dionaldo of Filipino Combat Systems, Gurus Edmond Wells and Mike Casto of Anjing Gembala Pencak Silat, (Darth) Maul Mornie of Silat Suffian Bela Diri, Professor Alessandro Ashanti of Full Circle Jujitsu, and Guro Jerome Teague of Applied Eskrima.

Also, thanks to each of you above for tolerating dozens of service dogs in training coming to class for obedience practice, distraction proofing, and socialization! In a way, many of you are directly responsible for the success of some of our dogs currently in the field.

Professor Alessandro Ashanti deserves special mention, as it was he who guided me through the weeks and months leading up to my manuscript submission, and dealt with all the writer's block, tears, and craziness during that time. He is an author hailing from four generations of writers. His experience, support, energy, and passion kept me moving forward to the final completion of this project.

Last of all, a massive and special thanks to the hundreds of dogs who I've lived with, loved, crossed paths with, and trained throughout the years, as I have learned something from each and every one of you, but especially Cheyla, Karma, Jitter (my soul dog), Angus, and Axel.

INDEX

NOTES

NOTES

NOTES

NOTES

NOTES